When the *Wicked* Seize a City

CHUCK & DONNA MCILHENNY
WITH
FRANK YORK

HUNTINGTON HOUSE PUBLISHERS

Huntington House Publishers
P.O. Box 53788
Lafayette, Louisiana 70505

Library of Congress Card Catalog Numbers
91-78342
Quality Trade Paper ISBN 1-56384-024-3

Dedication

To our children:

Erin, Ryan, and Megan: who have certainly "borne the burden in [their] youth," faithfully and without complaint . . .

"[We] have no greater joy than this, to hear of [our] children walking in the truth" (III John 4).

Contents

Foreword

If you want to know all about the homosexual movement—even more than you may wish to know—and how you, as a Christian should relate to it, this is the book for you.

In the chapters that follow, you will read of the struggles of the pastor of a small church and his family, living in the midst of San Francisco, a city captured and controlled by gay activists. You will read about what happens when they make an outspoken stand against great odds against the forces of evil.

You might think that after attempts to burn down their church, threats on the lives of their children, lawsuits, and innumerable other attacks, Pastor McIlhenny and his family would exhibit bitterness or hatred. Nothing like that is found in this book. While at every point abhorring compromise with sin, the book exhibits throughout a remarkable compassion for those enslaved by the sexual movement which falsely promised them freedom.

It is one of a kind; it should be read by every thinking Christian.

DR. JAY E. ADAMS
PROFESSOR, PASTOR, AUTHOR,
COUNSELOR

Acknowledgments

Donna and I want to express our appreciation for the love and support our own congregation has extended to us throughout the years, especially in the past year while we were writing this book.

We may be a small congregation, but the Lord has used this little group of Christians to further the message of the gospel and to uphold the cause of righteousness amidst a wicked and perverse generation.

In the words of Ecclesiastes: "This wisdom I have also seen under the sun, and it seemed great to me: There was a little city with few men in it; and a great king came against it, besieged it, and built great snares around it. Now there was found in it a poor wise man, and he by his wisdom delivered the city. Yet no one remembered that same poor man. Then I said: 'Wisdom is better than strength. Nevertheless, the poor man's wisdom is despised, and his words are not heard. Words of the wise, spoken quietly, should be heard rather than the shout of a ruler of fools. Wisdom is better than weapons of war; but one sinner destroys much good'" (Ecc. 9:13-18).

This little church that God has preserved through the years is that poor wise man.

God bless the congregation of the First Orthodox Presbyterian Church of San Francisco.

We also want to express our appreciation for the love and support of our families throughout the years. Most especially, we would thank our parents, who, by God's grace, were faithful in fulfilling the admonition of Scripture as found in Deuteronomy 6: "And you shall love the Lord your God with all your heart and with all your soul and with all your might. And these words, which I am commanding you today, shall be on your hearts; and you shall teach them diligently to your [children] and shall talk of them when you sit in your house ... when you walk ... lie down ... and rise up. When

ix

Acknowledgments

your [children] ask you in time to come ... 'What do the testimonies ... statutes ... and judgments mean which the Lord commanded you?' ... you shall say to [them], ... the Lord commanded us to observe these statutes, to fear the Lord our God for our good always and for our survival. And it will be righteousness for us if we are careful to observe all this commandment before the Lord our God, just as He commanded" (Deut. 6:5-7, 20, 24-25).

Our parents diligently taught us to love the Lord our God with all our hearts, souls, and might—at all times and in all areas of our lives. By careful instruction in God's Word and by constant godly example, they daily lead us in the way of Truth and thus prepared us to stand firm for Him. They gave us the greatest inheritance any parents could pass on to their children: Jesus Christ.

Introduction

Trial by Fire!

It was late, cold, and windy that evening of June 1, 1983. I had spent the evening at a meeting of the Crisis Pregnancy Center just forming in our area. Donna had been working and was late in getting to bed. I was dosing, half asleep, when Donna came into the room. As she got into bed, I turned off the lamp on the bedstand. What was that noise? It was a crackling sound. Could an electrical wire have shorted-out in the newly built roof over the alleyway between the church and house? I listened . . . the trash cans were banging together in the wind . . . was that the trash cans? Not to worry . . . .

All of a sudden, flames roared through the quarter inch glass of our second story bedroom window, licking up the curtains as it spread. So quickly it spread! So fast and furious! No time to put my clothes on, nor to reach for my glasses. I remembered that my father had trained us as kids that if there ever was a fire in the house, don't stop to pick anything up—just get out as fast as you can.

In the terror of the moment, our first thought was for the children in their rooms. It seemed such a long way down that hall to grab the kids from their beds. I dashed into the girls' room first and grabbed them, shouting orders at the same time: "Stay together in the hall—stay in the hall!" Both girls screamed and sobbed as I ran for Ryan's bunk bed in the far bedroom. I grabbed him from the upper bunk, twisting his little body into mine, and grasping the girls, together we made for the door. Donna had gone to the kitchen near the fire area to call 911. I yelled at her to get out immediately.

I opened the heavy front door of the closed-in porch into the cold early morning wind. The flames were spreading around the corner of the building from the bedroom side of the house into the ground floor of the church. All of us, in nothing but underwear, made for the car parked in front of the house. I literally threw the kids into the car. Donna had emerged from the house but on impulse had gone back in. "The children are cold—get blankets!" She did an "army crawl" into Ryan's room, ripped a couple of blankets from his bed, crawled back out the front door, headed straight for the car, and wrapped the children in the blankets.

Within minutes the fire engines came with sirens wailing and full regalia making for the house and church—fire hoses blasting and wielding axes on the church doors.

It had not been trash cans banging together in the wind that we heard that night, but the sound of two gasoline cans clapping together as someone deliberately set fire to the house and church.

They had finally done it. For years they had threatened to burn down the church and try to kill us—here it was! What more could they do? I was both terrified and delighted that they had done their worst to get rid of us and failed!

How did we get to this point in our ministry? How could a thing like this ever happen to a family in the United States? It seemed like a scenario from an occupied overseas country, but not America. You just don't do things like this in good ol' "God Bless America" land.

How could a little church of less than fifty people be enough of a threat to anyone to want us out of the way, or at least out of the city? The answer, to some extent, lay with the reputation San Francisco had become notorious for: homosexuality! In the 1960s, the hippies brought "free-love" and drugs to our city. Now in the 1980s, we were reaping the inexorable consequences of this "free-love" and promiscuity: A city dominated by legislated immorality. From the top down, the city was made to sin before heaven.

ONE

A City Besieged

The Gay Parade

". . . their words and deeds are against the Lord, defying his glorious presence. The look on their faces testifies against them; they parade their sin like Sodom; they do not hide it. Woe to them! They have brought disaster upon themselves" (Isa. 3: 8-9, NIV).

Have you ever attended a gay pride parade? Like most Americans, you probably haven't taken the time to see for yourself what homosexuals do at these parades. If your city does have a gay pride parade, it's unlikely that your local TV or radio stations or your local newspapers accurately describe what takes place at one of these events. TV stations certainly couldn't show what occurs and newspapers could get into trouble with subscribers for detailing gay sexual perversions that take place publicly.

Tragically, because of a media mesmerized by the gay agenda, most people are ignorant about homosexual activities, because very few media outlets accurately portray how gays act in public and private. The person who does describe homosexual behavior sounds as if he's writing a pornographic novel. It is this widespread ignorance of homosexual behavior that causes many to uncritically accept the idea that we should tolerantly and even lovingly embrace homosexual behavior as if it were just another lifestyle.

In the next few paragraphs, we're going to take the time to describe for you—as tactfully as possible—what occurred at the largest gay celebration in the world—the Gay Freedom Day Parade. The parade is held in San Francisco during Gay Pride week with over two hundred thousand watchers lining the parade route. This is by no means an exhaustive look at what occurred, because the parade lasted for several hours! By the way, all San Francisco parades begin at 11 a.m. on Sunday morning—traditional worship time for the church. We're doing this to make you aware of what has happened to San Francisco and as a warning that this is what can happen to your community if you fail to understand the gay propaganda agenda for homosexualizing the country.

The Gay Freedom Day Parade is an annual event in San Francisco and in many other major cities around the U.S. It is held to celebrate the Stonewall riots, when patrons of a gay bar in New York City fought with police in June of 1969. (We'll detail more of what happened at Stonewall in the next chapter.)

Gay Pride—Gay Depravity

The parade begins with an army of lesbians riding motorcycles, proudly calling themselves Dykes On Bykes, in varying degrees of dress and undress. Picture a colorful float slowly moving down main street. The float is filled with men and women gyrating to raucous music. The lesbians are smeared with paint and are topless. A gay man is dancing wildly to the music and shoving his hand down into his pants. Another man is clothed only in a g-string. The flap which covers his rear end is a miniature American flag.

Walking down the street beside the floats are a number of men dressed in women's nighties, pantyhose, and bright blue or red wigs. Dancing among the men is a bald-headed woman, naked from the waist up, with square pasties over her breasts. Another man stops to pose for a video camera. He's wearing a pink evening gown and has curlers in his hair.

Lying on the sidewalk near the curb, a long-haired man in shorts has pulled his pants down and is kicking his legs in the air as though he's trying to attract attention. Standing in the crowd, two gay lovers fondle one another, unconscious of the peering on-lookers. (Tourists from the "Bible-Belt" either react in horror or join the festivities—giggling—admiring the sense of uninhibitedness of San Franciscans!)

Back in the parade, an obese lesbian, naked from the waist

up, shows off to the crowd. She's wearing hiking shorts and boots.

Walking through the crowd are two men dressed in black leather and silver-studded jock straps. These are members of the sado-masochistic element in the gay culture. The man trailing behind the first man has a dog collar around his neck. His "master" is holding his "slave" chained to the collar. This is what is called "B & D" for "bondage and dominance," another sex fantasy in the subculture.

A group known as the Radical Fairies marches proudly down the street, and several of them are carrying a ten-foot long python or boa constrictor. Another group called NAMBLA, North America Man/Boy Love Association, a group of homosexuals that advocates sex with consenting minors, marches as respectably as every other group advocating sexual lawlessness.

Not long after they pass, a man strolls by with a sign which says, **"God Is Gay."** He is quickly followed by half a dozen lesbians from a group known as SLUTS (Seminary Lesbians Under Theological Stress). Various gay church groups pass by identifying their affiliations with traditional mainline churches such as Presbyterians, Lutherans, Roman Catholics, etc.

On the curb, two young men in their twenties lay down in the street and simulate oral copulation with each other. The crowd cheers enthusiastically. Such freedom!

Amazingly enough, in this parade various political candidates for office, state and local, follow these expressions of bizarre behavior, publicly declaring their tacit approval of what "gayness" means in San Francisco. You ask, "where are the police in all this?" Most definitely their presence is seen. For the first time, the new police chief is a participant in the parade, riding in an open-top car, waving to the crowds, ushered on both sides by his lesbian and gay officers. Indecent exposure laws lapse into outmoded times, far too archaic for the enlightened minds of liberal San Francisco. Laws governing public morality are simply suspended for the day in deference to the gay community. At the end of the parade route, a recruiting table is set up to enlist homosexuals into the San Francisco police department. The police department has a policy of non-discrimination in the hiring of homosexuals and lesbians, along with racial minorities.

All of these events occurred in the light of day on what we

Christians call the Lord's Day—Sunday. Is He watching? Or has He abandoned San Francisco to its own little temporal world?

The Truth Needs to Be Told

We realize what we have described is very offensive, but the Christian community cannot continue to remain ignorant of what immoral behavior "gay rights" brings to a city.

What has happened in San Francisco is a grim look into the future of what lies ahead not only for other cities, but for the US health care system, schools, the media and the church herself.

Ministering in this city for nearly two decades, we have witnessed and, in our feeble way, opposed the immoral revolution that, in such totality, is unprecedented anywhere else in the United States (although Los Angeles is not far behind).

A coup d'etat of decadence has occurred in San Francisco. There literally is a new rainbow flag that periodically flies above city hall announcing the new nation—"Queer Nation." An entire culture has been developed, emanating from the bizarre sex habits of those calling themselves gay and lesbian, and has seized control of the power centers of the city, leaving behind moral and traditional values. Straight society, as the hippies used to call it, is now out of power and without influence—living on the fringes of society.

A Gay Political Machine Rules San Francisco

The wicked have truly seized our city. It is estimated that over one hundred thousand homosexuals live in San Francisco—up to 20 percent of the voting population is gay. They have moved here from around the country to accomplish a very simple goal: to create a "model" city, ruled by a militant homosexual political machine. From their base of operations here, they hope to spread their control to other cities. Allegedly, key leaders of two of the most radical homosexual groups, ACT UP and Queer Nation, have recently moved from San Francisco to San Diego to begin building a political movement in that city. I know this sounds absurd, but by the time you finish reading this book, we believe you'll be convinced that the homosexuals mean business. No amount of red-necked incredulous laughing will stop the downward plunge to moral chaos. The gay machine is serious!

As an economic group, it is extremely powerful. Unlike the heterosexual community, gays and lesbians aren't normally "burdened" with such responsibilities as children, nor do they spend their time engaged in such activities as supporting the nuclear family and related issues. Many of them do spend time helping fellow homosexuals who are dying of AIDS, but their focus is primarily on gaining political power and passing legislation that provides them with special privileges not granted to the "straight" community. They are politically aggressive and view politics as seriously as the committed Christian views his relationship with Jesus Christ.

They desire nothing less than to have you—by force of law—accept their sexually perverted lifestyle. Their way to power is through the political system. They're talented and ruthlessly aggressive in the pursuit of their goals.

Power through Intimidation

One of the most revealing articles ever written about the objectives of the gay rights movement comes from *Guide*, a homosexual magazine. The article, "The Overhauling of Straight America" (November 1987), goes into considerable detail about how gays will conquer straight America through a combination of propaganda and vilification. The authors, Marshall Kirk and Erastes Pill, outline several strategies designed to weaken family-oriented America. Among them are:

1. Desensitization. "To desensitize the public is to help it view homosexuality with indifference instead of with keen emotion." The authors say it's imperative that gays talk about their gayness as much as possible on TV and radio until people become indifferent to homosexuality. Straights will eventually be desensitized to the point that homosexuality will be viewed as just any other lifestyle. The use of the term "lifestyle" itself lulls the moral sensibilities to include them along side other normal lifestyles.

2. Portray gays as victims, not as aggressive challengers. "In any campaign to win over the public, gays must be cast as victims in need of protection so that straights will be inclined by reflex to assume the role of protector."

3. Give the protectors a just cause. "Our campaign should not demand direct support for homosexual practices, but should instead make anti-discrimination as its theme."

4. Make the victimizers look bad. "To be blunt—they must be vilified. . . . The public should be shown images of ranting homophobes whose secondary traits disgust middle America. These images might include the Ku Klux Klan demanding that gays be burned alive or castrated. . . ."

The article goes on to describe a media campaign to promote homosexuality and to defeat the straight world. Marshall Kirk has since expanded this article into a book, "After the Ball," which is a tactical manual on how to seize power.

Where Is the Church?

Perhaps in no other city in the country is there such a clearly marked distinction between spiritual light and spiritual darkness as there is in San Francisco.

Gay activist and San Francisco supervisor, Harry Britt, a former Methodist minister, has openly stated that we're involved in a spiritual warfare. We couldn't agree more. In attacking opponents of "domestic partners" legislation (which give official governmental sanction to same-sex relationships), Britt said, "This campaign is a spiritual war . . . our enemies are saying they want the authoritarian, man-on-top, woman-on-bottom world" (*San Francisco Bay Guardian*, 2 August 1989). What is occurring in San Francisco is literally a battle for the souls of men and women, boys and girls—the soul of a city.

What is the San Francisco gay community saying to those of us who call ourselves Christians? It is saying with boldness and without shame, "We are here, we are queer. And we won't go away!"—the slogan of the radical group Queer Nation.

But San Francisco's gay culture is saying much more. It is saying we should be forced through raw gay political power to yield to homosexual demands. One of the primary goals of the gay rights movement is the silencing of the Church and any other opposition it may have. Unfortunately, here in San Francisco, it has readily achieved that goal through terrorism and intimidation.

As a minister and his wife working in this city since 1973, the Lord has given us many opportunities to speak for righteousness and biblical morality. For such threatening speech—

according to the gay community—we have experienced repeated
attacks against us, our children, and our congregation by militant gays. We have been subject to two lawsuits brought by a
homosexual church organist and later by two lesbians. By God's
mercy, we won both lawsuits, but it cost tens of thousands of
dollars. Our home has been subject to a firebombing, vandalized and graffitied numerous times; we have received multitudes of obscene phone calls and death threats; and for the
sake of the children, we've been forced to flee the city in fear
for our lives on several occasions.

Ignore the Message—Attack the Messenger

It is part of the gay agenda to "vilify" anyone who stands
against political normalization of a sexual behavior that is so
clearly condemned in the Bible and in nature.

In a city billed as a refuge of "civility and tolerance," San
Francisco is meanly intolerant of anyone who opposes the gay
rights movement. The most often used method of silencing the
opposition is to accuse the person of being a homophobe or
homophobic. The term has been used over and over again in
both the gay press and the liberal media to label anyone who
would dare oppose sexually perverted behavior. It is used much
like the word "McCarthyite" was used in the past to ridicule
anyone who expressed a concern over Communist subversion
in this country. This labeling or "name calling" often leaves the
gay "rights" opponent sputtering and trying to explain that he
does not hate nor is he afraid of gays.

Yet just the opposite is true; many homosexuals are actually
heterophobic. Many are afraid of straights— calling them "breed-
ers" and resentful of the nuclear family: the man-woman-child
family. Psychologist and author Dr. Frank du Mas, in his book,
Gay Is Not Good, notes that although the gay population is only
around 2-3 percent, gay men are afraid of straight women (who
account for more than 50 percent of the total population), and
they fear heterosexual men as well. This means that homosexuals are fearful of more than 95 percent of the population.
According to du Mas, "It seems to us that the conclusion is
inescapable: Homosexuals are far more prejudiced and discriminatory against a far larger proportion of the population
than are heterosexuals. If we further assume that heterophilia
(love of the opposite sex) is the natural order of mammalian

animals, then heterophobia is pathological. The homosexual's heterophobia is sociopathic" (Frank du Mas, *Gay is Not Good* [Nashville, Tenn.: Thomas Nelson Publishers, 1979].).

Unfortunately, however, there are individuals who *are* fearful of and even hate homosexuals. Some Christians have the idea that homosexuals are so sinful that they're beyond God's redeeming grace. We had a minister acquaintance tell us that if he found out that a homosexual was merely sitting in his service, he'd have the ushers throw him out. That kind of attitude is totally unscriptural and just provides the gays with ammunition to condemn the whole church for being hateful and homophobic. Homosexual behavior is no worse than any other sexual sin. The adulterer and homosexual both need the same sovereign saving grace of God in Christ to bring them to repentance. Both can avail themselves of God's mercy and forgiveness.

No Compromise—But Compassion

We already know what the critics of this book will say. They will, of course, immediately brand the messenger as homophobic, mean-spirited, intolerant, uncompassionate, and bigoted. They will accuse us of being hateful to AIDS patients. So called gay "Christians" will attack us for allegedly misinterpreting the clear teaching of Scripture that homosexuality is an abomination to God and that those who commit homosexual acts are damning themselves to hell.

The message of the Bible is irrefutable. It condemns homosexual acts over and over again in the Old and New Testaments. Unlike the issue of abortion, the Bible literally and clearly forbids homosexuality. Although we believe that abortion is wrong and that the Bible condemns it, still, the Scriptures do not explicitly condemn abortion as it does homosexuality. We cannot turn to a passage that says, "Thou shalt not commit abortion." Whereas on the topic of homosexuality, the Bible does say that such acts are an abomination to the Lord and are forbidden. At the same time, the Bible's message, God's message, graciously offers the hope of redemption and deliverance to the homosexual just as explicitly (1 Cor. 6:9-11).

The book of Romans contains the clearest New Testament condemnation of homosexual behavior. Romans 1:18-29 says:

"The wrath of God is being revealed from heaven against all the godlessness and wickedness of men who suppress the truth by their wickedness, since what may be known about God is plain to them, because God has made it plain to them.

"For since the creation of the world God's invisible qualities—his eternal power and divine nature—have been clearly seen, being understood from what has been made, so that men are without excuse.

"For although they knew God, they neither glorified him as God nor gave thanks to him, but their thinking became futile and their foolish hearts were darkened. Although they claimed to be wise, they became fools, and exchanged the glory of the immortal God for images made to look like mortal man and birds and animals and reptiles.

"Therefore God gave them over in the sinful desires of their hearts to sexual impurity for the degrading of their bodies with one another. They exchanged the truth of God for a lie, and worshipped and served created things rather than the Creator—who is forever praise worthy, Amen.

"Because of this, God gave them over to shameful lusts. Even their women exchanged natural relations for unnatural ones. In the same way the men also abandoned natural relations with women and were inflamed with lust for one another. Men committed indecent acts with other men, and received in themselves the due penalty for their perversion.

"Furthermore, since they did not think it worthwhile to retain the knowledge of God, he gave them over to a depraved mind, to do what ought not to be done."

It doesn't get much clearer than that. God specifically condemns homosexual behavior, but still loves the sinner. As I have often said to our congregation and friends: homosexuality is not the unpardonable sin. As repugnant as their behavior and attitudes may be, homosexuals are not beyond the power of God to bring them to salvation in Christ.

Our message to homosexuals in San Francisco has always been the same: you must repent from your sinful ways and turn to Christ for forgiveness of sins.

Unfortunately, this message sounds hateful to many, but it is the only message consistent with the Word of God. Proverbs 27:5-6 says, "Better is open rebuke than hidden love. The kisses of an enemy may be profuse, but faithful are the wounds of a friend." Although the gays in San Francisco may not believe it, we consider ourselves their friends—faithful friends. As friends, we believe it is our duty before the Lord to warn them of the dangers of their destructive lifestyle, which will ultimately lead them to death at an early age.

Many years ago, we ran into a former classmate of ours from Moody Bible Institute. Unbeknown to us, he'd moved to San Francisco not long after we were called here. We were downtown one day and were startled to see him walking hand-in-hand down the street with his gay lover. After some small talk, we invited him to attend our church. He immediately agreed, but made a point of bringing his gay lover with him.

One of the first things he said to us was, "I don't want you to condemn me. I would like to attend your church, but I won't argue with you. I'm gay and that's it." For the next couple of years we both prayed for him and his friend. We told him on several occasions, "We can't love you apart from what Christ has said. If we don't love you in Christ, we'll be loving you unto death. We have to encourage you to leave the homosexual lifestyle because you're sinning against God and your neighbor." The good news is that he eventually did repent and come out of the gay scene to become a recommitted member of the Body of Christ. We eventually encouraged him to leave the city for safer ground, not to be in the way of temptation living amidst his former gay friends.

Tragically, recent newspaper reports indicate that the younger, more militant gays are continuing to engage in high risk sexual activities, in spite of their knowledge of the AIDS virus. An article in the *Washington Post*, 24 June 1990, for example, points out that "gay and bisexual men under age 30 are twice as likely to transmit the AIDS-causing HIV virus—than older men."

A year later, the situation has not gotten any better, in spite of millions of tax dollars spent on AIDS education since 1980. According to a *Washington Times* article, a study conducted by the San Francisco Health Commission showed that young gays were ignoring warnings against "unprotected sex." The article states in part: "The first study found that 24% to 42% of young homosexual men were found to engage in unprotected anal intercourse . . . It was higher in the youngest age group—the opposite of what we expected," said Dr. (George) Lemp (of the

San Francisco Department of Public Health AIDS office). "The trend is of concern."

"The second new San Francisco study found that, despite the 1980s media blitz, high percentages of minority men—of all ages—still practice unsafe sex.

"Researchers discovered that 12% of surveyed homosexual American Indians, 40% of homosexual Filipinos and 50% of homosexual Latin men engage in at-risk sexual behavior. Earlier findings revealed that 32% of African-American men have unprotected sex" (*The Washington Times*, 6 June 1991).

It is sad to realize that a majority of these young men will die in their mid-thirties of a terribly painful, wasting disease—a disease that turns them into living skeletons. Yet, thousands of these young men will die prematurely because of their deviant sexual behaviors. These men continue to defiantly march to death much like lemmings over a cliff.

Hate the Sin, Not the Sinner

In spite of all that we've experienced as a family and church at the hands of gay and pro-gay activists, we have attempted, to the best of our ability and by God's grace, to show them the love of Christ.

David Hummel, a lay-Episcopal parson, considered himself a gay Christian. Several years ago, David carried the sign "Thank God I'm Gay!" in the Gay Pride Parade. He saw no inconsistency with his behavior and what Scripture teaches. We spent many years warning him to turn from his sinful lifestyle and flee to Christ before it was too late.

Through the years, we told David that we'd be here for him if he contracted AIDS. I asked him to call me if he should contract the virus and that we'd do whatever we could to comfort and provide for his needs.

After resisting our efforts for years, the sad day eventually came when David called, reporting that the doctors had diagnosed him with AIDS. He had both Kaposi sarcoma and pneumocystis, two of the more devastating diseases resulting from immune deficiency syndrome, and was going into the hospital for treatment. He asked me to come visit him. We prayed, I read Scripture to him. However, as to whether he ever turned from his homosexual lifestyle, we don't know for sure. He'd never tell us. Now he's in the Lord's hands. In a wheelchair and with an oxygen mask covering his face, David led a procession of people with AIDS in the 1987 Gay Pride Parade. A few weeks later, David died.

A year ago, we received a phone call from a young man we'd taught in our youth group at a church in southern California. The teen-ager had grown up to become a successful aide in the California legislature; he had also secretly imbibed the gay subculture, unbeknown to his family and friends. It had finally taken its toll. He was dying of AIDS at the age of thirty-three. Stan knew he was dying. His call was not one of desperation. He wasn't looking for a quick-fix solution for his problem—a miracle to save him from the inevitability of dying. No, Stan's call was one of responsibility. He knew he had to get right with the Lord. On several occasions, we visited with him at the nursing home in Sacramento, where he lived out his few remaining days. Unlike David, he repented of his sin and found forgiveness in God's grace. His close friends organized a memorial service for him in a church near the capitol building. I preached the sermon. Although his death seemed premature and a tragic waste to us, Stan had made his peace with God. He was ready to go home to be with the Lord; and we were confident that, as with all repentant sinners, the Lord met Stan with open arms and said "well done My good and faithful servant, enter into My rest."

As we write this, there's a man in our own presbytery who just learned that he has the HIV virus. I went to his mother's home with him to break the news to her. This young seminarian was afraid that the church community would not understand, but he knows that if anyone is equipped and called to minister to him, it is the Church of Jesus Christ—our congregation and his own.

Throughout the years, we've attempted to share the gospel with AIDS patients in our local hospitals, but we have been continually rebuffed by so-called Christian gays and San Francisco politicians. A few years ago, I had a private conversation with Supervisor Harry Britt about visiting and ministering to AIDS patients. Supervisor Britt told me that I could minister to them only if I would change my message. Drop the "sin" issue! I would not be welcome to minister to any AIDS patient in the city hospital unless that message changed. To date, the local general hospital's policy has required that all those wanting to minister on the AIDS ward take a counseling course originally sponsored by the Episcopal Diocese. In this course instructors discourage the use of the Bible in ministering to any AIDS patient.

Currently, I am a board member of the Christian AIDS Council, a small organization begun by various evangelical pastors and layman. The Council's purpose is to show people with AIDS that conservative Bible believers care about the needs of these individuals no matter who or what they are. As a council, we have had limited opportunities to pray with and comfort those in need.

Although we've been generally hindered in reaching AIDS patients, we have had the opportunity to minister to individuals, and our church women's group regularly gathers canned foods to donate to the local AIDS Food Bank. This effort was done jointly with the Sunday School children. The food stuffs are collected, various Scriptures are printed on labels, and the children paste the labels on the cans and boxes. The food is then delivered to the food bank. Ironically, Donna, who works at what could legitimately be termed a "liberal" law firm, asked her coworkers to donate food to help those dying of AIDS and was firmly rebuked by her coworkers. She eventually stopped trying to collect food at her office because of the callous response. Though the world loves its own, when in need, the world just as readily turns its back on its own with the same hardness of heart it shows toward the gospel. As one coworker said to Donna, "they made their own bed, let them lie in it!"

Showing Christ's Love

Donna was at work one day talking to a woman who was reacting to the news that the rear window of our car had just been smashed by vandals. Another incident in a long list of senseless harassment. She said to Donna, "You must really hate whoever is doing this to your family." To which Donna replied, "Actually, no. At times I'm afraid of them, and at times I'm angry, but hatred consumes the hater. They hate us. I can only pity them." If we hate our enemies, we become as our enemies.

In dealing with the persecution, the fear, and the vandalism, we both realize that we have to love them in Christ, regardless of what they do to us.

If you get involved in opposing immorality in your community, you, too, have to love them, in spite of what they say or do to you. It's not easy by any means, but love, as a fruit of the Holy Spirit, is the only answer if we are going to persevere. It really does take the love of God shed abroad in our hearts to continue to stand against the wiles and crafts of Satan in this spiritual warfare.

We've learned that even when you have the best of motives and attempt to help gay men, they'll probably still hate you. However, it's still your responsibility and privilege to love them for Christ's sake. Unless that be the core of your ministry, you will fail, and you will eventually become resentful and spiteful.

All of us have a responsibility to witness the truth of the gospel to gays and to help them leave that "death-style." Regretfully, the Church has in many ways failed in its duty—not only in this area of concern—but in many other areas as well.

Our goal in San Francisco is to keep on doing what we've been called to do until the Lord leads us elsewhere. We know that as long as we're faithful to what He has called us to, He will protect and vindicate us, even though the world may never appreciate or understand such out-of-this-world motives or the stubborn stand we've taken.

We believe that what has happened to us and to our family is only a foretaste of what will happen to you, your church, and your community if you fail to aggressively win them to Christ in every area of life. We must oppose all such legislated immorality by the force of love for Christ and His Kingdom.

We are called to be salt and light, says Jesus. But, if the salt loses its savor—if we refuse to get actively engaged in our society at EVERY LEVEL—our salt will be useless and will be trampled underfoot by men.

It is our duty as Christians to work to preserve decency and law and order based upon the foundation of the Gospel of the grace of God (Ps. 11:3-4). We are not simply called to preach the gospel and wait for a rapture to take us off the "sinking ship" of failing human culture. Jesus' own prayer in John 17 is that we "would not be taken out of the world but that we would be kept from evil. . . ."

We're afraid many in the Church have forgotten their Church history. The gospel message not only changes individuals but also changes whole societies, whole nations as well. The

Christian is not simply to possess the knowledge of God in his heart and keep it to himself. He is to put his faith into action: feeding the poor, working for prison reform, caring for unwed mothers, and, yes, helping AIDS patients through the dying as well as the living process for Jesus' sake.

This book is not simply the story of how the McIlhennys have been persecuted by militant homosexuals. It is not written to elicit pity for us. We're writing this as a wake up call to a sleeping Church. Either the Church wakes up and gets involved in society at large, or we face incredible persecution at the hands of individuals and governments (city, state, and national) who hate the God of the Bible and want His people and message destroyed from the earth once and for all. How often has the world attempted to do that and miserably failed? Either the Church becomes militant in its opposition to sin, and aggressive for righteousness and healing, or we will see the collapse of our entire culture into a hedonistic nightmare—with deadly consequences for millions.

TWO

The Calm Before The Storm

When I received a call to become pastor of the First Orthodox Presbyterian Church in San Francisco, Donna and I weren't really that excited about the prospect. It was 1973, and I was assistant to the pastor of a church in Garden Grove, California, near where my father was pastoring a Baptist church. We were fairly content where we were and didn't think there was any need to relocate to northern California.

Actually, at that time, I wasn't sure I wanted to continue serving as a pastor. Although I certainly had no desire to leave the ministry, with my training from Moody and my growing love for reformed theology, I was much more interested in becoming a teacher in a school or seminary. I had very strong leanings toward the academic life, rather than the pastorate. To me, the thought of being a seminary professor was appealing. It appeared to be a relatively peaceful life, and I thought it would also be non-political. However, in spite of these academic yearnings, I accepted the call to the church in San Francisco. I assumed I'd gain some useful experience as the senior (and only!) pastor of a small church and that that knowledge would come in handy should I ever become a seminary professor.

I had spent my childhood in Portland, Maine, where my father pastored the largest Baptist church in the state. This was during the 50s and early 60s. In his denomination, my father was known as an expert on church growth and development. He had managed to increase his congregation from four hundred to fourteen hundred in less than ten years. Those accustomed to mega-churches may not find that impressive, but for New England that was quite an accomplishment.

We were living in Maine during the early days of the civil

rights movement, and Martin Luther King's name was just starting to make the headlines. As the civil rights movement gained momentum, a number of activists began arriving in the state to help organize the Bible-believing Black community.

During this period, my father was asked if he would allow a black man to stay at the house for a time. Dad refused to do so, not because of any racial antagonism, but because, as a pastor, he didn't want to get involved in politics. His reaction reflected the general attitude of most evangelical churches during that era. There was a widespread belief that church members, and especially the pastor, were only on this earth to get souls saved and ready for heaven. Nothing else mattered very much. The liberal churches had long since abandoned any concern for personal salvation through faith in Jesus Christ, and emphasized social action instead of soul winning. They eagerly embraced civil rights activism as a redemptive process.

As good Baptists, however, we stayed away from being involved in the political world and spent our time in soul-winning service. Unfortunately, our culture went into a tailspin during the rebellious years of the 60s; and most churches, or Christians in general, had little impact on the culture at large during that time.

Although I wasn't aware of it at that time, I now know that a faulty view of the church's role in society had infected Christianity, leaving it powerless—not only to impact personal salvation and holiness, but to make any impact on the world for the sake of the gospel. Theologian Francis Schaeffer and others have written eloquently on this defective view of Christianity and the need for us to recover our roots as movers and shakers in this world.

Like myself, Donna also grew up as a "preacher's kid." Her father, Doug Fisher, was a Baptist minister in Chicago. Although we didn't meet until our Moody days, we had very similar backgrounds as "p.k.'s" growing up in the 50s. Unlike my father, Donna's father was not a pastor all his career. As a multi-talented man, he also was involved with a variety of evangelistic enterprises: musician with Moody radio (WMBI); coordinator for evangelistic rallies for Chicagoland Youth For Christ; a founding member of Youth For Christ International (YFC); and he was also active in setting up the YFC evangelistic crusades in post-war Europe, out of which came the Billy Graham evangelistic team. In the 50s and 60s, his ministry turned toward the pastorate. He also became involved in coordinating both African-American and Caucasian evangelistic committees in the Baltimore area for joint evangelistic efforts. He was never confronted with political issues as my father was in Maine. Though they lived in Chicago, with its notorious reputation for "machine" politics, the city still seemed to be administered with a conservative "moral" mindset. Evangelism was the theme of his ministry—not politics or social action. In those days, the country was still assumed to be predominantly Christian in its consensus, and there appeared to be no need for pastors to become politically involved. Politicians were at least nominally Christian, and no apparent threat to the status quo loomed on the horizon as a serious threat—least of all homosexuality.

Moody Bible Institute Gets Shaken Up

Donna and I attended Moody Bible Institute in the mid 60s and became gradually sensitized to the importance of Christians being involved in politics and culture. With the civil rights movement in full swing and Vietnam war protestors marching in the streets, even Moody was infected with a spirit of revolution. When we were there, Moody still officially reflected the "don't get involved in anything" philosophy of the earlier days of Evangelicalism, but black students on campus were beginning to make their presence and concerns known. They were no longer content with the status quo. They were beginning to challenge the school's policy against interracial dating.

I can remember sitting in chapel one day hearing a young man pontificating about the "blackness of sin" and exhorting us to remain pure. An irate black student got up in the middle of the auditorium and started protesting the speaker's choice of words—chastising him for linking "blackness" with sin. This was at the time of the "black is beautiful" era. We were shocked at the black student's response, but some of us felt he had a valid point. This unusual event at Moody eventually led a group of us to stand in solidarity with the black students on a number of other concerns. It was also an event that gently nudged us into considering the importance of being socially involved in our fallen world.

While at Moody, we spent a good deal of time studying the great theologians, including John Calvin. Calvin's message came through loud and clear: Christians are to have an affect not only on individuals, but on the society as a whole. We were certainly not here just to spend our lives waiting impatiently for the rapture.

My political awakening continued as we went on through the turmoil of the 60s, which culminated in such major events as the assassinations of Martin Luther King and Bobby Kennedy, the Kent State shootings, and Woodstock. But even through those events, we stayed relatively apolitical in our practice.

It wasn't until I arrived in San Francisco that we finally realized the importance of Christians being involved not only in politics, but also in every aspect of God's creation and culture. We began to realize that we were called to a *city*—not just a congregation.

Our baptism of fire into the world of politics took place in 1978 when we were sued by our church organist whom I had fired after discovering that he was a practicing homosexual.

The Revolution Begins

There are two years that have great significance for the gay rights movement: 1969 and 1973. These are important historical markers in charting the sexual revolution that has taken place in the United States and especially in San Francisco.

A routine police raid on a New York homosexual bar in Greenwich Village in June of 1969 set off a homosexual rebellion that is still growing in strength. The police raided the bar because they had been tipped off that illegal sexual activities were taking place inside. Instead of quietly giving up, the militants in the bar started swearing at the police and threw bricks and bottles. The Stonewall Riot (as it has been called in gay folklore) is considered to be a turning point in radicalizing the sexual revolution. Violence and intimidation were to become standard practice among many militant homosexuals.

Of course, as I've already explained, 1973 is significant for us because it's the year we moved to San Francisco. Ironically, at the same time, the modern gay movement began to take root in the political arena of San Francisco. After all, San Francisco has been known historically as the "Barbery Coast" or "Babylon on the Bay." The first topless bar was opened in San Francisco in 1965. The hippie movement, love-child/peace-movement, relocated from Berkeley to the Haight-Ashbury neighborhood of San Francisco. This same neighborhood was to become the drug-infested hippiedom for the psychedelic movement—"make love, not war!" San Francisco was ripe for the homosexual movement to emerge. Love was more important than traditional marriage values. Live and commune together, but don't license it.

Storming the American Psychiatric Association

Nineteen seventy-three also has significance for the entire gay rights movement. In that year, the homosexual militants literally bullied the American Psychiatric Association into removing homosexuality as a mental illness from the Diagnostic and Statistical Manual of Psychiatric Disorders (the DSM). This manual is what psychiatrists and psychologists use to define and categorize various forms of mental illnesses and sexual perversions.

Ronald Bayer, a pro-homosexual psychiatrist, wrote an entire book on how the homosexuals strong-armed fellow professionals into redefining a mental illness or sexual perversion into a normal behavior. In *Homosexuality and American Psychiatry, The Politics of Diagnosis,* Bayer recounts how the gay rights movement targeted the APA in 1970 for repeated verbal and physical assaults at its annual conventions:

> . . . the American Psychiatric Association became the target of homosexual attacks in 1970, . . . when gay activists in San Francisco saw in the presence of the APA convention in their city yet one more opportunity to challenge the psychiatric profession. . . . With the APA designated as a target, gay groups thought the country could direct their wrath against a common organization foe. (Ronald Bayer, *Homosexuality and American Psychiatry, The Politics of Diagnosis* [New York: Basic Books, Inc., 1981].)

In May 1970, the gays and militant feminists disrupted their first APA convention with guerrilla theater and shouting matches. Their target at this convention was researcher Irving Bieber who was sitting on a panel discussing transsexuality and homosexuality. According to Bayer, "His efforts to explain his position to his challengers were met with derisive laughter. Since the norms of civility were considered mere conventions designed to mute outrage, it was not difficult for a protester to call him a 'mother ———.' . . . This verbal attack with its violent tone caused Bieber considerable distress" (Ibid., 102-103).

The attack against the APA continued year after year with the psychiatrists increasingly fearful of what was going to happen at each convention. Bayer speaks approvingly of the shouting matches and threats of violence as the only way the homosexual could gain a hearing.

By 1972, the homosexuals were allowed to have their own panels during APA conventions, and most of the opponents of gay aggression had been silenced.

In 1973, the gays worked with several influential members of the APA in redefining how homosexuality was dealt with in the DSM. One of their closet allies was Dr. Judd Marmor. In October of 1980, Dr. Marmor, who was then running for president of the APA, testified at the first Congressional Sub-Committee hearing on gay rights. (Out of nine witnesses, I was the only one testifying against the proposed legislation (See Congressional Record, 96th Congress, H.R. 2074). . . "to prohibit discrimination on the basis of affectional or sexual orientation, and for other purposes" p. 64ff.) Through the influence of the National Gay Task Force, the APA sent out a letter to its members urging them to support a change in the definition of homosexuality in the DSM. The gay task force helped draft the letter, bought the APA mailing list, and mailed it to thousands of psychiatrists.

Through intimidation by the militant homosexual community, the definition of homosexuality was changed from that of a mental disorder to what was then called "ego-dystonic homosexuality." This meant that if a person was disturbed by his homosexual tendencies, then his condition should be treated. If, however, he was satisfied with his condition, then no treatment was necessary. The definition was changed for political reasons, not because of any new scientific revelations about the origins of homosexual behavior. This change in definition in the DSM gave homosexuals the legitimacy they'd been seeking for so many years. They could now say the APA had declared their behavior to be normal.

Dr. Charles Socarides, a well-known psychiatrist and author, was one of the few men willing to publicly oppose the politicizing of his field by the gay rights movement. He once wrote that "[i]f such changes [the redefining of homosexuality due to political pressure] are due to social and/or political activism, neither the goal of individual liberties nor the best interests of society are served. These changes would remove from psychoanalysis and psychiatry entire areas of scientific progress, rendering chaotic fundamental truths about unconscious psychodynamics as well as the interrelationship between anatomy and psychosexual identity" (Charles Socarides, "The Sexual Deviations and the Diagnostic Manual," American Journal of Psychotherapy, Vol. 32 [1978]: 414.). Socarides would today be called a homophobe by gay rights activists, but his writings about homosexual behavior are filled with references to compassion and understanding for those suffering from this particular sexual orientation disturbance.

One of my great concerns is that if a militant group of homosexuals can pressure the American Psychiatric Association into redefining a mental disorder or sexual perversion into a normal behavior, what can prevent any other militant group of sexual deviates from having their particular form of perversion "redefined" in the same manner?

If this sounds absurd, consider the views of a couple of so-called experts on child sexual abuse who think that pedophilia (a condition where adults are sexually attracted to children) is a "sexual orientation"—not a sexual perversion.

Behavior Today magazine reported in 1988 that Dr. Sharon Satterfield, a recognized expert on child sexual abuse, had suggested in a speech that pedophilia might be an orientation, rather than a perversion. According to *Behavior Today*, "In the final analysis, the difference between sexual orientation and deviance may not be a scientific judgment, but a reflection of what society finds acceptable or repugnant" (*Behavior Today* [5 December 1988]: 5.).

Also, in a 1989 issue of *Journal of Sex Education & Therapy*, Dr. Joan A. Nelson wrote an article entitled, "Intergenerational Sexual Contact: A Continuum Model of Participants and Experience," in which she advocates a new view of child/adult sex as a positive experience. She even goes so far as to suggest that pedophilia be referred to as "visionary" rather than a perversion.

Will we someday see the "normalizing" of bestiality or child abuse—just as we have seen the normalizing of homosexual behavior? The possibility certainly exists.

A few years ago, I was asked to be on a local TV talk show

called "People Are Talking." The guest was an Episcopal priest, pastor of the oldest Episcopal church on the West Coast. His notoriety stemmed from his defense of homosexual marriages, having performed them for years in defiance of his own denominational standards. To date, the Episcopal church does not endorse such marriages, but there is a "ritual" for the blessing of same-sex unions. Father X's congregation has a high concentration of homosexuals and lesbians. Throughout the years, this priest has been known to be quite radical in his advocacy of sexual freedom. I was asked to be in the audience for balance since I am known as the local "fundamentalist" preacher. As the show progressed, Father X arrogantly rejected the biblical account of the creation of Adam and Eve, denied the literal understanding of God's original creation of one male and one female, and clearly rejected God's concept of holy matrimony as the only standard for marriage. One lady in the audience expressed her extreme dismay that a "preacher of the gospel"—as he referred to himself—could so casually reject the clear meaning of the biblical account of marriage and family. He boldly pronounced to this distraught lady that the Apostle Paul was simply wrong on the subject! A gasp rose from many in the audience over his blatancy.

My usual practice at these shows is to wait until just before the end to make my challenging remarks. Finally, the moment came for me to interject my differing opinion. I did it by way of asking a couple of questions: How would he counsel certain problem areas of sexual freedom? (He had stated earlier that, although homosexuality was fine and acceptable, incest was obviously harmful—however, not necessarily wrong.) I asked how he would counsel a father and son in a homosexual relationship? He stopped, thought, and then hesitatingly answered that he'd never run into a situation like that and didn't know quite how to answer. The show immediately came to an end at that point. Break for a commercial! It was my intention to demonstrate that if homosexuality is acceptable, then there's no reason to reject incest—except out of mere prejudice against this type of "sexual orientation."

Later, I made an appointment with Father X to discuss my point more at length. As we sat in his office, I argued the scriptural case that all sexual sins condemned in the Bible are of one piece, one context. To excerpt one sin from the list of sins is arbitrary. There's no reason to except any one particular sexual sin as opposed to another. The list of sexual sins all hang together or all fall apart. I told him frankly that his advocacy of homosexual marriage was in fact tantamount to accepting incest as permissible too! He unabashedly agreed. To him, incest was not wrong. In some cases it may be harmful, but not wrong! Wow, was I floored! This confession came from the lips of an ordained minister of a church of Jesus Christ. Ministers making confessions such as that make what Jim Bakker and Jimmy Swaggart did look like Sunday School pranks!

With ministers like Father X, why be afraid of the homosexual community on the outside? No wonder immorality is so rampant in our city! No wonder the Church has lost its potency. She has fallen for the idolatry of the times. This church—more like the "synagogue of Satan"—has succumbed to the seduction of pagan faith. I couldn't believe my ears, and I told him so. I left that office trembling inside for the impending judgment of Christ on the church in San Francisco. "Judgment must begin in the house of God . . ." (I Pet. 4:17). (It was this episcopal diocese from which the notorious Bishop Pike came thirty years ago. Bishop Pike was himself a denier of traditional values and also the doctrine of the trinity.)

Another trend is occurring among homosexual psychiatrists, which could eventually have serious repercussions on our rights to free speech. A number of these psychiatrists are seriously proposing that "homophobia"—the supposed fear of homosexuals—should be considered a mental illness and should be added to the DSM. Again, as absurd as this might sound, the 13th National Gay and Lesbian Health Conference, held in New Orleans at the Hyatt Regency in July 1991, had a workshop on this topic.

At this conference, Dr. Hilda Hildago, a professor of Public Administration and Social Work at Rutgers University, New Brunswick, N.J., held a seminar entitled, "Homophobia: a Public Health Hazard." The conference seminar described the workshop this way: "This workshop will examine heterosexism and homophobia as socially transmitted mental health diseases that affect all members of the society." Heterosexism is a gay-created term, which is used against those who think that only men and women should be sexually attracted to one another.

This trend of redefining sexual perversion to normalcy is getting even more bizarre. This same conference sponsored a workshop entitled, "Normalizing S/M: A Non-DSMIIIR Approach." The workshop was given by Arlene Istar, a staff member at Choices Counseling Associates in Schenectady, New York.

S&M, in case you're unfamiliar with the term, is sado-masochism, a practice that combines sexual behaviors, plus inflicts pain as pleasure. San Francisco has a number of S&M parlors, where men and women can actually rent torture chambers to whip, beat, and humiliate their consenting sexual partners.

Arlene Istar's workshop was designed to present S & M as a normal sexual behavior, even though the current DSMIII apparently still considers this abnormal sexual activity. According to the catalog, "[t]his workshop is an attempt to explore s/m as a normal healthy sexual identity, despite the DSMIIIR assessment of it as psychosexual disorder."

This description of the seminar from the catalog is poorly written but should give you an idea of what is seriously being proposed among homosexuals: "The role of the Lesbian community's analysis of s/m as patriarchal male domination and politically incorrect, and the Gay men's community celebration of s/m, ignoring all political analysis of their sexual behavior (before the AIDS epidemic that is), will be discussed in light of the clinical communities' complete lack of any serious discussion beyond heterophobic condemnation."

It may still be a few years before S&M is removed as a psychosexual disorder from the Diagnostic and Statistical Manual. The danger of gays and lesbians having "homophobia" defined as a mental illness should be obvious: Anyone who then opposes the gay rights movement could legitimately be considered to be suffering from a mental disorder. Businesses and schools could establish policies requiring "counseling" for those who suffer from this newly defined mental illness. As we'll see later, there is already a move to have any anti-homosexual statements considered "hate crimes" punishable by fines or imprisonment.

At the end of 1990, the San Francisco Police Department started a "hate crimes" unit. A meeting of the police chief and the unit officers was scheduled with those who were known to be victims of hate crimes. Donna and I were invited to attend. After the last attack against our family in March 1990 (which will be more fully documented later), Donna wrote a letter to Mayor Agnos documenting, in legal brief style, the crimes that have been committed against our family in the past ten years. On the basis of Romans 13, she appealed to him as God's "minister for righteousness" to protect our family. Consequently, our name was referred to Police Chief Casey, and we were included among those considered to be victims of hate crimes.

At the meeting we found ourselves seated among members of committees, and sometimes legal counsel, representing various minority community groups including: Asian, Hispanic, Gay and Lesbian, African-American, Jewish, and the handicapped. It was noteworthy that Donna and I were the only couple representing one individual family at the meeting. We were somewhat surprised that we were the only family that had personally experienced so many crimes over the years without redress or relief of any kind. And that, to date, no one had been apprehended for any of the crimes including the firebombing, continuous death threats, vandalism, graffiti, or even the latest smashing of our bedroom window with hammers in the middle of the night. What was glaring to us was that the others at the meeting represented community *groups* which were victimized, but we were the *only individual family* that has been continually victimized.

As each group asked their questions for clarification, an obvious conflict of interest began to form. Was there a conflict between the interests of the gay community and their hate crime victim status, and our interests and hate crime victim status? The dilemma arose for two reasons: 1) that a portion of the gay community, albeit a radical portion, had made their participation in crimes against us quite obvious to the public, and 2) most importantly, could the definition of a hate crime be interpreted in such a way that the mere preaching of the Bible against the homosexual lifestyle be considered a hate crime against the gay community? I worked up enough courage to ask the chief, "being Christians and knowing our stand against homosexuality, how would the Unit differentiate between what I say the Bible says about homosexuality and how the gays accuse us of perpetrating hate crimes against them by way of our message?"

The chief really had no answer. He attempted to give some response but the answer still remained nebulous to us. If the message of the Word of God is that homosexuality is sin and an abomination before the Lord, wouldn't the preaching of this message in itself constitute a crime against homosexuals? Therefore, mustn't we curtail our message in case unthinking and misguided biblicists mistake the prohibitions of Scripture for endorsements to attack gays and lesbians?

Also, it should be noted that "hate crimes" legislation can work both ways. Christians could use it against those who speak threateningly against them! As far as I am concerned, it is useless legislation—more thought-control legislation than anything. Crimes committed against anyone, gay or straight, are wrong—whatever the motive.[1]

San Francisco Supervisor Richard Hongisto proposed that an ordinance be passed requiring any civil service worker (police, fire department, etc.), who spoke against any minority, including the gay community, be demoted. The question arises: What would constitute speaking against a minority, and whose standard would be used in such determination? Several pastors went to city hall to protest this proposal. We spoke publicly at a hearing and also privately to some supervisors, voicing our moral concerns that Christians would be discriminated against because of their biblical views on homosexuality.

It's important for us to realize the power of Psalm 11:4: "If the foundations be destroyed, what can the righteous do?" Hate crimes must be rooted in the law of God as found in Scripture, or there really is no SURE foundation. We have to realize that as Christians, unless the Word of God—the commandments of God—is foundational to our society and its laws, then there is no knowing what hate means or what crime means. Hate crimes legislation does not distinguish between religious language, i.e., what the Bible teaches, and offensive harassment threats. It will be left to the courts to autonomously judge whether such language is "threatening" and therefore constitutes a crime. This could eventually prevent a pastor from preaching against homosexuality from the pulpit for fear of being fined or imprisoned.

It seems that the inmates are running the asylum. What the gay rights militants have accomplished in the psychiatric and psychological community is like something out of *Alice in Wonderland*, where everything is upside-down or backwards.

---

[1] In San Francisco, a business may fire someone for ineptitude, and that person can invoke the "hate crime" law for redress. He can claim he was fired because of homophobic motives, and, so, seek damages.

I've taken the time to give some background on how homosexuals bullied the members of the APA and how they are working to have homophobia declared a mental illness because, whether you want to or not, you will eventually have to deal with the gay rights movement. It may first appear as a "human rights ordinance" at your local city council; or it may turn up as a pro-homosexual teen counseling center at your local junior and senior high school, or, perhaps, as a safe-sex education program for your children, teaching them that homosexual sex and same-sex partnerships are just as "normal" as heterosexual marital relationships. ALL of these things are in effect in San Francisco at the present time. Regardless of how it comes to your community, you and your children will eventually be *forced* to submit to the homosexual agenda—or face legal sanctions.

If the gay rights activists can't win through the legal system or through influencing public school policies, they will use their time-honored techniques of fear, death threats, and physical violence against their opponents. These techniques are constantly used in San Francisco and wherever the gay movement wants to seize power.

A Quiet Life

When Donna and I arrived in San Francisco in 1973, we had no idea what lay ahead of us. The church I pastored had been around for a long time, but the pastors before me had not stayed more than an average of five years. In fact, the pastor before me had only stayed nine months before he was asked to leave. It was a small congregation filled with predominantly older members. We were the youngest couple in the congregation. During those early years, Donna and I did our proper churchly duties: preaching, visiting the sick and elderly, working with what youth we could muster, etc. We were following the philosophy of typical 50s evangelism: keep your Christianity within the four walls of the church. Don't let it seep outside those walls to change the world. And, heaven forbid, don't ever get involved in the political system. It's a waste of time and money.

Such was our disposition until 1978. That year we decided

to hire a new organist to play at our Sunday morning services. When we learned he was a homosexual, I asked him to step down as organist. That event changed our lives forever. We learned the hard way that we had to be involved in the world—even in the political world—especially when the politics of this world reach into the domain of the family and the Church.

THREE

This Is No Joke: You Are Sued . . .

For the last eighteen years, whenever the opportunity presents itself, Donna and I have tried to get acquainted with new pastors when they arrive in San Francisco. After some small talk, we often ask them a pointed question to see how they will react: "Are you planning on getting involved in this city, if necessary politically—either as an individual or through your church body?"

The answer they give is invariably the same, year after year: "No, that's not my calling. I'm called to the ministry, not to get involved in politics."

We then go on to explain that what's happened in San Francisco is that morality—concepts of right and wrong—has been politicized by the radical gay movement. And, furthermore, whether they want to or not, they will eventually have to get involved in some way in the political and social institutions within this city.

We make it very clear to them that if they're going to be true to the Word of God—if they're going to faithfully preach and teach their congregations how to act in this fallen world—they will inevitably find themselves clashing with secular humanism, the dominant religion of San Francisco.

We attempt to explain to them that the gays in San Francisco (as well as other enclaves of immorality) pose a far greater threat to the health and safety of the traditional family than the abortion industry. That may come as a shock, but hear me out.

The gays in San Francisco, unlike those in the abortion industry, have developed an entire culture based on their perverted sexual habits with same sex partners. They have gay teacher's organizations, Queer Scouts (a.k.a. The Boy Scouts), a Gay Men's Chorus, newspapers, restaurants, ocean cruises (publicly advertised as such at the rail and bus stops), gay political organizations, and much more. This gay-created culture has become as all encompassing as a ghetto within the larger community. You can actually drive (or walk) into the "Castro District" with gay shops and businesses abounding within an area of a few city blocks—the same as "Chinatown" or "Japantown," which are legitimate subcultures within the city limits.

Militant homosexuals view themselves as creating a new civilization in San Francisco. They're more zealous than an evangelist in spreading their gospel to other cities and towns. Queer Nation, the most violent of the gay rights groups, for example, has its own flag. (They view themselves as a separate nation, much like in the movie, "Alien Nation.")

In 1991, homosexual militants lobbied the Board of Supervisors (our city council) to declare San Francisco a "sanctuary" where homosexuals and lesbians from around the country and the world, under threat of legal persecution, could look to San Francisco as "the City of Refuge for the sexual minorities." There has also been talk of radicals lobbying the California legislature to make sure that only gays represent the gay "district"—legislative district—in San Francisco. Nothing has come of this yet, but the intent and political machinery are there.

As we try to explain these things to new pastors, there's a certain number who respond with alarm and concern. Others simply decide to "stay out of politics"—even though the whole definition of right and wrong has been politicized and relativized by homosexuals in our government and public school district.

When we came to San Francisco in 1973, we were of the "in the world but not of the world" attitude regarding political involvement, as was the majority of the Christian community. However, as the Lord would have it, we were jolted into reality in 1978 and our lives (as well as our theology) have not been the same since.

It all began when we were looking for an organist for our worship service. It was our custom to either hire or ask Christians (whether members of our congregation or not) to play the organ. A nice Asian couple in our church said they knew a fine young music student named Kevin Walker who might fill our need. Kevin and I talked about the needs of the church and the job description in the worship service. He gave me his personal testimony of faith in Christ, having grown up in a Bible believing household in Michigan. His testimony was much the same as ours. We had no reason to suspect anything odd or unusual about his Christian life or walk at that time.

That same year, March 1978, the Board of Supervisors had quietly passed the sexual orientation ordinance (now known as the "gay rights ordinance"). This ordinance essentially began with the preface: "to discriminate on the basis of sexual orientation poses a substantial threat to the health, safety, and general welfare of the City and County of San Francisco." In effect, the ordinance protects gays and lesbians from discrimination in the work place. Donna and I had paid no attention to the law and were busy doing what Christians do in the church—ministering to and fellowshipping with their own. Since then, I've had the opportunity to go back over the news clippings describing the passage of the ordinance. There were only two letters to the Board of Supervisors protesting the possible infringement upon church and state issues if the church was not exempted in the law. One of the letters was from a gay minister who pointed out this possible constitutional conflict.

As I mentioned earlier, a few years prior to hiring Kevin, Donna and I ran into an old friend from Moody Bible Institute who had moved to San Francisco and became caught up into the homosexual lifestyle and subculture. After much personal and spiritual struggle, Bruce eventually came out of the gay community, became a recommitted Christian, and industrious member of the church.

In August 1978, Bruce informed us that Kevin was gay! "Great!" I thought to myself, "this is all we need!" How do I handle this? What will be the reaction of the congregation?

I knew from Scripture what needed to be done. In obedience to Matthew 18, I privately went to Kevin's apartment in the Castro district to confront him with this rumor. He readily admitted he was a practicing homosexual, living with his lover in that apartment, and that he saw no inconsistency with his lifestyle and what the Bible said about homosexuality.

For nearly two hours we had a calm but intense discussion about the Bible and its proscriptions, which clearly forbid homosexual behavior. In response, Kevin repeated the gay theological line, which rejected the statements of the Word of God or else reinterpreted them to allow for certain kinds of homosexual acts! He still maintained that he, as a homosexual, was a born again Christian, living within the bounds of God's law.[1]

I ended the conversation by telling him we wouldn't allow him to continue as church organist if he were going to maintain his homosexuality. I did, however, extend an invitation for him to attend church. Before leaving, he handed me the church's organ music and key, and we seemed to part as friends.

When I got home, Donna told me that Kevin had just called to request that I publicly announce to the congregation that he had been fired, and why. Immediately I got suspicious! Why would he want me to expose him to public ridicule or condemnation? This didn't seem to be a matter that had to be shared with the whole congregation in the worship service. I never did announce to the congregation why Kevin was fired. On that Sunday morning, I simply told the congregation that he'd been dismissed and that if anyone wanted to know why, they could speak to me privately.

One church-attender, a retired police officer, asked me later why I'd let Kevin go. When I told him, he became frightened and warned me that I could get into serious trouble because of what I'd done. The recently passed gay rights ordinance protected individuals such as Kevin from job discrimination based on their sexual practices. I had naively "broken" the law! I was mildly concerned, but didn't think anymore would come of it. Kevin and I had been on good terms, so I had no fear of retaliation.

I was wrong. A week later, we got a phone call from a lawyer, Don Knutson, head of a newly formed gay rights law organization, the Gay Rights Advocates. Knutson briefly warned me that I had violated the city ordinance and would be taken to court. "Is this a joke?" I asked him. He replied, "I can assure you this is no joke. You'd better get a lawyer." END OF CONVERSATION. I never did speak with him again.

---

[1] Later in the lawsuit, we saw a letter that Kevin's mother wrote to him, pleading with him to drop the suit. It was remarkable that his parents, for the most part, sided with our church and against their own son. None of Kevin's family knew about his chosen lifestyle before the lawsuit, so it was a double blow: his homosexuality and suing the church. It was a moving letter of a mother's love for her son and her greater love and loyalty to Christ. During the writing of this book, we have tried to find out where and how Kevin is and also to contact his family. We have been unsuccessful in both endeavors.

After I hung up the phone, I was trembling inside and felt absolutely frantic. Fear gripped me, which I couldn't shake. I knew I had to get a lawyer and fast. We hadn't been sued yet, only warned, but I had to contact a lawyer quickly in order to prepare for the eventuality.

What in the world had I done? What terrible crime had I committed? How was my congregation going to react to the news that their pastor was being sued for firing a homosexual? When I told our elder and the congregation, a shock wave went through the church. The elder was terribly upset at what I'd done. He told me I should have found some other reason to fire the organist. He reminded me that other members of the congregation, as well as himself, owned homes and land that he feared would be jeopardized if we lost the suit. His suggestion was that since Donna and I did not own a home (we lived in the parsonage) or any other property, we should somehow absolve the church of any liability, take the lawsuit on ourselves personally, declare bankruptcy, and the church would reimburse us for any loss we incurred. "After all," he said, "you don't own anything, so you have nothing to lose." How true, and at that moment, what a blessing it was *not* to be encumbered with material possessions that might have deterred us from taking this stand! The elder had much to lose—as did the rich young ruler.

The elder's compromising attitude incensed me and made me more determined than ever to defend myself and the church from Kevin's threatened lawsuit. Not surprisingly, this attitude prevailed among a majority of the congregation. The young pastor had finally overstepped his bounds! Many had believed that I was too big for my britches anyway.

Just the threat of a lawsuit caused dissension in the congregation. It virtually turned into the young members versus the older members. Sundays became the hardest day of the week to face. The older faction of the congregation would not speak to us. Mondays became the best day of the week because it was the furthest away from Sunday! Finally, after one Sunday evening service, Jean, one of the faithful few, broke the deafening silence. She took Donna aside after the service and tried to explain the feelings of the people. She said, "we're not strong . . . people are afraid . . . we're spiritual babes . . ." What an indictment on a generation who had professed Christ all their lives! "For everyone who partakes only of milk is not accustomed to the word of righteousness, for he is a babe. But solid food is for the mature, who because of practice, have their senses trained to discern good and evil" (Heb. 5:13-14). I believe Jean understood this and thus raised the spiritual need of the congregation.

The session (the elder and I) was stalemated. I called for a meeting with a committee of the Presbytery that was specifically designed to help in dilemmas such as we were experiencing. The committee's own report was revealing about the split in the session and the congregation. One paragraph of their report read as follows: "One major concern at this point is the existence of a division within the congregation (and session) as to the propriety of the action taken in firing the organist. All agree that the man could not continue as organist while a practicing homosexual, but some feel that *he should not have been fired until some other reason could be found to let him go, thus removing the danger of a lawsuit* " (emphasis added).

In the end, the elder and members found that, by law, they could not simply excuse themselves from the suit. It should be noted, however, that no member of the congregation, including the elder, suffered any financial loss as a result of the lawsuit. And, although individual members contributed to the lawsuit, some at great sacrifice, not a penny of "church funds" was contributed for their own defense.

I believed it was time to go—the pastorate here was too much. I had removed Kevin from participating in the worship because of immoral behavior, and here I was defending my actions against my own session and congregation! As I look back on it now, I can truly thank the Lord that I hadn't first thought to take it to the session for approval, considering the spiritual condition of our church. Satan had attacked the heart of our church with fears of a lawsuit and possible bankruptcy. There's nothing like fear to paralyze your motivation for the work of the church.

By the fall of 1978, nothing had happened. But we were still unnerved by what might happen and the delay just made it worse for all of us. Unfortunately, the elder and I continued to be split over this issue. In fact, earlier that year, the elder had resigned, but the Presbytery itself overruled our division and warned us to "get over our differences" and be united.

While all of this turmoil was going on, I started to get some interesting phone calls from people who claimed they were students doing research on the Orthodox Presbyterian Church in America. It seemed odd that I should be receiving these calls at this particular time. I became convinced that these were researchers working for Knutson's law firm. They were trying to get as much intelligence information as possible on our theology and membership requirements in preparation for the pending lawsuit.

The division in our session became so serious that, by March 1979, I decided to quit and take the chapel work we had started a few years before in Marysville/Yuba City, California. I felt the spiritual difficulties in San Francisco too great to continue with the congregation. I'd already done some part time pastoring at the Marysville/Yuba City work and felt good about leaving San Francisco. In the Spring of 1979, Donna and I let it be known that we were leaving and began looking forward to moving to the quiet suburbs of Central California.

"Are You Charles McIlhenny?"

On 14 June 1979, a fellow drove up to our house next door to the church, knocked on the door and asked, "Are you Charles McIlhenny?" I told him I was, and he handed me three summonses. I was caught totally off guard. Not only was I being sued, but our church and the entire Presbytery (ten other churches in northern California) were being sued for allegedly violating the gay rights ordinance. We were given thirty days to respond or else default and lose the case.

My reaction was rather unusual. Instead of panic, I was exhilarated! I was thrilled! I ran to Donna and showed her the summons. "This is fantastic," I told her. "What an opportunity to share the gospel." I had visions of being interviewed on NBC, CBS, and in the newspapers, boldly sharing my faith and decrying the injustice that had been done to us and our church! See how far the homosexual community had gone! Now maybe people would wake up to the danger of a promiscuous society. I could see the headlines, "SMALL CHURCH PASTOR DEFENDS SELF AGAINST GAY COMMUNITY!" How naive I was!

Since the threat of a lawsuit had now become a reality, Donna and I felt a responsibility to stay with the San Francisco congregation; so we changed our plans to move away. (However, as a result of the lawsuit, more than half of the congregation left the church over the next few years.)

Now I really needed an attorney in earnest! I started calling some of my friends to see if they could recommend a good lawyer to help defend us. The lawyer I had contacted the previous year failed to return any of my repeated phone calls to him, and the thirty-day clock was running. Theologian R. J. Rushdoony recommended a man named John Whitehead. I'd never heard of Whitehead, but time was running out and so I took a gamble and called him. He was in the middle of moving his family from Ohio to Washington, D.C., where he hoped to get involved in working on religious freedom cases. He had been with a Christian legal group, but wanted to branch out on his own.

When I told John about the nature of the lawsuit, he was excited about the prospect of defending us. He immediately decided we'd go with a First Amendment defense. We would argue that our free exercise of religion had been violated by this ordinance—as indeed, it had.

We then got down to a discussion of how much I would have to pay him for his services. "How much will it cost?" I asked. "How much do you have?" he replied. "I don't have anything." "Fine," he joked. "It'll cost you as much as five hundred thousand, depending on how far we go up the appeal process." I said, "You're hired!"

The truth of the matter is that neither one of us had any money, but we agreed that we'd work those details out later. After talking to John, I went to a special meeting of our Presbytery, which had been called expressly to process my transfer to the new work in Marysville/Yuba City. By now, the news had gotten to the presbyters that we'd all been sued. I brought along a lawyer friend, John Stuebbe, to help convince the presbyters that now was the time to get an attorney for themselves and to act promptly. One presbyter at that meeting, who was a meticulous follower of Robert's Rules of Order, objected, stating that we had no business bringing up the legal matter at this special meeting. We'd have to call another meeting ten days from then to make it all "legal"—according to Roberts! I was fuming. I told them they'd better get their act together—and fast—because they only had two weeks left to respond to the summons and complaint. In very strong terms I urged them to waive the "Robert's" technicalities in the light of the urgency of the situation. I told them that it had taken me two weeks to find John Whitehead to defend me and the church. It was up to them to hire their own attorney if they didn't want John as well. Within a couple of hours and phone calls to Whitehead from the meeting, the Presbytery decided to retain Whitehead; and a committee was set up to follow the course of the suit.

In the providence of God, we couldn't have made a better choice than John Whitehead to defend us. Not only is he an excellent lawyer and a good friend, but our theological compatibility made for a good working relationship. John forged a team of lawyers to help us present the best possible defense for the Church of Jesus Christ. He laid down rigid conditions: 1) that he and he alone would direct the legal end of things, and 2) he had chosen to take the long-haul approach and build our defense on freedom of religion as framed by the First Amendment of the Constitution.

John assigned to me the job of raising money to fund the case. He called almost daily from Virginia to give me a list of people and churches to contact about the suit. The list was made up of potential donors who were interested in our case and its far-reaching implications for the rest of the church in general. Our case was unique in legal history in that, to our knowledge, it was the first time that immorality had taken on the church for fulfilling its biblical responsibility within the parameters of God's worship. The gates of hell were doing their best to break up the church from within and from without. Little did we realize in taking a minimal stand against the prevailing sin of the community how vehement the attack would be. The fact that they had taken on the Church of Jesus Christ was incredible to us. However, the consequences would be terrifying for them, whether they realized it or not. "Be not deceived, God is not mocked, whatsoever a man sows, that shall he also reap" (Gal. 6:7). "The gates of hell shall not prevail against [the Church of Jesus Christ]" (Matt. 16:18). Yes, the consequences would be terrifying.

As a result of endless lists of possible donors, Donna and I were on the phone for hours daily, trying to find people who were supportive of our plight. We didn't even own a typewriter at the time; we had no church secretary. We were it! Donna was working part-time at a Christian radio station throughout the summer to help make ends meet. I remember reviewing different form-appeal letters that various Christian organizations sent out in bulk. We decided not to commercialize or technologize our pleas for donations. The letters went out one by one.

For a couple of months, I was writing everyone I could, running back and forth from a copy business up the block, and taking care of our two youngest children when Donna was working. After telling a local pastor friend, Rev. Richard Jefferson, about our lack of office help, he recommended a young student from his church to help out. Tomigail showed up late in August to provide any help she could. She was a God-send. She took to our little ones immediately and was ready to care for them, as well as type letters and do the ever-growing duties of a church/legal secretary. Tomigail and her fiance, Mark, proved to be extremely loyal and brought us the comfort that both Donna and I really needed. To this day, no one knows the frustration of the suit itself, caring for three little children, having to learn how to run an office, and John constantly assigning us more people to phone and write. The congregation never knew all this. They expected me to keep up the normal routine of the pastorate despite the tensions of the case and the anticipation of the possible ramifications when this finally hit the secular press.

Our families proved to be super supportive. My dad was so excited about the case, right from the first ominous phone call, that he immediately offered to go to jail with me if that prospect became a reality! My father-in-law, equally excited and yet concerned for our safety, offered to either bail us out or move us all to Florida. However, we knew that we were here for the duration. We couldn't leave.

My father took our situation to his Conservative Baptist Association annual meetings and, within a few days, was able to orchestrate full denominational support and a multitude of Christians began to help finance the case. As a result of his pleas and various Christian magazine articles, checks began rolling in. By the end of July, we'd received more than three thousand dollars, and more was on the way. At its peak, we were receiving approximately ten thousand dollars per month from generous donors from all over the world. The Lord literally supplied the money from churches, individuals, and various organizations to help defend the church in San Francisco. Originally, back in 1978, the Presbytery had offered to help foot the bill, but the bill was too great even for them. Not one penny went to us personally. All donations were cataloged and receipted for the lawsuit and its expenses. The financial records were reviewed by the Presbytery, and were open to the public for scrutiny. We were concerned that there would be no impropriety regarding the donations. The thought of misappropriating funds reigned in my fears, keeping us open and aboveboard about the money. Later that year, Dennis Fullalove, an elder in our denominational church in South San Francisco, was appointed by the presbytery committee and hired by the Christian Rights Defense Fund (the title by which we were formally organized) to manage the finances. He became my assistant manager for the remainder of the lawsuit. Not only did Dennis bring relief to our responsibilities, but also great personal encouragement.

Donna and I were very much in need of personal encouragement. Along with the pressures of dissension in our congregation, raising funds for the lawsuit, the possibility of fines and/or jail, there were also those Christians who were highly critical of the stand we had taken, and who didn't shy away from letting us know.

This mindset also existed among some in our own presbytery and denomination. However, it must be said that there were those in our own congregation, in our presbytery, in our denomination, and in the Church at large, who greatly encouraged us and ministered to us at this time. (Thank you for binding our wounds and for giving a cup of water in the Lord's name.)

In July 1979, John flew to San Francisco to introduce himself to the Presbytery and the congregation, to answer their questions, and to allay their understandable fears.

In time, John and I decided that we'd go directly to churches around the country and ask them to help us. After all, our church was under attack. If other churches didn't stand with us, they'd be the next targets. If nothing else, their own self-interest should motivate them to get involved in this cause for religious freedom.

In the fall of 1979, John helped line up a number of speaking engagements in various churches throughout the country. Having already reached an agreement with my church that I would be there to preach on Sundays, arrangements were made for these speaking engagements during the week. What many in the church did not know was that I was speaking, debating, interviewing, etc., from Monday through Saturday in many states back East and up and down the West Coast. A few supportive pastors from our own denomination, Rev. Craig Rowe, Rev. Don Poundstone, Rev. John Mahaffy, Rev. Stan Sutton, Rev. George Miladin, and others, helped out tremendously by lining up speaking engagements on local radio and TV shows as well as churches and schools. Everywhere I went I brought along a slide show, voluminous notes, and a scrapbook of photos showing what had happened in San Francisco and to us as a result of the gay rights ordinance. I warned them that this was going to happen to them if they didn't wake up.

After an extensive speaking tour, I stayed for a week at John's home in Manassas, Virginia, where he coached me on constitutional law; and I instructed him in reformed theology and presbyterian church government. We spent hours at a stretch going over questions and legal points as John prepared to take the lengthy deposition of Kevin Walker. John was meticulous in his work. We also went over my own testimony. We wrote and rewrote it until it was cleanly crafted. Kevin's attorneys did not depose me. Instead they served me with interrogatories—a set of questions to answer. This gave us a wonderful opportunity to clearly present biblical and rational reasons why we had to dismiss Kevin.

The Day Approaches

In September 1980, John deposed Kevin Walker on his religious and political views. The following are portions of that deposition, which show how reprobate a man's mind can become when in rebellion against God and His law:

John Whitehead: What does the phrase "sexual orientation" mean?

Kevin Walker: Sexual orientation is simply one's—well, to be objective, it's just one's object of sexual attractive [sic]—in other words, what one is attracted to, sexually. That's what I would take it to mean sexual orientation.

Whitehead: Does that apply with sex with minors?

Walker: Excuse me?

Whitehead: Does that apply to sex with minors?

Walker: If one is attracted to a minor I suppose it could be, yes, applied to a minor.

Whitehead: Could it mean sex with animals?

Walker: Sexual orientation could, yes, sir.

As the deposition continued, John asks him to describe his feelings about a law that forces a church to hire someone it believes to be a practicing and unrepentant sinner. Kevin seems to be unable or unwilling to give a coherent answer:

Whitehead: If this ordinance applies to the church, would it force the church to end up hiring someone it considers a sinner?

Walker: I can answer. Yes, if the church holds that to be— homosexuality to be sinful in nature and the law requires that a person applying for a job be granted that job, provided they are qualified, then I supposed they would be forced to hire someone that they consider to be a sinner. Although legally . . .

Whitehead: I am just asking you what the church believes.

Walker: The church believes? I'm sorry. I have confused— you asked.

Whitehead: I think you have answered it. The ordinance applies to the employment practices of the church. This ordinance will make the church employ somebody it considers to be a sinner to play the organ.

Walker: It doesn't require them to hire somebody who is a sinner.

Whitehead: Again, the ordinance we are talking about it— talking about sexual orientation, which includes homosexuals.

Walker: I feel they are tying it to being a sinner.

Later in the deposition, John attempted to have Kevin clarify his position.

Whitehead: If this ordinance is standing behind the person applying, he said, 'Hey, I'm a homosexual, and I want to be the organist and part of the worship team, worship service,' will it [the ordinance] not force them to hire this person they consider to be a sinner?

Walker: I would think so.

A few minutes later, John asked Kevin point blank: "The fact is, in this case, to obey the ordinance means that the church must violate a fundamental tenet of their religious beliefs; isn't that true?" To which Walker replied, "I would—yes, it's true."

Without knowing it, Kevin Walker had said things that would eventually lead to his defeat. He had given John many good reasons why the case should be thrown out of court. The ordinance was clearly discriminatory against freedom of religious expression and was unconstitutional on its face as applied to the church.

As January 1980 approached, we were still waiting for a court date and trying, as much as possible, to stay out of the press. However, the media eventually did pick up on the story, but the angle was slightly skewed from what I had naively imagined. The headlines of the San Francisco Chronicle read: "Gay Man Defends Himself Against Firing . . ." The scenario, repeated continually in the press, was that of a struggling gay musician who was being persecuted by a rigid fundamentalist pastor. I was the "bad guy," the bigot, and meanly intolerant of the "sexual diversity" within our liberal city. I could see that an ungodly press would not give any benefit to the Christian Church! After all, what did I expect! This was San Francisco—not the Kingdom of God!

The story not only hit the front page of the Chronicle, but also local radio and TV stations. I can remember getting a call at six o'clock in the morning from KGO radio news reporter, Jim Dunbar, who wanted to know why we were even defending ourselves.

The interview went very well, in spite of my justifiable fear of being misquoted and smeared by a hostile press. Jim Dunbar finally asked me, "Don't you think you're rather old-fashioned, hanging on to this kind of ethic?" To which I answered, without hesitation, "Oh, yes, I think so. I think this biblical ethic goes back thousands of years. I think it's the only ethic that will ever last. It's eternal. We don't need another ethical standard. It's not going to do us any good. In fact, we don't even know where a new ethic would lead us."

The media attention stirred up a spiteful homosexual population in San Francisco. As a result of the news articles and radio interviews, we received obscene phone calls, dozens of threatening letters, pornographic materials mailed to us, and death-threats, some of which described the children in detail— their names, ages, what they looked like, where they attended school, and what sexually deviant acts were going to be performed on them before they killed the children. More than once we had to leave the city for safety.

God Deliver Us

As our March 1980 court date approached, John Whitehead and his team of attorneys, Susan Paulus and Tom Neuberger, were working feverishly to investigate the background of the judge who was to preside over the case. We needed to know as much about him as possible in order to properly frame our arguments. Rumor had it that our judge was more than slightly sympathetic to the gay rights movement—but this was more scuttle-butt than hard fact.

The day before our hearing, John and I went down to the judge's chambers to sit in on some other hearings and observe him in action. What we found, much to our surprise, was that the judge had abruptly gone on vacation! After weeks of preparation for a hearing before this particular judge, overnight, we were to plead our case before a different judge! The switch actually turned out to be advantageous. We subsequently learned that the new judge was known as a conservative Roman Catholic who possibly shared, or would at least be sympathetic to, our biblical principles.

On the Friday evening prior to our scheduled court appearance, we held a special service to ask God for His protection and guidance. Our tiny church was packed beyond our wildest dreams with supporters coming from all over. We had to outfit the place with several closed-circuit TVs to accommodate all the people.

We asked Dr. Jay Adams, a professor from Westminster Theological Seminary in Escondido, California, to give the message. Dr. Adams didn't hesitate one moment. From the beginning he had been an ardent supporter, and remained a good friend throughout.[2] At the meeting, Dr. Adams gave a challenging message to approximately four hundred people about how

---

[2] Dr. Francis Schaeffer, whom I never did get to meet, also unhesitatingly endorsed our cause and wrote repeatedly in support of us, even including us in one of his books, A Christian Manifesto.

important it was for Christians to stand up for biblical rights
and the rights of the church. His words were so inspiring that
we turned his sermon into a pamphlet and widely distributed it.

The hearing was set for 18 March 1980 at nine o'clock in
the morning. The courtroom was packed with homosexual
activists, Christians, and reporters. In fact, the room was so
packed that there was no place for Donna to sit; and a Christian
friend gave up his seat so she could hear the proceedings! T.V.
cameras were in the hallway outside the courtroom along with
many more Christians, some of whom were on their knees
praying during the entire hearing. When Kevin got off the
elevator, he was visibly shocked to see all the commotion.
There was no place for him to sit either; so another Christian
gave up his seat; and I ushered Kevin into the courtroom.
Before the hearing began, John, Susan, Tom, and I prayed in
the back corner of the courtroom. Attorney Mary Dunlap (who
has since become prominent in gay & lesbian politics in the
city) stood up and argued her case for fifteen minutes. John
then argued our side for fifteen minutes. It was over that fast.
Now all we could do was go home and wait for the judge's
ruling.

Before John left San Francisco that day, we discussed just
what to expect next. If we lost this judgment, we would go to
trial. This is what we expected. Whether we won or lost at trial,
John was sure that either side would appeal. We all assumed
that this case would go on for a long, long time—to higher and
higher courts—making for everyone greater and greater reputa-
tions! ("The plans of a man are in his mind, but it is the
purposes of God which will be fulfilled" [Prov. 19:21]. God had
other plans!)

The judge didn't waste time in reaching his decision. On 3
April 1980 (Good Friday) I received a phone call from a newsman asking me for a response to the judge's ruling in our favor.
That was the first I'd heard anything about the decision. Of
course we were thrilled! We'd actually won it by arguing our
protection under the First Amendment's free exercise of religion clause. We were also shocked that we had won a case of
this kind in San Francisco! In his ruling, the judge stated in
pertinent part:

The framers of the United States Constitution and the Bill of
Rights wrote the Free Exercise Clause to protect religious
beliefs that may not be followed by the majority, to allow
every person to obey his own conscience without interfer-
ence from the government.

Freedom of religion is so fundamental to American history
that it must be preserved even at the expense of other rights
which have become institutionalized by the democratic process. Whenever a court is asked to balance the right of one
individual against a conflicting right of another, it is a serious and difficult task. The United States Constitution and
the cases interpreting it make that less difficult in this case.

Defendant's motion for summary judgment is granted.

We'd won!

The Price of Victory

Our court victory had not been cheap. Although we were
vindicated, we had spent one hundred thousand dollars on this
case and nearly two years of time and effort. We counter-sued
to recover some of our costs. We eventually received seven
hundred dollars from the other side. Kevin, of course, had no
money—but he had received thousands of dollars worth of legal
help from the gay attorneys' association.

Kevin Walker and his gay rights attorneys filed an appeal to
a higher court, just as John had predicted. Now, we were back
on track and in the fight again! We were in this for the long
haul! Then—for some unexplained reason—they dropped their
appeal!

After all those months of preparation, speaking engagements, fund-raising events, stressful phone interviews, hate mail,
and long strategy sessions, it was all over. Just like that . . . we
had worked so hard for this victory! Now there would be no
legal precedent set! What, then, could be the significance of
this case?

The case was significant for several reasons: First, never
before had the homosexual movement directly attacked the
fundamental rights of a church. It is also significant that a city
government should pass a law (promoting immorality) that
failed to specifically exempt religious organizations.

The case was significant for John Whitehead, because it

provided him with invaluable experience in arguing First Amendment cases—and it helped to nudge him closer to founding The Rutherford Institute, one of the most effective, aggressive religious freedom organizations in the country. Since John defended us, his team of Rutherford Institute attorneys have fought similar battles all over the United States.

Most of all, the case was significant for us, because the Lord taught us a hard but wonderful lesson: in all things He, and He alone, will get the glory. He brought the lawsuit; He provided the funds; He made us able; and He won the victory in a way so totally unexpected by either side that no one but the Lord could claim the victory. We learned that God will get the glory—our responsibility is to give it.

> O give thanks to the Lord. . . . Make known His deeds among the peoples. Speak of all His wonders. Glory in His holy name; . . . Remember His wonderful deeds which He has done, . . . His marvels and the judgments from His mouth. Ascribe to the Lord the Glory due His name. (I Chron. 16, NASV)

This Lesson Prepared Us for the Years to Come

And what of Donald Knutson and the Gay Rights Advocates? Although no direct "cause and effect" result may legitimately be implied, it must be said that the words of Scripture remain true and God will not be mocked in His promises: "the gates of hell shall not prevail against [the Church of Jesus Christ]." In 1990, Donald Knutson died of AIDS. In 1991, the San Francisco and Los Angeles offices of the National Gay Rights Advocates closed as a result of bickering and in-fighting.

"It is a dreadful thing to fall into the hands of the living God" (Heb. 10:31, NIV).

We Won a Battle, Not the War

We were thrilled that we'd won, but we realized it was a small victory in what was going to be a very long war for control of our culture. Two diametrically opposed religions had clashed in the courtroom: secular humanism, the religion of our dominant American culture, and orthodox Christianity.

One or the other will eventually win. In light of God's

Word, we believe that it will be Christianity that will eventually win the world for Christ. I don't believe there is any compromise possible in this war. The gay rights movement is militantly intolerant of the Christian faith. Faith is totalitarian—it encompasses a whole world and life view. The "religion" of homosexuality clashes squarely and directly with the Scriptures of the Old and New Testament. One cannot hold sincerely to the teaching of the Word of God and to the faith of homosexuality even in principle—let alone in practice. As a lifestyle, homosexuality represents a holistic culture under the dominion of man in rebellion against God.

To speak of the faith-motive of homosexuality is not to say that one necessarily practices these unnatural sex acts as such, but it is to agree with the deep-rooted religious commitment to the so-called autonomy of the natural man. To agree with the homosexual lifestyle is to completely challenge the biblical definition of man, the family (the basic biological unit of human existence), marriage, children, parenthood, etc. The religion of homosexuality challenges the fundamental structure of morality, the nature of the Word of God, and civilization in general.

The gay rights movement argues "live and let live"; yet, because it is a holistic life and world view, it refuses such equality to those Christians who traditionally and convictionally believe and live by the Scriptures. Gays will agree to no compromise or peaceful coexistence unless Bible-believers keep the light of the gospel to themselves. A homosexual-dominated society cannot tolerate "archaic or old-fashioned" values. The enlightened society must establish its own morality, despite the disease-ridden course of its end.

We believe that the homosexual rights movement is God's judgment upon a fearful and ineffective Church which has not taken an active role in our society. It is our deserved chastisement for failing to minister to those suffering in this sin and failing to take seriously the needs of those individuals struggling in sexual sins.

Homosexuals have been the butt of jokes and humiliation for so long that Christians have failed to realize the seriousness of their personal and public rights as human beings. God created human rights. We stand for human rights, whether a person is a homosexual, adulterer, or whatever type of sinner he may be. Nobody escapes the indictment of the Word of

God, yet everybody under God's creation is divinely accorded respect and decency despite their sinful deviance: gay or straight. "[F]or all have sinned and fall short of the glory of God" (Rom. 3:23, NIV). Nobody is exempt from the scrutiny of God's Word. Nor, for that matter, is anyone exempt from the equal promise of eternal life for all who repent and believe the gospel. All men are created in the image of God and for that reason have divine rights protected by God Himself—that includes the homosexual. The Christian community, in all its spheres, ought to be the first to protect the human rights of homosexuals and lesbians. We ought to be at the forefront of defending them against unjust and iniquitous deeds, whether it's called gay-bashing or "sexual [unsafe sexual] orientation" ordinances. Only then will the Church be effective in ministering to the needy. The true Church brings healing through the gospel, which is not a pleasant "operation" to those who need radical spiritual surgery.

I don't credit the gay community for all of their political success. I blame the church for not standing for and maintaining the biblical message of morality in Christ. I blame the church for the moral depravity in this land, because pastors (including myself) and para-church leaders have too often failed to speak out against immorality in the public sector.

In our case, a victory was won against the gay rights movement in 1980, but our exhilaration was to be short-lived. It's as if the Lord said, "I'm not done chipping away those rough edges yet . . ." The gays were certainly not pleased and definitely were not done with us. We were to pay a price for our stand!

FOUR

Getting Hit From Both Sides

During those tempestuous years of the lawsuit, another conflict began to evolve. We naively thought that all Bible-believing Christians would support our stand, maybe not financially, but at least spiritually. We were to find that this would not be the case. This, perhaps, became our greatest grief. The split that we had experienced in our own congregation began to emerge in a much broader sense in the Christian community at large.

In the Spring of 1980, my presbytery allowed me to visit various other presbyteries up and down the West Coast to tell our story and to ask for financial support. It was a challenging experience for me, because I often found myself confronted by reformed pastors regarding the lawsuit and my public stand against homosexuality. A number of them engaged in heated debates over "my right" to fire Kevin because of his homosexuality. On one occasion, I remember being challenged by the question: "What distinction do you make between someone who is constitutionally homosexual, but who doesn't practice it, and someone who practices homosexual behavior?" My reply was that the Bible doesn't make a distinction between one who is a homosexual and one who engages in homosexual acts. It does, however, specifically condemn all sexual deviation from God's infallible standard. I certainly believe that a person who is struggling against homosexual tendencies and temptations is not necessarily engaging in sin. The Scriptures do not call one a murderer or thief or fornicator because he or she struggles with such temptations; we all have temptations, but it's when we give in to them in thought as well as deed that we're guilty of sin. It is the practice of homosexual behavior, whether in the private recesses of the heart or outwardly, that is forbidden in the Word of God. The Bible does not divorce the act from the sin. It does not refer to a person being homosexual apart from that person committing the act.

Another presbytery in our own denomination was split over whether they should support us ecclesiastically (not financially) or not. At their meeting, we were asked to give a presentation on the lawsuit, its ramifications, costs, and effect on our family. After both Donna and I spoke, several motions were offered, one in particular questioned whether, on the merits of the case, the presbytery should support the lawsuit. A lively debate ensued. When the smoke cleared, we found that we'd won their support on that motion by one vote (12 to 13): it was a shallow victory.

When I first went to visit these pastors and elders, I had naively assumed they would welcome me with open arms and gladly help with the financial burden. I was wrong. It galled me to think I had to defend my position on homosexuality among brethren of like-theology, and that many of those in the reformed tradition were hostile toward me. I felt as though I was being betrayed by those who should have been the most supportive of me. Donna and I were getting emotionally beaten up, not only by the gays, but by our friends.

In July, I was privileged to speak at the Reformed Presbyterian Synod, a gathering of more than four hundred church leaders, in Seattle, Washington. Their reception was very warm, and as a body, they agreed to join us in a "friend-of-the-court" brief on our behalf, if we should need such assistance. However, when an officer of the Synod originally called me to set up the speaking engagement, he made it quite clear that personally he did not agree with our legal defense. While he agreed that the organist should have been fired, he felt that a First Amendment defense was, not only "stupid," but wrong. However, he offered no alternative.

There were those who believed that homosexuality was a sin, but *separation of church and state* precluded us from defending ourselves over the issue. In other words, if in good conscience we could not reinstate the organist, which was one of the demands in his complaint, we should plead guilty, pay the fine, and/or go to jail. There were those of the opinion that since the organist claimed to be a Christian, this was a dispute between two "brothers," and the secular court should not enter into it. Therefore, we should settle the matter on a church level. (The fact that Kevin sued us did not seem to make much difference.) There were those who didn't even get to the issue at hand. They simply criticized us for living in San Francisco at all, seeing it was such a reprobate place. One such note came from a well- known Christian author who castigated us in such a crude manner that it deeply distressed Donna, and remains in her memory as one of the saddest moments over those years.

It was not the criticism that was so difficult to take. If a Christian perceives another brother to be in the wrong, it is that Christian's loving responsibility to bring it to his brother's attention. Disagreement among the brethren was not the problem. The hurt came with the manner in which criticisms were expressed. In these situations, the concern was more for "theological correctness" than giving the cup of cold water in the Lord's name. There was a lack of any expression of care for our welfare: spiritual or physical. "Go thy way . . . be warmed and filled. . . ." It was indeed a hostility that we had not expected and which caused profound discouragement.

In all fairness, I must say that we did receive a good deal of help from a handful of pastors. As was mentioned before, Dr. Jay Adams was one of our first supporters. In fact, he was the first to contribute to the Christian Rights Defense Fund and continued throughout to be an ardent supporter and friend. Many other pastors and friends encouraged us: Roger Wagner, Dick Miller, Carl Erickson and his family (who have continued to "bind our wounds" over the years), and many more. We are forever grateful to those faithful men and women who stood by us and prayed for us, and for the hundreds of Christians all over the world who wrote letters of encouragement and who helped us pay off the debt.

My reception before Baptists, independent Bible congregations, and charismatics was totally different from the treatment I received in reformed circles. I was overwhelmed by the nearly instantaneous support I received among these church groups. One of the pastors who was the most supportive was John MacArthur. During 1980, I received an invitation to speak at his church in southern California. At a normal Wednesday night prayer meeting, I gave a brief fifteen minute testimony before about a thousand listeners. When the offering was taken, I was shocked to find his church had given about five thousand dollars. It was overwhelming to me to see such a positive response. On another occasion, Donna and I spoke at Tim LaHaye's Scott Memorial Baptist Church in San Diego. They were very gracious and wholeheartedly supported our stand.

As time passed, we came to find that "theological correctness" was not the only reason for part of the Christian community to oppose us. Mere association with us brought fear to some.

At the time we were served with the summons and complaint and the lawsuit became a reality, Donna was working part-time as secretary and receptionist for one of the local Christian radio stations. When she told the station manager that the lawsuit was no longer a threat but was indeed a reality, he immediately expressed concern. I had voluntarily been doing a couple of regular radio programs at the station for a few years—quite a while before firing Kevin. The programs I did had nothing to do with the subject of homosexuality; however, his concern was that the notoriety I might receive as a result of the case would focus unwanted attention on the station. They were afraid that if I were kept on the air, the gay community might find out and either cause legal trouble for the station or, using FCC rules, demand equal time for their religious opinions.

That very same day, a phone call came from the owner of the station to the manager. Donna connected the call. Within just a few minutes, the station manager came out and in a very nervous way told Donna that I was to be taken off the air immediately. He attempted to explain their reasons. Among the myriad excuses given, one stood out as the real impetus: they were afraid that if they kept me on the air, they could be in danger of losing a 25 million dollar organization. ". . .And, if the station is closed down, we would have no witness here in San Francisco." This certainly was a message to the gay community, one they love to hear, but not one that will bring them to Christ.

That was a very difficult situation to deal with. We were fearing the unknown of what lay ahead with the lawsuit and the gay community, how to hold the church together, how to pay for everything . . . but to find that "guilt by association" with us was the thing that some Christians feared the most was difficult indeed. In all good conscience, Donna could not remain at the station, and she quit her job.

"The fear of man brings a snare . . ." (Prov. 29:25, NASV).

Shortly after having been taken off the air, we received a letter from Dr. Joel Nederhood of "The Back To God Hour." Enclosed was a transcript, in tract form, of a program he had recorded called "The Normal Church," which was scheduled to be aired on Christian stations across the country. "The Back To God Hour" was and is a regularly scheduled program on this station. Dr. Nederhood was extremely supportive and, in his program, eloquently presented that our actions in dealing with the homosexual organist was the way the "normal church" should act when confronted by such obvious sin. He also graciously provided an unlimited supply of the tract to distribute when we spoke in various places to raise money.

Donna knew that the station's policy was to make every effort to preview all programs scheduled to go on the air. We fully expected that for one reason or another, "The Normal Church" would not be aired in San Francisco. However, in God's providence, the tape was not previewed and was aired as scheduled. It was strange to listen to that program on the station that had just taken a stand so diametrically opposed to us and to the point of view of the program.

At this same time, our first child, Erin, was ready to start school. Donna had been scrutinizing several "Christian" schools in San Francisco. Of all the Christian schools she investigated, there was only one that believed in a biblically-based, thoroughly Christian approach to education. That school was San Francisco Christian (SFC). She immediately signed Erin up for SFC.

The following Sunday, a member of our church (who himself had formerly lived the gay lifestyle) informed Donna that he knew one of the teachers at SFC. Our member claimed that during his time in the gay community he had known the teacher, and that the teacher was or had been a homosexual. Donna's reaction was at the same time skeptical and frustrated. It seemed that the topic of homosexuality followed us wherever we went and touched every area of our lives.

Donna called the school administrator, Mr. Jack McBirney. She explained to him that while not wanting to falsely accuse anyone, she had to bring the accusation to their attention. It was clear, especially in our immediate situation, that we could not send Erin to SFC if these accusations were true. Mr. McBirney, in a characteristic graciousness that we came to know so well over the years, promised to investigate. Over the next couple of months, he and the school board had several meetings with the teacher and with our church member. Based upon the testimony of both men, and after much prayer and counselling with the teacher, the board felt it necessary to ask the teacher not to continue at the school in his present spiritual state.

No one was happy about the situation. It was a painful process to go through—for everyone. It also put the school in a very dangerous legal situation. If we, as a church, could be sued for firing our organist, based on the city's sexual orientation ordinance, how much greater jeopardy could a school be in if sued over the same type of issue. Mr. McBirney had started the school himself and had maintained it over the years as both a ministry and a labor of love. When Donna asked Mr. McBirney if he realized the precarious legal position the school might be in by taking this action, his quiet but confident reply was "if there's an enemy in the camp, the Lord will not bless." SFC didn't stop to count the cost.

"In quietness and in confidence shall be thy strength" (Is. 30:15, KJV).

It was both amazing and encouraging to us that a tiny Christian school had enough confidence in the Lord and obedience to His Word to take such a painful action, while a multi-million dollar radio station was so concerned about the mere possibility of "trouble" that they were afraid to be publicly associated with us. To date, both organizations are still in full operation. The radio station suffered no "trouble," and the school experienced no legal repercussions. The school continues a faithful witness; the station continues a witness that includes as its official policy no public or private involvement of any kind, with political issues such as abortion or homosexuality.

However, in San Francisco, a policy of political non-involvement does not and cannot relieve a Christian, Christian organization, or church of taking a political stand. Because the politics of San Francisco are most predominantly controlled by the religion of homosexuality—or more fundamentally the religion of humanism—so, politics become religious. Thus, religion, by default, becomes political. Case in point: Under FCC rules, the radio station has a responsibility to meet the need of the community it serves. This includes putting regular public service announcements on the air. Presently, this station is airing a public service announcement that encourages parents to support the San Francisco public schools. The dilemma: 1) Last year a counselling program was officially put into effect in the San Francisco public schools for "self-identified" lesbian and gay teen-agers. The counsellors are exclusively gay and lesbian adults; 2) with the approval of the School Board, condoms are freely distributed in all the public high schools; 3) "safe sex" (AIDS) classes are being taught, which present homosexuality as a viable alternative lifestyle and give actual instructions on how to have "safe" homosexual sex, and 4) the Boy Scouts of America were officially banned from the San Francisco public school system because of their stand against homosexuality.

In San Francisco, any community organization that not only condones but advocates such programs for teen-agers, makes a political and religious statement. And, any public service announcement aired on a Christian radio station in support of that community organization is also a political and religious statement: is it a statement for Christ or against Christ? There is no neutral ground here.

Many Christians have blithely accepted the secular notion of separation of church and state, i.e., the state sets the boundaries of the church. Consequently, we have thrown out God's infallible standard of separation of church and state—the Bible. God sets the boundaries in all of His creation: sacred or secular. One need only read Romans 13 to recognize God's authority over the civil magistrate. Be he Christian or non-Christian, he is called a "minister of God for righteousness."

The Christian (individual, church, or organization) has been called to "always [be] ready to make a defense to every one who asks you to give an account for the HOPE that is in you . . ." (I Pet. 3:15). The consequences of that answer may be terrifying, but the blessings are far greater.

Why write about these situations? Why not "let sleeping dogs lie"? Donna and I have agonized over this question. We still have contact with most of these brethren mentioned above. Why, then, fan the flames? The reason is not to point a finger at any individual or organization. If that were the case, we would have to point a finger directly in our own faces. The Lord woke us up to our own apathy and selfish ease of comfort by thrusting us into a "no turning back" situation and then causing us to stand. It was of God's doing—all of His grace—never of our own strength.

The incidents described above only bring to light the apathy, arrogance, and fear that exists in the Christian community, which dilutes, and sometimes quenches altogether, the gospel message. First, we are so arrogant in our own "personal relationships" to Jesus and in our "biblical correctness" (as if we've merited the first and accomplished the second by our own effort) that we are apathetic to those in society around us who are desperately in need of Christ. Even those involved in Christian political issues are often more interested in preserving a moralistic "way of life" than imparting the message of eternal life to the lost. Second, we are so afraid of losing our comforts and wealth that we shrink back from owning up to Christ when the opportunity presents itself. Philippians 1:29 tells Christians that "[they] have been granted for Christ's sake, not only to believe in Him, but also to suffer for His sake. . . ." I don't mind the privilege of believing, but I'm not so sure I'm interested in the privilege of suffering for Christ's sake!

Sometimes, by His grace, God "paints us into a corner," and though our desire is to run, He makes us stand. So, it was for Esther . . . so it was for Daniel. Donna and I remember and were profoundly affected by the martyrdom of the five missionaries by the Auca Indians in Equador during the 1950s (*Through Gates of Splendor*, by Elizabeth Elliott). Those men not only lived for Christ, but were willing to die for Him as well. We only need to read *Fox's Book of Martyrs* to see how the saints have suffered for Christ's sake over the centuries to hang our heads in shame for the very little we have endured for the Lord. We need to remember Christians such as these, and ask ourselves, what is our calling in Christ?

"Am I a soldier of the cross, a follower of the Lamb, and shall I fear to own his cause, or blush to speak his Name?

"Must I be carried to the skies on flow'ry beds of ease, While others fought to win the prize, and sailed through bloody seas?

"Are there no foes for me to face? Must I not stem the flood? Is this vile world a friend of grace, to help me on to God?

"Sure I must fight if I would reign: Increase my courage, Lord; I'll bear the toil, endure the pain, supported by thy Word.

"Thy saints, in all this glorious war, shall conquer, though they die; they view the triumph from afar, and seize it with their eye.

"When that illustrious day shall rise, and all thine armies shine in robes of vict'ry through the skies, the glory shall be thine."

Isaac Watts.

Getting Hit from Both Sides

In our feeble attempt to maintain unity in our congregation, we had earlier instituted a series of prayer meetings where we'd meet every night for one week each month in someone's home just to pray together. Whatever else we needed, we certainly needed prayer. Nothing unites and comforts God's people more than praying together. These meetings helped to restore the needed unity, but one of our biggest foes remained a prominent member! He steadfastly refused to meet at these prayer meetings.

Our family continued to be terrorized daily by death threats over the phone and through the mail. Preaching each Sunday was a nerve wracking experience for both Donna and me. When new people attended the service, there was always the question in our minds: were they visitors or protesters? If Donna could not identify everyone in the congregation during a service, she was constantly on edge, wondering whether someone was going to pull out a gun and follow through with their threats to kill me. After all, just the year before, a member of the board of supervisors had shot and killed the mayor and a homosexual supervisor at city hall; and the People's Temple/ Jonestown massacre had occurred. (People's Temple was homebased in San Francisco just a short distance from our church.) San Francisco seemed to be identified not only by sexual immorality but also by violence.

A number of suspicious characters began to come to our services during this time. Two men showed up one Sunday morning. One was neatly dressed in a suit, while the other was in "leathers"—a well-known identification with the homosexual community. They made themselves quite obvious to the congregation by sitting down in the very front of the church. Not knowing their intentions, nor wishing to cause a stir, I ignored them as best I could. It was communion Sunday, which presented another dilemma. Should we dispense with the Lord's Supper for that Sunday? Would they take the communion? If the elder and I refused them, would they disrupt the service entirely or even become violent? Not wanting to turn the worship into a spectacle, we simply warned the congregation what it meant to "partake worthily" and left the decision whether to eat and drink between them and the Lord. As the elements were passed, the well-dressed gentleman did partake; the "leather" man did not.

As was my custom at the end of each service, I stood at the door and greeted the parishioners as they left. The two men made a beeline for me. Neither one would shake hands with me. However, one spoke up and said that they just came to see a real-live, anti-gay minister in action! Then, I knew their intentions for sure.

Sometimes, protesters would come into the service dressed in "punk"-style garb, with hair that was either dyed garish colors, spiked, half shaved off, or shaved off altogether. Others came in "drag"—men in dresses with make-up on their faces. (Considering what is condoned in public here, by this city's standards, it could be said that an element of conservatism was present in these protesters in that they were clothed at all!) Sometimes, they sat quietly and wrote protestations and obscenities in our psalters and pew Bibles. Other times they would stand up, walk around, slam windows, and/or verbally protest while I was speaking. It was difficult to preach, knowing angry protesters were in the audience. I had mixed emotions about their being in the service. I was anxious because I was never sure what they might do in the midst of my preaching. They were disruptive, abusive, and terrorizing. Would they rush the podium and assault me? Would they provoke a fight as they had been known to do? I never knew. On the other hand, I was reminded that we were in San Francisco for precisely that reason—to give the message of the gospel to a lost and dying society. How could I object? This was my calling and the church's calling before the Lord. It has always been my desire that something I might say would bring them to a saving knowledge of Jesus Christ. We continue to pray that perhaps one out of all those who have attacked us and protested against us over the years might come to know Jesus as Lord and Savior.

As I look back on those days, I realize that I was a bit arrogant about the whole situation. Maybe it was a John Wayne movie type of mentality, but I didn't worry that much about being assassinated. I didn't realize how much danger I was really in. I've been taught some humbling lessons in the years since. Today, I'm far more apprehensive because I know the enemy means business. Still, the messenger for Christ is not above the "destiny" of his Lord in being put to death for testifying to the gospel. God doesn't promise to keep us alive— He promises us eternal life. That is not heroic—that is God's grace.

By the fall of 1980, my travelling schedule was wearing thin for all of us. My prolonged absences from home were increasingly difficult for the family. Because of the constant harassment we were experiencing, Donna was understandably afraid for the safety of all of us—especially the children. Fortunately, whenever I was gone, one of the young men from the church would graciously stay with my family for their comfort and protection.

Even though I was receiving dozens of invitations to come and speak at churches around the country, I finally decided to refuse all future engagements for the sake of the family and my ministry.

Called to Testify

By this time, I had become the officially designated resident "homophobe" of San Francisco. I continually received calls from newspaper, radio, and TV reporters wanting comments on gay rights activity in the city. It wasn't a position I wanted to be in, but when called upon, I tried to present a credible, biblically-based opposition to the homosexual movement.

In September 1980, I received a phone call from an attorney in Washington, D.C., representing the minority (Republican) side of the House of Representatives' Committee on Labor Relations. He informed me that the Subcommittee on Employment Opportunities of the Committee on Education and Labor was planning to hold a hearing on H.R. 2074, the subject of which was: "TO PROHIBIT DISCRIMINATION ON THE BASIS OF AFFECTIONAL OR SEXUAL ORIENTATION,

AND FOR OTHER PURPOSES." It was, in effect, the same "sexual orientation" law under which we had been sued, only on a federal level. The proposal was to add sexual rights, which meant gay rights, to the already-existing Civil Rights Act. Homosexuals would be added as a legitimately protected minority. The hearing was scheduled for 10 October 1980 in San Francisco.

The attorney wanted to know if I could recommend someone to testify against the gay rights proposal. I called a few friends, one of whom was R. J. Rushdoony. He wasn't available, but suggested I testify. To help me compile a detailed report on gay rights, he put me in touch with Garret Buddhing, a fine Christian attorney based in Sacramento.

Garret and I spent weeks going over the economic, social, medical, and biblical reasons why homosexuals should not be accorded minority status under the current Civil Rights Act. After dozens of hours of research, writing, and briefings, we completed a lengthy report to present to the committee.

The hearing was held in the state building, downtown San Francisco. What better place for such a momentous (and unadvertised) hearing, which would radically alter the fundamental idea of legitimate civil rights! My mom and dad flew up from Long Beach to give us moral support. Donna, who was now teaching at the Christian school, decided to bring her class to the hearing.

There were eight witnesses testifying in favor of the bill. Among these were California assemblyman Art Agnos, who ten years later became a one-term mayor of San Francisco; Dr. Judd Marmor, a key sympathizer to the gay agenda at the meetings of the American Psychiatric Association; and Cecil Williams, the ultra-liberal pastor of Glide Memorial Methodist Church in San Francisco. Mr. Williams was apparently chosen to balance my "fundamentalistic" opposition to the amendment.

I was the only one to give testimony in opposition to the proposed gay rights amendment. As I rose to speak, I was literally shaking. It was frightening to be before a panel of congressmen, most of whom were pro-gay, and all of whom were very hostile toward me. Looking back on it, I don't think I gave a very good presentation, but at least there was some token opposition to the proposal. (". . . it pleased God by the foolishness of the preaching to save them that believe.") (I Cor. 1:21)

I read just a portion of my report and then was subjected to a torrent of mocking comments, laughter, ridicule, and insults from members of the committee. Never before had I been subjected to such public humiliation as I was at that hearing. The treatment I received was so demeaning that a staff attorney for the Democrats came to me afterward and apologized for the congressmen's obnoxious and unprofessional behavior. I was even approached by a representative of the National Gay Task Force who, although he didn't come right out and apologize to me, was clearly sympathetic because of the unfair treatment I had received. Garret Buddhing spoke sympathetically to Donna after I testified, apologizing for the fact that she had had to witness her husband being made to look such a fool in public. Donna's reply was quick and sharp! She said, "Our calling as Christians is to be 'fools for Christ's sake' (I Cor. 4:10). If Chuck has appeared the fool for giving a faithful witness for Christ, then praise the Lord! Personally, I have never been prouder of him than I am right now!" It is not enjoyable, but it is indeed a privilege to be "granted to suffer for [Christ's] sake" (Phil. 1:29).

The introduction to my report before the committee was entitled: "The Emperor Has No Clothes." It compared the gay rights movement to the old story about a vain emperor who, in his seeking to appear wise, was instead fooled by some thieving tailors who wanted nothing more than to abscond with the king's money. The following is part of my statement: "Once upon a time there was an old vain Emperor who was approached by some clever philosophers. They suggested to the Emperor that they could weave a magical cloak that could discern who was wise and who was foolish. Although the cloak would be expensive, for what it could do, it would be worthwhile.

"Because of the magical makeup of the thread, only the wise and sophisticated could see it. The Emperor ordered the weaving to be done only to realize that he himself was foolish and unsophisticated, for he saw nothing as they fitted him with his new cloak.

"Not wishing to embarrass himself and reveal his stupidity, he expressed his delight in such a wonderful garment. On the day of the royal procession, the whole town came out to praise the Emperor for his new glorious garment. Everyone joined in admiring the magical cloak, lest they be branded fools and unsophisticated themselves. Then a little boy in his childish way cried, 'The Emperor has no clothes.' The little boy had told the truth and revealed his foolishness. The Emperor and the crowd were exposed by the unsophisticated remark of the boy.

"We would love to have a magical garment or magical glasses that we could put on and discover the wise from the foolish. There is no such magical apparatus. The Bible plainly says that homosexuality is immoral. I am here to say that the Gay Rights Movement has no clothes on.

"To be sophisticated and avoid political suicide you must bow to the latest cry of 'discrimination'. The word itself has become the shibboleth of political wisdom and expedience. The cry of 'discrimination' is like the Emperor's magic garment. Those that see it are wise—those that don't are foolish. Those that kowtow to it get elected; those that don't—fade away.

"The Gay Rights Movement has no clothes on. It is a hoax—perpetuated to protect the special interests of a single group of people who have chosen an immoral lifestyle."

*****

I then went through economic, health, and social arguments why homosexuals should not receive special protections under the Civil Rights Act. In my conclusion, I discussed the gay rights ordinance that cost me, my church, and presbytery over one hundred thousand dollars and two years of agony. I concluded my opening statement by saying: "Homosexuality, not heterosexuality, poses a substantial threat to the health of this city, the moral as well as the physical health. This ordinance in San Francisco has cost me and my church approximately $100,000 in terms of a lawsuit defending our Constitutional right to discriminate.

"This is a moral issue and it puts an unjust burden upon individuals, businesses, and organizations that believe that moral issues should not be legislated against. I, for one, would discriminate against immorality; but whether I chose to or not, it is not the province of the state government to dictate what moral matters I consider relevant or not. God's Word alone dictates moral matters. It is the responsibility of government and its citizens to uphold morality and decency. In this matter of sexual preference, I have a constitutional right protected by the First Amendment to discriminate against immorality.

"I respectfully urge the members of this committee to reject this proposed legislation."

The proposal was never acted upon, but year after year, a federal gay civil rights bill is reintroduced in Congress and is gaining more support every year.

Gay Economic Power

My report to the committee also included statistics showing that the homosexual community is not and never has been an economically oppressed "minority." If anything, the statistics show that the average homosexual couple has a far better standard of living than the average American family. Why? Because two same-sex individuals, usually professionals, don't have the responsibility of raising and caring for their own children. They can spend all of their money on themselves and their own causes—and they do.

Some of the statistics I presented to the committee came from reputable business publications, as well as from the homosexual press. They are as follows:

• the average income of a gay household of 1.4 persons is $23,000

• the income of a gay household is roughly 50% above the national average

• 70% of the gay community are college graduates

• 97% of the gay community are employed

• 84% of the gay community are regular voters

• It is estimated that gays control 19% of the spendable income in the U.S. ("A Big Push for Homosexuals' Rights," *U.S. News & World Report*, 14 April 1980.)

The following are taken from a survey in the *Advocate*, a weekly gay magazine:

• 79% of the gay community uses commercial airlines and averages four trips a year.

• 80% of the gay community owns at least one car.

• 80% of the gay community orders drinks by brand name.

According to *Business Week*, 3 Sept. 1979: ". . . homosexuals have established dozens of Chambers of Commerce and other business and professional organizations to further one another's economic interests." The publisher of the *Advocate* bragged that, ". . . we're everywhere, and we're the most affluent of any minority."

The 1980-81 Gay Phone Directory indicated that homosexuals spend an average of five hundred dollars a year on clothing. How many of us have that kind of spendable income for our clothes?

However, that was 1980. What about the 1990s? Has there been a decline in the standard of living for gay men and lesbian women? Not according to a survey completed in 1991 by a Chicago-based polling organization, Overlooked Opinions.

The 27 August 1991 edition of the *San Francisco Chronicle* reported that as of 1989 the figures are:

- Average Incomes:

Gay male households:	$51,000.
Lesbian households:	$45,937.
All households:	$36,520.

- Percent of households with income over $100,000:

Gay male households:	15%
Lesbian households:	3%
All households:	4%

- College graduates—among people over 25

Gay male households:	62%
Lesbian households:	59%
All males:	24%
All females:	17%

- Top industries for lesbians and gays

Education:	8.4%
Publishing:	6.9%
Social Services:	6.8%
Finance/Insurance:	6.5%
Medicine:	5.6%

- Percent that voted in the last presidential election

Gay male household:	87%
Lesbian households:	82%
All males:	56%
All females:	58%

The 18 July 1991 *Wall Street Journal* carried an interesting article that detailed gay affluence. It pointed out the following statistics:

• 49% of gays hold professional/managerial positions, compared to 15.9% for the national average.

• 57.8% of gays are wine drinkers, compared to 21.5% for the national average.

• 26.5% are frequent fliers, compared to 1.9% for the national average.

• 59.6% are college graduates, compared to 18% for the national average.

These statistics come from the Simmons Market Research Bureau, Inc., and the U.S. Census Bureau.

In fact, the total homosexual market is estimated to be around $400 billion. To me, that certainly does not indicate economic deprivation or widespread discrimination that poses substantial hardship on the gay community! (I wonder where conservative Bible believers fit into this economic spectrum!)

There is no reason that homosexuals should receive special legal protections as a minority group. To give protection to a sexual behavior is to demean legitimate minority groups who have been oppressed or denied their rights because of their skin color, their place of national origin, race, or sex. Some have argued that religious freedom sets up a potential paradigm for sexual preference rights because religion is a "chosen lifestyle" and so would be comparable to the chosen lifestyle of homosexuality. If religion, as a chosen lifestyle, is a protected freedom under the First Amendment, so homosexuality, as a chosen lifestyle, would be a protected freedom. If, then, homosexuality is protected by the First Amendment, what is the need for this new legislation? Then it becomes a matter of special-interest legislation, which irrationally favors a specific sexual deviant behavior. And, if this particular behavior is protected, why not any and all deviant behavior?

When we begin handing out special legal protections for sexual behaviors, we're opening up a Pandora's Box of social and legal problems. Why should pedophiles (individuals who enjoy sex with children) be denied the right to practice their sexual orientation—as long as the child consents and it does not "hurt" him. But, then, what does "hurt" mean, and when is a child able to consent or just say no? After all, this is a sexual behavior. What about bestiality, necrophilia (sex with the dead), and all other forms of "sexual orientation." If we are going to protect one deviant sexual behavior, we should probably legalize them all.

Does it matter any more?

FIVE

Gay Power

To understand how the homosexual community took over San Francisco, it's necessary to go back to the 1970s—and in particular—to 1977 when openly gay candidate Harvey Milk was elected to the San Francisco Board of Supervisors. (The board is the ruling "city council" of the city and county of San Francisco.)

Milk's election is touted in gay folklore as the first time an openly gay man was elected to a public office in the entire country. It was a fluke because it was one of the few times in San Francisco's history that the election of supervisors was limited to districts. In other words, it was not a city-wide election; therefore, people could only vote for candidates from their own district. Being gay, and in the "gay" district, Milk handily won. He was not elected by a majority vote of the whole citizenry of San Francisco, but by the overwhelming number of gays in his district. A year after Milk's election, the city reverted back to city-wide elections for all candidates.

At the same time Milk was elected, George Moscone, a radical liberal, became mayor. Another candidate for the Board of Supervisors at that time was Dan White: ex-cop, ex-fireman, husband and father, a conservative Roman Catholic from a conservative district. He came into office as a "Mr. Clean." Many conservatives in the city were looking to White as a possible mayoral candidate in future elections. Dan White was going to be the man to provide some opposition to the radical left policies of George Moscone.

Regrettably, White became increasingly frustrated as a supervisor. He just couldn't seem to accomplish any of his objectives, because he was usually outvoted by the liberal majority. Less than a year after his election, White resigned in disgust. His friends were shocked and dismayed, and they urged him to reconsider. They argued that White's resignation simply paved the way for Mayor Moscone to appoint another radical liberal to fill the vacancy. That was not what the conservatives wanted to happen!

White reconsidered and on 27 November 1978 he went to city hall to ask for his seat back on the Board. But White came prepared to do more than ask the mayor for reinstatement. He was armed with a gun. He entered city hall through a window, probably to avoid being searched for weapons. According to press reports, he first went to the mayor's office and argued for reinstatement. Reportedly, Moscone refused, telling White that that very day he planned to announce White's replacement to the Board. White pulled out the gun and killed George Moscone. He went out the side door of the mayor's office, and down the corridor to Harvey Milk's office. Apparently, he blamed both Moscone and Milk for his problems and frustrations with the Board of Supervisors. His aim was deadly, and Harvey Milk apparently died instantly. Dan White called his wife and told her what he had done. Later in the day, she accompanied him to the police station where he turned himself in.

The city went into shock. Supervisor Dianne Feinstein announced the assassinations at a press conference: "As president of the Board of Supervisors, it is my duty to make this announcement: both Mayor Moscone and Supervisor Harvey Milk have been shot and killed . . . the suspect is Supervisor Dan White."

As a result of this double killing, Feinstein automatically became Mayor and Dan White was brought to trial.

In May 1979, a jury found Dan White innocent of first degree murder because of an apparent "diminished capacity" mental condition. When the gay population learned that he might serve no more than seven years for killing two men, they went berserk. On the night of 21 May 1979 hundreds of angry homosexuals stormed city hall, set fire to trash cans and parts of the building, set police cars on fire, broke windows, and injured scores of policemen. That night became known as the "night of gay rage" or the "White night riot."

This violent reaction and its aftermath were documented in a 1980 CBS special called "Gay Power, Gay Politics." In this frightening documentary, reporter George Crile interviewed

one of the leaders of the homosexual community named Cleve
Jones. At the time, Jones was a top legislative aide to then state
Assemblyman Art Agnos. Crile asked Jones whether he regretted what happened the night of the rioting at city hall. Jones
answered smugly, "I'm not going to apologize for what happened that night. Part of me didn't want it to happen, but part
of me was celebrating. Because I knew that nobody would ever
again underestimate the rage that we can muster."

George Crile noted in his report that just two months after
this violent homosexual rampage, Dianne Feinstein found herself campaigning for reelection. With an estimated 15 percent
of the population in San Francisco being homosexual, she
knew she couldn't ignore such a large voting block. However,
she had made the dangerous mistake of criticizing San Francisco gays in an article in the *Ladies Home Journal.* She said they
should observe community standards in their sexual behaviors
and not try to push their lifestyle on others. This seemingly
innocent comment turned the gays against her. Her opponent,
Quentin Kopp (who is now a California state senator from the
San Francisco Area), was not trusted by the homosexual community. The gay strategy was to field their own candidate,
David Scott, who would draw away enough votes from both
candidates to force a run-off election. And, that's exactly what
happened.

Suddenly, Dianne Feinstein decided she desperately needed
the homosexual vote. She appealed to David Scott for his en-
dorsement. As a good-faith gesture, she attended a drag queen
ball where she was photographed with "Michele," the city's
most famous transvestite. She appeared before a group of
homosexuals and officially apologized for being "insensitive" to
their needs. She promised to appoint a gay to the police commission and to make other political appointments in proportion to the gay population in the city. By caving in to gay
militancy, she finally won their support. David Scott became
her constant companion as she travelled through the city, court-
ing the homosexual vote. She even campaigned in "leather
bars"—havens for gays who enjoy sado-masochistic sexual activities.

In the run-off election on 11 December 1979, Feinstein
overwhelmingly defeated Quentin Kopp and remained in office. She had learned an important lesson: if you want to get
elected in San Francisco, you have to have the gay vote. Once

in office, she kept her promises. She appointed a lesbian to the police commission and gave other appointments to homosexuals as positions became available. With her help, homosexuals were entrenched within San Francisco city government.

A Bitter Prophecy

At the conclusion of "Gay Power, Gay Politics," the camera shows thousands of homosexuals gathered at the civic center for a candle-light vigil in memory of the deaths of Moscone and Milk. As Cleve Jones stands before the crowd on the steps of city hall, he shouts: "How many of you have heard from behind, 'Hey, faggot, hey dyke,'. . . That is why we are here tonight. That is why we marched on Washington. That is why we will keep on marching. It will be a long struggle. And we will have leaders and slogans and martyrs aplenty. But let no one misunderstand. We are deadly serious. We are growing in power every day that passes. And we will not be stopped."

As I've reviewed this documentary in recent months, I am amazed and saddened at the accuracy of Jones' statement. Little did he know that less than a year after his speech, the first cases of AIDS would appear in New York and California. He was right. There have been and will be "martyrs aplenty," multitudes of young men in the prime of life dying for their "faith" in such unprecedented sexual freedom!

The word "martyr" means witness. Make no mistake about it—homosexuality in San Francisco is more than what two people of the same sex do. It is a whole way of life, or death if you please, which proselytizes the "worship of the creature rather than the Creator." It is the religion of self-worship having its foundations laid upon a particular type of bodily function. The gay philosophy is the natural outworking of the "Playboy" philosophy of the 60s and the Hippie ideology of the 70s. It is a deadly paradigm of how far men and women are willing to go for self-gratification. The sexual aspect happens to be the most bizarre aspect of their faith. According to the Apostle Paul, sexual sins above all other sins desecrate the body most offensively. Gays and lesbians are more dedicated to this "witness" of their faith than most Christians are to their faith in Christ. Homosexuals must distinguish themselves in every area of their lives by their peculiar "sexual preference" in order to establish their own identity.

Example: In 1990, the first lesbian was seated as judge on the bench of the California Superior Court, for the city and county of San Francisco. The headline in one legal newspaper read: "Making History: The First Openly Lesbian Jurist Defeated An Incumbent For Her Seat"—not "Donna Hitchens Becomes Judge of the San Francisco Superior Court." What identified her as a front page celebrity was not becoming a judge of the California Superior Court, but her being a lesbian/judge. In other words, it was her chosen sexual behavior that made her judgeship noteworthy, not her professional abilities. She is known first as a lesbian, and then as a superior court judge. Why is this distinction necessary? If her sexuality were that of God's creation ordinance, there would be no need of such labeling. The headlines have never been "Heterosexual Ms. So & So Becomes Judge . . ." That kind of identification is unnecessary! But, for the gay community, it is necessary that they be identified in every area of their lives as being homosexual. Because their "sexual orientation" is such a blatant perversion of God's creation order, they lose their creaturely identity and so they must distinguish themselves by that very perversion. Here again is the sadness of the gay community: that they are identified in every area of their lives by a particular sexual activity.

This is a clash of faiths, a clash of cultures, a clash of two whole societies: one that is based on man's law "of himself, by himself, and for himself" versus God's law founded on revealed truth in creation and the Word. Politicized gays are not ashamed to fight for their faith and utilize whatever resources they can to promote their "religion of mother earth." The homosexual movement is the natural outgrowth of secularism come into its own! The Apostle Paul described "the worship and service of the creature" in terms of homosexual/lesbian behavior (Rom. 1:24-27). Its militancy and surprising social success can only be explained in terms of a fundamental religious drive for ultimate autonomy from the God "who is, who was, and ever shall be. . . ."

Perhaps "martyr" is not accurate enough to describe the character of the gay population. "Victim" may more accurately describe the plight of homosexuals trapped by this insidious lust. They are victims of their own unbridled passions and blinded by a lifestyle that promises them freedom, but only delivers death. It is only the gospel of Christ and His salvation that delivers from this bondage. The Christian alone, equipped with the power of redeeming love and the Word of God, has the gracious antidote to this licentious "disease" of ultimate self-worship and self-gratification. The good news is that homosexuality is not irreversible, nor is it the "unpardonable sin," nor is it an irrecoverable deathstyle. GOD LOVES TO SAVE HOMOSEXUALS. "It is a trustworthy statement, deserving full acceptance, that Christ Jesus came into the world to save sinners . . ." (I Tim. 1:15, NASV).

Where is the Church? Where are the Christians? The gay community puts us to shame. They're not afraid to speak up for their faith, nor to evangelize—even in the public schools. Don't be fooled, the Bible-believing community is not immune from the judgment of God simply because we're biblically correct in rejecting homosexual behavior. We've got the divine sovereign medicine for this population of young men and women dying needlessly for their cause. Unless we spread the really good news of deliverance from this bondage to sexual self-gratification, the Church is in for severe judgment. No more mocking of homosexuals, no more parodying them as limp-wristed effeminates, no more unmercifully castigating them as hopelessly perverse. We need a Christ-like attitude of compassion as well as a sense of holy justice in order that they be saved. ("Create in me a clean heart and renew a steadfast spirit within me . . ." [Ps. 51:10, NASV]). We need to re-evaluate what it means to be salt and light in this world and get back to what preaching the gospel really means. What Martin Luther said to his generation so clearly applies to ours:

> If I profess with the loudest voice and clearest exposition every portion of the truth of God except precisely that little point which the world and the Devil are at that moment attacking, I am not confessing Christ, however boldly I may be professing Christ. Where the battle rages, there the loyalty of the soldier is proved, and to be steady on all the battlefield besides, is mere flight and disgrace if he flinches at that point.

San Francisco Today

Our city is greatly influenced from top to bottom by the gay political mindset. Lesbians and gay men are in key positions of authority. Art Agnos, our former mayor, has been a hero for the homosexual cause ever since being in the California legislature. Our Board of Supervisors has three openly self-identified gays on it: Harry Britt (former Methodist minister), Carole Migden, and Roberta Achtenberg (whose lesbian lover is Municipal Court Judge Mary Morgan). There are at least three other members of the Board who are rumored to be closeted gays.

The Police Department:

It actively recruits homosexuals, and new officers must undergo sensitivity training for all minorities—including homosexuals. The department had one homosexual chaplain for the gay constituency on the force. He recently died of AIDS. One of the police commissioners, Gwenn Craig, is a long time gay activist.

The Public School Board:

It is dominated by the gay agenda on both the junior high school, senior high school, and junior college levels, even though homosexuals are not a numerical superiority. Ramone Cortines, the former Superintendent of Schools, is sympathetic to the gay cause and authorized free distribution of condoms to combat AIDS among teen-agers and supported a "Project 10-like" counseling program for self- identified gay and lesbian teens in the schools. Board members usually vote unanimously for pro-gay initiatives whenever they are presented to the board, even over public protestations by parents. Parents whose children attend the public school system in San Francisco are powerless when it comes to the institution of any gay-related program.

The Fire Department:

It has a lesbian commissioner as a liaison with the gay community. Just recently, Mayor Jordan appointed a well-known drag-queen (from the Imperial Court) to the commission (San Francisco Examiner, 24 Feb. 1992).

The Health Department:

It has an obvious interest in health consequences of homosexuals. Sexually transmitted diseases are notoriously high in
San Francisco and are excessive in the gay lifestyle. There is an
understandable preoccupation with handling AIDS and other
gay-related diseases.

The Religious Community:

Judaism

San Francisco Chronicle, 26 June 1990. "Reformed Jews To
Accept Gay Rabbis," "Calling for an end to 'condemnation of
homosexual behavior by the Jewish tradition,' the nation's largest branch of Judaism voted yesterday to welcome gay men and
lesbians as rabbis."

San Francisco Chronicle, 24 May 1991, "Gay, Lesbian Jewish
Conference: 500 People Registered For Conference In S.F.
This Weekend." "Lesbian and gay life in Israel, gay Jewish
fiction and how to start a gay Jewish organization are among
the topics to be explored at the 12th International Conference
of Gay and Lesbian Jews in San Francisco this weekend. . . . The
biennial conference is being held at a time when many religions, including Judaism, are re-examining their traditional
antipathy to accepting open lesbians and gays as members—and
leaders—of their congregations. . . . More recently, about two
dozen lesbian and gay rabbis from across the country sent an
open letter to Jewish publications in which they made a plea for
tolerance. 'It is time to be accepted for who we are: committed
Jews and rabbis who are also lesbians and gay men.'"

Episcopalian

San Francisco Examiner, 1979, "Gay Atheists vs the Church,"
"Grace Cathedral, for instance, has made itself the bastion of
gay Episcopalianism in San Francisco, to include the establish-
ment of a 100-member gay orchestra and choir to concertize on
Gay Freedom Day. Father William Barkus of St. Mary the
Virgin Church has brought his considerable eloquence and

theological erudition to the cause of reconciling gays to Christianity." (In 1990 Father Barkus died of AIDS.)

San Francisco Examiner, 2 March 1991, "Episcopal Celibacy Rule May Be Lifted." "New York: An Episcopal Church panel opened the door to the ordination of non-celibate homosexuals to the priesthood by recommending that ordination decisions be left to individual dioceses. [Bishop George N. Hunt] said this was the 2.5 million-member denomination's long-time tradition until the church's governing convention specified in 1979 that it was inappropriate to ordain people who habitually had sexual intercourse outside marriage. The new proposal, issued Thursday, would have the net effect of nullifying the 1979 action, Hunt said, 'I think the church is ready to take a little more progressive stance,' he said."

Presbyterian Church (USA)

San Francisco Examiner, 14 March 1991, "Report On Sexuality Stirs Up Denomination: Presbyterians Mull Gay Ordination, Unmarried Sex." "A report endorsing the ordination of practicing homosexuals and the practice of sex outside marriage is causing a furor in the Presbyterian Church. The report was prepared by a task force on human sexuality, which voted in February to pass its recommendations on to the church's General Assembly. . . . Most task force members say the report presents a sexual ethic that focuses on justice. But opponents, . . . say it ignores the Bible. 'The moral norm for Christians ought not be marriage, but rather justice-love,' the 200-page report states. 'Rather than inquiring whether sexual activity is premarital, martial or postmarital, we should be asking whether the relationship is responsible, the dynamics genuinely mutual and the loving full of joyful caring.'. . . Opponents of the report argue that its recommendations disregard traditional Christian morality in favor of the values of modern society."

Newsweek, 6 May 1991, "Roll Over John Calvin: The Presbyterians Rethink The Sexual Revolution." ". . . until now no Christian denomination has seriously considered the wholesale rejection of traditional sexual ethics as outdated and oppressive—much less blessing homosexuality, fornication and other behavior that it once found sinful. That, in sum, is the challenge facing the Presbyterian Church (USA) from a highly controversial report on human sexuality to be debated next month at the church's general assembly. . . . Fundamental to the committee's argument is the assumption that sexual gratification is a human need and right that ought not to be limited to heterosexual spouses or bound by 'conventional' morality. . . . 'Gays and lesbians are feared,' the report argues, 'because erotic passion between persons of the same gender is a sharp break with socially conventional patterns of male dominance and female subordination.'. . . Noting that a third of all Presbyterians are single women and men, the report warns that the unmarried will ignore the church unless the clergy cease their 'painful' assumption that singles should remain celibate. Christians 'must become the church for and of the marginalized,' the report argues, meaning lesbians and gays, sexually active singles, women in general plus those males who exercise 'little power.'. . . Thus, for a denomination that has already declined by a half million members over the last two decades, the report sounds a call for widening the circle of faithful—not with children, but with nonreproductive gays, lesbians and heterosexual singles who practice 'safe sex.'"

Lutheran

San Francisco Chronicle, 19 July 1990, "2 S.F. Lutheran Churches Suspended—Gay Clergy—Discipline Board's Action Concludes Trial." "Two dissident San Francisco congregations were suspended from the Evangelical Lutheran Church in America yesterday for defying church policies prohibiting sexually active homosexuals in the clergy. St. Francis Lutheran Church and First United Lutheran Church were suspended . . . for the highly publicized ordination in January of a gay man and lesbian couple as assistant pastors. . . . Church officials stressed that homosexuals are still welcome as members of the Lutheran church and that they could be accepted as clergy if they agreed not to be sexually active."

San Francisco Sentinel, 14 February 1991, advertisement section: "St. Paul Lutheran Church (Oakland); Sunday Worship & Communion, 10 a.m. St. Paul is a member of Lutherans Concerned (the Lutheran Gay/Lesbian Caucus) All are welcome. . . .

Methodists

San Francisco Chronicle, 14 February 1991, "Methodists Rethink Beliefs On Gay Sex." "United Methodist Church officials have recommended that the 8.9 million-member denomination throw out a controversial church tenet that homosexual lovemaking is 'incompatible with Christian teaching.' During a meeting in San Francisco in November, committee members reported that an overwhelming majority of those testifying at five public hearings wanted to soften the church's condemnation of gay sex and remove barriers keeping 'self-avowed, practicing homosexuals' from becoming Methodist ministers. The new statement replaced those prohibitions with the admission that 'the present state of knowledge . . . does not provide a satisfactory basis on which the church can responsibly maintain a specific prohibition of homosexual practice.'"

The responsibility for the moral condition of San Francisco today lies at the feet of the religious community. More specifically, it lies at the feet of the "Bible-believing" Christian churches who have done little or nothing to turn the tide of this immorality.

Politics

In the 1991 mayoral campaign, all five candidates for mayor were firmly pro-homosexual in their political as well as moral stance. An article in the 26 September 1991 issue of the *San Francisco Sentinel* detailed the pro-gay positions of the candidates as follows:

• Art Agnos, incumbent for re-election. His "pluses" were listed as: "Has empowered the gay and lesbian community with appointments to key staff positions and commissions. Longtime record of support as Assemblyman and Mayor. Authored "AB1," original gay and lesbian civil rights bill in Sacramento" (pg.25).

• Angela Alioto, who gained the support of Board of Supervisor [gay] members Carole Migden, Harry Britt, and Britt's former legislative aide, Jean Harris.

• Tom Hsieh, supervisor and architect. Hsieh eagerly endorsed same-sex marriages, worked as a campaigner for the Jesse Jackson campaign, and has many ties to the gay community through the Rainbow Coalition.

• Richard Hongisto, City Assessor, former supervisor, one-time sheriff of San Francisco County. Dubbed the "straight Harvey Milk" for his thirty years of support for gay causes. Hongisto has advocated gay marriages for twenty-five years.

• Frank Jordan, ex-Police Chief for San Francisco. Hailed as being "fairly progressive. Hired first [police commission] liaison to [gay] community. Created First Hate Crimes Unit in major California city." Jordan also actively recruited and promoted gay officers and started a "sensitivity training" program to create understanding for those dealing with AIDS.

A group of evangelical pastors met with candidate Jordan in September before the 1991 election to see how we could fit into his agenda or how he could work with us. Having known him on other issues, several of the pastors came to the meeting ready to cast their lot with him. As police chief, Jordan had been open to "Cops for Christ," had displayed sympathy that no other city official had shown toward the violence our family had experienced and, according to one reliable source, had even made a "profession of faith" in Christ. Knowing this, along with the fact of his conservative Roman Catholic background, many of the pastors felt that we, as evangelicals, could, and even should, support his bid for mayor. They felt since he was a "nice guy" and sympathetic to our issues, that we should support him as the "lesser of two evils"—or in our city the lesser of five evils! Before Mr. Jordan arrived at the meeting, I challenged that idea.

I spread out on the table in front of the pastors a collection of articles that Donna and I had saved from the gay newspaper. They confirmed Jordan's public support of homosexual issues, his participation in the Gay Freedom Day parade (with all its public indecencies and obscenities), his support of AB101 (the state Assembly's gay-rights proposal) and the money his campaign had pledged toward the passage of that law. It was my conviction we ought to confront him with these statements and seek some kind of rapprochement with him. Still, some were going to support him no matter what sentiments he had about homosexuality or abortion, both of which he publicly supported. Ironically, most of the ministers in this group were the same ones that had worked so hard against the passage of domestic partners legislation (same-sex marriage) in the city for the past three years! (We will discuss domestic partners later.)

When Mr. Jordan arrived, his campaign manager, Jack Davis, was with him. Davis, a conservative Republican, soon proclaimed unabashedly his homosexuality and pro-gay agenda. This didn't sit well with some of the pastors. However, some argued that Davis was hired as a professional, not because he was gay! (Exactly the argument used by the gays when pushing through an anti-discrimination law! Some of the ministers bought the argument.) Interestingly, it never occurred to any of the ministers that if Jack Davis were there exclusively in a "professional" capacity, WHY had he found it necessary to begin by so vehemently declaring his homosexuality? To de-sensitize—to set at issue his homosexuality versus what the ministers knew the Bible had to say about homosexuality. If the ministers rationalized the issue, as in fact some did, he would have them in his camp. How easily we fall into the snare of the enemy when we compromise God's Word.

At the beginning of the meeting, I asked Mr. Jordan what his ultimate standard for morality was. Davis, immediately jumped into the middle of Jordan's answer and proceeded to berate me (and the ministers), branding us homophobic and prejudicial against his candidate simply because I asked this "set up question." He went on to say that Jordan had no obligation to answer; nor did we have a right to ask the question. In Davis' mind, the question was irrelevant and calculated only to be inciteful. The ensuing tirade between Davis and the ministers went on for about thirty minutes. Davis berated the ministers, the ministers defended themselves. I was so upset at being interrupted and insulted by Davis in such a manner that I didn't press my question—at least, not then. I was completely let down as to Davis' response and at Jordan's lack of response and control over Davis. A number of the pastors demanded an apology from Davis right then and there or they weren't going to continue. However, there was no apology, my question was left suspended, and Jordan continued talking about more innocuous issues.

Toward the end of the meeting, I had regained enough of my composure to ask my question again, only this time more directly. I first thanked Jordan for the care and concern he (as police chief) had personally shown for our family over the years when we were attacked, but told him that I wanted to know clearly whether he believed that homosexuality was immoral. I thought I'd ask it that bluntly because I had nothing to lose; the fire had been set—the flames raged, and now my decision about Jordan was essentially sealed. He agreed that it was a difficult question to answer, but the essence was that homosexuality was no crime and that what "people do in the privacy of their bedrooms was none of the state's business." I did not pursue nor attempt to argue with him. He knew as well as I that homosexual sex acts go on publicly in San Francisco in the parks and around the city. It is a bogus argument that in this city sex acts are private and consensual. Consensual—maybe— but private, inside, out of the public eye . . . No. He had been the police chief. He knew. Public homosexual behavior and other sexual perversion had been documented by the CBS special already mentioned, "Gay Power, Gay Politics," and many other media entities. Needless to say, I was grieved with his answer. He supported homosexuality—gay rights. That was the official line of the "conservative" candidate of the city.

There is no neutrality here in any area of life. The god of homosexuality makes the same demands as the God of the Bible—either you're for Me or against Me. Christian, there is no middle road. No area of non-involvement. No ignoring sin in hopes that it will just go away. "Choose this day whom you will serve" . . . ask the Lord to make you a lighthouse in your community . . . and prepare for battle.

SIX

Gay Lifestyle—Gay Deathstyle

"Do not lie with a man as one lies with a woman; that is detestable" (Lev. 18:22, NIV).

> The wrath of God is being revealed from heaven against all the godlessness and wickedness of men who suppress the truth by their wickedness, ... For although they knew God, they neither glorified him as God nor gave thanks to him, but their thinking became futile and their foolish hearts were darkened. ... Therefore God gave them over in the sinful desires of their hearts to sexual impurity for the degrading of their bodies with one another. They exchanged the truth of God for a lie, and worshiped and served created things rather than the Creator—who is forever praised. Amen. Because of this, God gave them over to shameful lusts. Even their women exchanged natural relations for unnatural ones. In the same way the men also abandoned natural relations with women and were inflamed with lust for one another. Men committed indecent acts with other men, and received in themselves the due penalty for their perversion. (Rom. 1:18, 19, 21, 24-27, NIV)

These passages quoted from the Old and New Testaments are just two of many that could be cited to show how God feels about homosexual behavior. Homosexuality is a heterosexual sin. It is a perversion of heterosexuality in that it violates both God's creation and His clear instructions about the relationships between men and women in our society.

God's plan, of course, is for men and women to have sexual relationships within the context of holy matrimony. All extra-marital sexual liaisons are condemned as sinful and a perversion of His plan for mankind.

In Leviticus, the Lord clearly lays out His regulations on sexual relationships. He condemns sexual intercourse between

parents and their children; He condemns adultery; He condemns sexual liaisons between close relatives, animals, and
same-sex partners. On a more practical level, God's prohibitions against same-sex relations just makes good sense because
of the health consequences and the emotional scars it leaves on
those who live that perverted lifestyle.

It is necessary for you to understand exactly what the gay
lifestyle is all about. It certainly is not about two people of the
same sex "loving" one another. A mother loves a daughter, a
father loves a son, two sisters love one another. These are not
homosexual relationships. A man may love another man, or a
woman another woman, however, "loving" another person of
the same sex is not the issue. Homosexuality is about degrading
sexual behaviors that often result in the spread of serious
venereal diseases and death through AIDS. The homosexual
community would have us believe that theirs is simply a relationship of mutual "love" for one another. Again, this is a
"desensitizing tactic" to obscure the real issue: the act of homosexual sex. A loving relationship between two people of the
same sex does not become a homosexual relationship until and
unless homosexual sex is desired and/or practiced. That is the
very thing that distinguishes and defines the gay lifestyle—the
act of homosexual sex. Gay sexual behavior needs to be exposed, so you can better understand the insidious and calculated cover up of the gay rights movement.

However, in light of Ephesians 5, we are told that Christians are different from the rest of the world. We are not to let
"immorality or any impurity . . . even be named among you as
is proper among saints" (5:3-4). The idea that such sins not
even "be named" is more than referring to, identifying, and
labeling particular sins. These sins are not to be charged—
"named"—to us. In Christ, we are saints. Paul goes on to set at
variance the life of the saint compared to the life of the unbeliever. He states categorically that "no immoral or impure person . . . has an inheritance in the Kingdom of Christ and God
. . . therefore, do not be partakers with them . . ." (5:5-6). This
was our former life, but it no longer is. The punch line is that
not only are we forbidden to practice sins of sexual impurity,
but that "we must expose them; for it is disgraceful even to
SPEAK of the things which are done by them in secret . . ."
(5:11-12). However, the word "expose" (used in the NIV, NASV,
NKJV, etc.) does not mean to "detail-expose" as in "to dis-

close," but rather to "expose" as in "bring conviction" upon those that do such things.

Even in its description of the debauched practices of the Canaanites, the Bible does not give explicit descriptions. It uses "euphemistic" expressions such as "don't lie with a man as with a woman," or "do not uncover the nakedness of . . ." to suggest the heinousness of their sins. These are the most graphic terms that are used to warn us to flee these sins. The Bible uses the term "abomination" to describe and expose the wickedness of these sins.

John the Baptist "exposed" (same word) the sin of Herod when he merely described it as "having his brother's wife" (Mark 6:18). There was no need to detail the debauched sex practices of Herod and his paramour in order for them to be "exposed" as the sinners that they were. It was enough that "having his brother's wife" was against the law of God.

As much as we might want to reveal to the world the disgusting and degrading habits of the sexual sinner, we are forbidden. We may think that if we merely describe their heinous acts of degrading debauchery, we will effectively turn people off to such sins, or that we will incite the Christian community to fight those who practice and advocate such a degrading, disease-ridden lifestyle. However, we are convinced from the Word and the example set forth in it, that speaking of these sins in detail is not the answer. It is only the Spirit of God that quickens our sense of justice and incites holy indignation against such debauchery. The "naming" of them in a list does not inflame holy passions, but more dangerously taunts and teases our own sensual passions. We may be immediately "turned-off" by such explicit descriptions, but the subtleties of our sin nature and the craft of Satan combine as a powerful and deadly force that eats away at our own saintliness. We become desensitized to such sins; we become enamored with the bizarre; we then find them disgustingly attractive in a perverse sort of way. And, surprisingly, we may eventually be tempted to fantasize about them in the privacy of our own minds. The lust of the heart works an insidiousness that ensnares us; and before we know it, we are caught like a bird in a trap!

Donna and I have seen some of these things that God refers to as "abominations" and we are not the same. We have grappled with the propriety of including these things in this book. ". . . Whatever things are pure, lovely, admirable, excellent or praiseworthy, think about such things" (Phil. 4:8). We realize that we will be criticized on both sides, 1) by those who don't think that any description of the gay lifestyle should be revealed because of its basic offensiveness, and 2) those who will feel we should tell the truth, the whole truth, and nothing but the truth in all its graphic and disgusting detail. There may be a legitimate forum for that, but we have decided that this book is not that forum.

We have three teen-agers who have lived with, been exposed to, and have an experiential knowledge of the gay community and its practices that few Christians of any age have. We do not feel it proper nor God-honoring to expose them to the most graphic of homosexual behaviors. We have Christian parents who faithfully raised us in the Lord and thus prepared us to do spiritual battle in San Francisco. We have siblings and their families who have stood by us, loved us, and prayed for us over the years. We have a responsibility to our families that they be able to read this book with a clear conscience before the Lord.

The Lord awakened Donna and me to the gay political movement, the heinousness of homosexual behavior, and our responsibility in Christ to respond by thrusting us into this life in San Francisco—and keeping us here. Our families do not need to be awakened—they have lived it with us. But what of the Christian community at large? As Donna has researched the materials that we have accumulated over the past eighteen years in preparation for this book, frustration has raised its angry head! She has momentarily wished that all bible-believing churches across the United States could be made to read just one edition of the gay newspaper freely distributed throughout San Francisco (including in front of city hall) in hopes of exposing the heinousness of the sin to a sleeping Christian community. However, we know that it is only the work of the Holy Spirit that will awaken the hearts of Christians, Christian churches, and Christian organizations to their biblical responsibilities in this regard.

The following is a description of the homosexual lifestyle, its behaviors, diseases, and its political goal to hide the reality of this lifestyle from the straight public. As you read it, remember that whenever a gay rights, sexual orientation law is passed on a city, state, or federal level, it is not minority civil rights that are being protected, but a particular sexual behavior. And not only do these laws legislate immorality, they are also very costly in terms of employee benefits, and long-term health care costs.

We hope the "exposure" is given within the boundaries that Scripture has set for us.

The Gay Way of Life and the Gay Way of Death

As I mentioned in an earlier chapter, gay strategists Marshall K. Kirk and Erastes Pill encourage gay activists to discuss gay rights as often as possible, but discourage any open discussion of gay behaviors. According to Kirk and Pill, "In the early stages of any campaign to reach straight America, the masses should not be shocked and repelled by premature exposure to homosexual behavior itself. Instead, the imagery of sex should be downplayed and gay rights should be reduced to an abstract social question as much as possible. First, let the camel get his nose inside the tent—and only later his unsightly derriere!" (Marshall K. Kirk and Erastes Pill, "The Overhauling of Straight America," Guide Magazine [November 1987]: 8.)

The worst thing that could happen to the gay rights movement is for the average American to understand exactly what kinds of behaviors homosexuals engage in. As Kirk and Pill readily admit, most Americans would be repelled by what is obviously perverted behavior.

A look at the personal section of any gay newspaper, especially those in San Francisco, reveals a variety of bizarre sexual practices. These behaviors are obviously abnormal and usually result in the spread of exotic venereal disease from one person to another.

According to Roger Magnuson in "Are Gay Rights Right?"—The Berean League, January 1988, "San Francisco alone has seen a venereal disease rate 22 times the national average since gay rights laws were passed in our city. There's been a 100% increase in the spread of infectious hepatitis A; a 300% increase in hepatitis B; amoebic colon infections increased 2,500%; venereal disease clinics see 75,000 patients every year, of whom 80% are homosexual males; 20% of them carried rectal gonorrhea" (p. 17).

As long ago as 1980, San Francisco Health Department officials were vexed over the rise of syphilis cases in the city. An article in the 24 April 1980 edition of the *San Jose Mercury News* pointed out that the national rate for syphilis was 11 cases per 100,000; in California, the rate was 18.6 per 100,000; in San Francisco the rate was 240 per 100,000: more than twenty times the national average. According to clinic director Dr. Irvin Braff, the "problem is due to generally active people having multiple sex partners."

In an article entitled "Gay Times and Gay Diseases," in the August 1984 issue of *The American Spectator*, syndicated columnist, Patrick Buchanan, and medical researcher, Dr. J. Gordon Muir, detailed how gays are spreading venereal diseases. They discuss the spread of AIDS through multiple partners, and then go on to describe what is known as the "Gay Bowel Syndrome," the name of a group of rare bowel diseases spreading through gay urban communities. They include:

• Amebiasis: a parasitic colon disease which causes dysentery and sometimes liver abscesses

• Giardiasis: a parasitic bowel disease which causes diarrhea

• Shigellosis: a bacterial bowel disease which can cause severe dysentery

• Hepatitis A: a viral liver disease spread by fecal contamination.

According to Buchanan and Muir, San Francisco saw a fourfold to tenfold increase in gay bowel diseases beginning in 1977. "The incidence of shigellosis and hepatitis A in men 20 to 29 years of age is now six to ten times that of men or women in any other age group." say the authors.

"It is self evident, that gay sexual practices are an assault upon the ecology of the human body, that the gay communities of America's cities are polluted with disease. With respect to AIDS, there exists a potential for disaster," say Buchanan and Muir.

A former member of our congregation contracted hepatitis through homosexual behavior. Even after leaving that sinful lifestyle behind him, he suffered from recurrent bouts of hepatitis and suffered the devastating effects it had on his body. As has been said before, Donna and I have witnessed and continue to see death by AIDS. There is an anger that wells up in us. The sufferings caused by these diseases and death by AIDS are painfully tragic, but when they are the consequences of a "chosen lifestyle," they become bitterly foolish and unnecessary!

Multiple Sex Partners

AIDS and numerous venereal diseases are rampant among the homosexual population, primarily because homosexuals engage in unsafe and abnormal sexual practices—and because they are promiscuous as well.

A 1972 Centers for Disease Control study, mentioned in an article entitled, "The Gay Dilemma," in *Psychology Today*, January 1984, notes that 50 percent of the male homosexuals surveyed have had over five hundred different sexual partners. The article also points out that AIDS victims have had an average of eleven hundred sex partners ("The Gay Dilemma," *Psychology Today*, [January 1984]: 56.).

Homosexuals Jay and Young, in the *Gay Report* quoted one homosexual as saying, "I believe my estimate of 4,000 sex partners to be very accurate. I have been actively gay since I was 13 (thirty-one years ago.) An average of two or three new partners per week is not excessive, especially when one considers that he will have ten to twelve partners during one night at the bather" (Jay and Young, p. 250).

With such extreme promiscuity among homosexuals, it is little wonder that AIDS has spread so rapidly through its population.

In the 4 July 1991 issue of the *San Francisco Sentinel*, a self-identified HIV positive reporter wrote an article called "A Weekend of Uncontrolled Restraint: AIDS and Gay Day." From his perspective, he describes the celebrating of the gay community the night before and the day of the Gay Freedom Day Parade:

> Happily, the 102 degree fever that I had . . . dissipated into a pool of sweat on my sheets, and I was feeling much healthier. . . .
>
> . . . I returned to the street to find crowds even larger (and drunker) with exhibitionists flashing the crowd drawing as much attention (and more enthusiasm) as the entertainment . . . . But when I looked at the writhing masses, ... I couldn't relate. . . .
>
> I spent most of the rest of the evening looking for signs of PWA's [people with AIDS] in the crowd. Were we out, enjoying this precious opportunity, or were we at home, leaving the uncontrolled folly of the evening to those who

still could forget? Except for a few T-shirts, . . . I saw no signs of the disease that has changed our community forever. My plans to go with friends to some hot new sex clubs (yes, PWA's do go to sex clubs) deteriorated into a desire to sleep, both for my health and to escape my sadness.

Despite my intentions, I ended up sleeping poorly. (Don't you just hate when tricks don't get the hint to leave and then snore?) But when I looked out at what was definitely going to be a rare, glorious, hot San Francisco day, I got psyched anyway. It was as if nature had lifted the veil of tears that so often seemed to cover our lives and cajoled us towards the sort of behavior that the gay community should be proud of! . . .

At the civic center, I was pleased to see several PWA's walking around having fun, shirts off despite huge molluscum or the theatrical favorite, KS [Kaposi Sarcoma] lesions. I felt happy, included, part of it all. . . . On the way home, . . . we passed a young Latino with an unbelievable butt . . . who practically ran over us trying to walk, gawk and remove his shirt at the same time. He seemed very interested in us both, so since he was just my friend's type, I offered my place for some fun. [He] came over, but my friend clearly changed his mind, . . . and both [he] and my friend left for separate destinations. . . .

Lying in bed, I heard the doorbell and my roommate tell [the young Latino], who had returned, that I was asleep. Before I could put my shorts on and catch him, it was too late. I went back to bed, thinking it was just as well, and finally drifted off to sleep amidst a dreamed sea of drag queens, scientific abstracts, yellow shorts, summer days, etc. They flowed by just as silently as my battery-powered clock tracked the minutes and a sinister virus reproduced inside of the miraculous cells of my immune system, both marking an inevitable march to a shared fate that is too horrible to be real, to real to be ignored.

Even with the knowledge of being HIV positive and knowing the deadly consequences of the AIDS disease, this kind of promiscuity continues. However, the truly tragic thing in this article is the eternal lostness and sense of hopelessness of the writer. Christ is his only answer.

The act of homosexual sex is as abnormal a process as someone deciding to eat food only through his nose. It could be done, but it wouldn't be considered normal in any sense of the word. It would be absurd to "accept" or to provide legal protections for an eat-through-your-nose movement (no matter how much self-gratification and fulfillment they claim such behavior brings to them!). It is equally ridiculous to legalize a movement that bases its existence on the practice of engaging in abnormal sexual practices. Yet, that is precisely what the gay rights movement wants.

Tuberculosis Outbreak Is Linked to AIDS

There is an alarming increase in the number of tuberculosis cases, primarily in Miami and New York City. According to the New York City Health Department, from 1980 to 1990, the annual number of cases jumped from 1,514 to 3,520, with a 30 percent increase in 1990 alone.

In November 1991, tuberculosis killed thirteen people in New York state prisons. Twelve of those individuals were HIV positive prisoners. Of those, four were being treated at the University Hospital of the Health Science Center in Syracuse, New York. A prison guard who had been assigned to guard these four inmates also became infected with TB and died. Syracuse hospital officials tested their workers and found that fifty-two of them were infected with the TB virus, although none have (at this writing) come down with the disease.

A 12 September 1991 article in the *Bay Area Reporter*, reported that doctors are seeing an outbreak of a new drug-resistant strain of TB among AIDS patients in New York and Miami hospitals. One doctor who treated AIDS patients at St. Claire Hospital in Manhattan has already died of TB. The article points out that the Centers for Disease Control in Atlanta has located three hospitals in New York where drug resistant TB strains are multiplying among patients. This apparently follows a 1988 TB outbreak in a Miami hospital. In all, 147 patients at four hospitals have been infected with TB. Of those, 141 were HIV positive patients (*Bay Area Reporter*, Vol. XXI, 37 [12 Sept. 1991]: 1, 27.).

The 1 February 1992 edition of the *San Francisco Examiner* reported that "the Board of Supervisors, worried about a tuberculosis rate in San Francisco that is five times the national average, will hold a hearing Tuesday on combating the very contagious disease. The hearing is spearheaded by Supervisor Angela Alioto, . . . Alioto is most concerned about the recent discovery of a strain that is resistant to anti-TB drugs. 'There is no doubt in my mind that if these recent disclosures are not attended to immediately, TB will become the epidemic of the '90s,' said Alioto. 'What's happening now reminds me so much of the early days of AIDS.'"

The article went on to say that a representative of the Department of Public Health "attributed the higher-than-average tuberculosis rate in San Francisco—33 total cases—to 'the rise of TB among people with HIV.' Alioto said New York recently opened its first sanitarium to combat the disease, which is transmitted easily when an infected person coughs."

In other words, as a result of their deficient immune systems, HIV positive people and AIDS patients are contracting this new strain of TB at an alarming rate. However, unlike AIDS, this tuberculosis is not passed on by unsafe sexual practices, IV drug use, transfusion, or the like—all of us are susceptible. The fear is that because of their weakened immune systems, this strain of TB will ignite among HIV/AIDS people, and explode into an epidemic that could have serious repercussions for the general public. The argument that a person's private practices, whether it be unsafe sexual behavior or IV drug use, does not affect anyone else but that person, is a farce that has been played on the American public. All of society suffers the affects of immoral behavior.

The health costs associated with the AIDS epidemic are going to be astronomical. According to AIDS expert Shepherd Smith, in *Christians in the Age of AIDS*, the U.S. Army has estimated that the cost of caring for one AIDS patient from the time of infection through symptomatic AIDS is around $250,000.

"The hospital requirements of AIDS patients are significant and largely unpredictable. Estimated costs for this care for 1990 approach $5 billion and could grow to over $10 billion by 1993, when AIDS cases in that year alone may exceed 100,000" (Shepherd Smith, *Christians in the Age of AIDS* [Wheaton, Ill.: Victor Books, 1990], 63.).

Insurance companies are estimating that AIDS-related claims will cost them $50 billion during the 1990s. According to Smith, this increased financial burden " . . . will fall on public financing of health care, potentially raising everyone's tax liability. We will increasingly see uninsured risk pools established by states, and the federal government taking action to provide treatment centers for persons infected" (Ibid.).

What does the future hold for San Francisco's gay population? In the 16 March 1990 issue of *JAMA* (*Journal of the American Medical Association*), a group of doctors have predicted that ". . . the number of AIDS cases in San Francisco by 1993 is expected to be between 12,349 and 17,022, with between 9,966 and 12,767 cumulative deaths" (p. 1497).

Public Sex

As much as homosexuals argue their right to engage in perverted sex in the privacy of their own homes, the truth of the matter is that they quite often choose to engage in sexual behaviors in public places. They often meet for anonymous sex in such places as public restrooms at bus stations, libraries, rest stops, or service stations, in public parks, on beaches, on street corners, and in pornographic bookstore peep show booths called "Glory Holes."

The gays have effectively taken over various parks in the city (Buena Vista, Lincoln, parts of Golden Gate Park), especially at night. Several years ago, the city closed the Buena Vista park to automobile traffic; and now homosexuals have free run of the area for anonymous sexual encounters—not the place for family or church picnics! And, with so many homosexual officers on the police force and a "hands-off" city hall policy, arrests are not made for such indecent exposure.

Reading the Gay Press

There are two main topics in gay publications: politics and sex. A "subtopic" of both main topics is disease. For the homosexual community, disease is not only sex-related but also a political issue. Donna and I periodically read gay newspapers for two reasons: 1) self-preservation, and 2) political awareness.

• Self-Preservation: Years ago, after the lawsuit, we developed a few acquaintances in the gay community. They were homosexuals who, although they totally disagreed with our

biblical position on homosexuality and our opposition to the
gay movement, took it upon themselves to "befriend" us to the
extent that they would argue the "religion of homosexuality"
versus biblical Christianity. They also felt a responsibility to
keep us informed of the political climate of the gay community
and any imminent danger that our family might be facing.
(This is how we knew when to get the family out of the city for
safety's sake.) Since then, all these men have died. One was
found in his apartment several days after he died. He was a
minister and prominent (but antagonistic) member of the gay
community. The papers only reported that he was found and
that his death was a "mystery." To this day we do not know how
he died. The other men with whom we had contact have all
died of AIDS. Now we have no "inside" information about the
community nor when we may expect any protesting or violence
against us. Consequently, we read the papers to find out the
emotional climate of the community and the possibility of
danger for us.

• Political Awareness: The politics of the gay movement are
definitely reflected in their newspapers. They keep their community well informed of any pending gay rights legislation,
whether on the city, state, or federal level. This information is
conscientiously kept out of the secular/straight press until after these laws are passed, and it is too late for any opposition to
such legislation.

You can't really understand what the homosexual lifestyle
is all about until you know what's being written and advertised
in these gay publications. We can assure you, it's a world you
never knew existed; and in this city it is legally protected and
advertised. We do not advise that you regularly read gay literature—its insidious immorality is oppressive to the Christian
spirit and can seduce your own sense of morality. We have,
however, taken just one typical newspaper, the *Bay Area Reporter*, dated 12 September 1991 for a cursory review.

The cover story deals with the increasing spread of tuberculosis among HIV-infected hospital patients in New York and
Miami. A secondary story describes how Amnesty International,
a human rights group, has agreed to include homosexual sex
on their list of "protected rights." Another article describes the
effort of pro-gay School Board members to oust the Boy Scouts
of America from local schools, because the national headquar-

ters of the Boy Scouts excludes homosexuals as scout leaders or scouts.

On the editorial page is a diatribe against the nomination of Clarence Thomas to the Supreme Court. An accompanying guest editorial is written by Matthew Coles, an attorney for the American Civil Liberties Union of Northern California. Coles, an open homosexual, is urging Governor Pete Wilson to sign AB101, the gay rights bill, which would have legitimized homosexual behavior and effectively restricted the religious freedom of Christian radio and TV stations, bookstores, and other non-ecclesiastical Christian businesses. (Thankfully, Wilson vetoed the bill, but not for any principled reason. We'll discuss AB101 in a later chapter.)

One of the saddest pages in a gay newspaper is the evergrowing list of obituaries of young to middle-aged men who have prematurely died of AIDS. In this particular issue, there are fourteen deaths. Most of them were in their thirties and forties. One in particular is striking because it describes the death of a transvestite, who moved to San Francisco in the late 1970s. Leon "Dolli Levi" Standord, died on 22 August 1991 of an AIDS-related disease. Standord worked at a San Francisco law firm but was better known in the gay culture as the "Princess of St. Petersburg." According to the obituary, Leon will "always be remembered as that little blonde who walked the [gay pride] parade route wearing those big 'Dolli Levi' hats."

Moving through the political news and obituaries, you eventually come to the entertainment section and personal advertisements for sex partners. In the entertainment section, you'll find dozens of ads for dial-a-porn services tailor-made for homosexual men. There is an advertisement for an exclusively gay cruise line with a picture of two men enjoying each other "on board" ship.

On the following page, there's an advertisement for "Leather Headquarters," a store featuring the latest in sado-masochistic and bondage and dominance paraphernalia. Also, every week there is an entire page devoted to the latest news for "Leathermen" of the gay community.

Each page gets progressively more bizarre. The personals section is worse. It is simply too explicit to describe. Here is a sample:

• "Secret God's Church: Ancient Phallic Rites of Gnostic

Christianity: An Orgy of Brotherly Love. Males 18 & Older Welcome."

• "Cross-dressing can be fun and fulfilling. Why hide it in the closet? Express your creativity and be a whole person by learning everything from make-up to mannerisms. With a little help you can be as socially accepted as I am."

• "HIV positive and masculine, good looking black wants . . ."

HIV positive . . . wants . . . what?!

These papers convey two conflicting messages: that gay sex is dangerous to your health and at the same time, it's up to you to do as you please—there is no absolute standard from God about the kind of enjoyment you can have. Such political and social sexual freedom leads to this wedding of contradiction in our society. Sooner or later, the contradiction will be resolved in favor of death unless the law of God prevails and is received by faith in Christ.

Conclusion

You only have to read one of these papers to sense the emptiness and tragedy of the gay lifestyle. It is by no means "gay." It is a life filled with anger, lust, venereal diseases, pain, loneliness, and early death from a number of wasting diseases. The tragedy is that it is so unnecessary. Militant homosexuals are so caught up in their drive for political power to protect their "rights" to self-gratification that they can't see how their sexual behaviors are literally killing them. The obituaries tell the story, yet the personal ads show there are men so driven by their lust that they will knowingly risk death for it.

We cannot help but feel a deep sadness for men and women who have been so enslaved by their sin. However, at the same time, we realize that we cannot remain quiet while militant homosexuals pursue political power and preach sodomy in our public schools in the name of "safe sex." We cannot allow them to perpetrate their "death-style" among our children—nor can we acquiesce to their push for absolute control of our major social and political institutions.

As Christians, we feel a sense of anger at the media and other institutions popularizing the gay philosophy and style of living. Yet, we also must have a deep sense of sorrow for those trapped by their sexual lusts without hope of deliverance. The gospel of Jesus Christ is the only hope for such prisoners. Gay men or lesbian women do not have a corner on imprisonment in their sin; the gospel of sovereign grace breaks the prison bars of sin and hopeless despair for all of us. The message of our holy God is that He is abundant in loving kindness and mercy to save all that call upon Him in sincerity for deliverance and a changed life, a real life of holiness. A clean life in the truest sense of the word is available for any man, woman, or child who in simple and childlike faith, by the Spirit of God, receives the good news that their old life can be broken and replaced by a new life of forgiveness in full and pardon complete.

SEVEN

"Fire, Get Out!"

It had been three years since the lawsuit . . . three frightening and difficult years. The end of the lawsuit was the beginning of relentless intimidation for our family. We had crossed the homosexual community and, for some, there would be no "forgive and forget."

The harassment started. Rocks, beer bottles, beer cans were thrown through the church windows on many occasions. Swastikas were carved in the church doors and drawn on our house. A window in our car was smashed out. Graffiti was sprayed-painted all over the church, house, and sidewalk. Anti-Christian, pro-homosexual leaflets were scattered around the neighborhood calling us Nazis, bigots, anti-gay, etc. Demonstrators would come into our Sunday services and disrupt the worship by writing protests in the hymn books or, at times, by vocal protests.

Having people come in and disrupt the services in this manner was also frightening, as we were at the same time receiving frequent death threats. These days you don't know who has a gun and who is just crazy enough to use it! One time a man came pounding and spitting on our front door in the middle of the night, screaming, "We're going to get you McIlhenny—we're going to kill you politically!" We were verbally threatened outside the house on the way to our car. There were daily—24-hour-per-day—telephone calls. They began with screaming and obscenities. They graduated into phone calls describing our children—by name, appearance, where they attended school, when they got out of school, and what sexually deviant behavior was to be practiced on the children before killing them. There were also calls of an obscene seductive nature.

This kind of harassment continued for a full three years. I guess the telephone calls were really the worst of it. At least three times, the death threats became so severe that we flew the children down to Los Angeles to stay with relatives. Whenever well-known TV preachers from other parts of the country would say or do anything about abortion or homosexuality on their programs, we would suffer the consequences from the homosexual community. We had no bars on our windows at that time—no gates, no guard dog—we didn't even have an answer machine to take the brunt of the calls. We had nothing but the Lord.

Then on 31 May 1983 at 12:30 a.m., someone actually attempted to follow through with their threats to kill us. I'll let Donna describe the events of that night and the period following:

Fire and Fear

It had been a long day at the law firm where I work, and when I got home it seemed that I had a hundred different things to do before going to bed. It was nearly 12:30 a.m. by the time I locked up for the night and headed for bed. The children had already been asleep for hours, and Chuck had gone to bed shortly before me.

As I crawled into bed, I heard what I thought were the garbage cans banging together in the fierce May wind. Experience had taught me to check out any strange noises; however, I was so exhausted that I simply listened for a moment and then lay down to sleep.

The church and the house are right next door to each other, attached by a small alleyway. Our bedroom was right next to the alleyway. As I lay down, I was looking toward the alleyway window. I saw something flicker, and before I could even wonder what it was, a huge ball of fire roared up the alleyway wall and burst through the window into the bedroom, breaking the quarter inch pane of glass.

I yelled at Chuck to get the kids. He was out of bed and down the hall to their rooms in a flash! I heard him barking orders at them, and in just seconds, they were lined up on the sidewalk in front of the house like three little troopers.

As Chuck got the children, I ran for the phone in the kitchen and called 9-1-1. (I was firmly reprimanded by the firemen afterwards—always leave the house first and then find a phone to call.) By the time I hung up the phone, smoke had begun to fill the house.

I ran out the front door and found the children out on the sidewalk shivering from the wind and cold. On impulse, Chuck had grabbed his keys from the nightstand by the bed before racing down the hall to rescue the children. We piled the kids into our car; and Chuck moved the car across the street, away from the front of the house and the fire. In the meantime, my motherly instincts got the best of me; and I did another foolish thing: I went back into the house and, doing an army crawl to stay under the thick smoke, made my way to Ryan's room and pulled a couple of blankets from his bed to wrap around the children. By the time I crawled back out the front door, I'd inhaled so much smoke that I coughed up what looked like black dust for days afterward.

Ironically, after we were all outside the house, we heard the smoke alarm go off in the hallway by the girls' bedroom.

The fire trucks arrived within minutes of my call. Some manned the hoses and some began chopping at the church doors with axes. Even though the strong winds were whipping the flames around, the firemen were able to extinguish the blaze before the entire house and church had gone up in flames.

Our next door neighbor, Dr. Steve, came rushing to our aid. He got a pair of his own pants for Chuck to put on and took me over to his house to call some of the men in the church to tell them what had happened. I also called a couple in our church, Joyce and Scott Cox, who lived nearby. Scott came to the house immediately and took the kids back to their apartment where Joyce settled them down and made a place for us to sleep on their living room floor.

Up until this time, we did not know that the fire had been deliberately set, but somehow I had that frightening feeling. After the fire was out, I asked one of the firemen how it had started. I thought perhaps the main electrical fuse box, located in the alleyway, had been the cause. Or perhaps I should say, I hoped it was the cause. However, when the fireman showed me the two charred gas cans and told me that this was indeed arson, the real seriousness of our situation struck me. I was filled with terror. I asked whether this had merely been an attempt to scare us—somehow it was just too terrifying for me to comprehend that someone had actually tried to kill us, especially little children! The fireman replied: "The intent was to kill. It's as if someone pointed a gun in your face and pulled the trigger . . . only, in this case, the gun misfired!"

Even with all the death threats that we had received by phone and mail, it truly was unbelievable, unreal, and absolutely terrifying that someone would actually follow through with such threats. It was almost like being in the midst of a fantasy—like being a character in a T.V. movie—BUT THIS WAS REAL! It's such an unstable feeling and next to impossible to describe. I was unable to comprehend or grasp the fact that it actually happened.

Scott came back after dropping the kids off at his apartment to see if he could help us pack some clothes or salvage things. Of course, there was no electricity (all the main wiring had been burned out), so, equipped with a flashlight, the three of us went back into the house. The arson investigators had arrived on the scene and were sifting through the debris over in the church. As we went through the smoke-sooted rooms, we trembled with the words of the Psalms on our lips. Chuck's recollection was Psalm 46, "God is our refuge and strength, a very present help in trouble, therefore, we will not fear . . ." I remember walking through water and chunks of glass back down the dark hallway where just an hour or so before the children had been screaming and crying in terror, and repeating the words of Psalm 23 over and over again, ". . . yea, though I walk through the valley of the shadow of death, I will fear no evil, for Thou art with me . . ." Oh, but I was afraid!

We alternated between humming, singing, or reciting the words we could remember, thanking God that He had delivered us and that we belonged to Him. Our lives were in His keeping. We were at His disposal!

We packed a few things for ourselves and the kids and went to Scott and Joyce's for the night.

To date, as of the writing of this book, nothing has been turned up by the police and fire department investigations as to who may have set the fire. No leads, no clues, and no person has ever been questioned!

Chuck and I thought it best to keep things as normal as possible for the children; after taking them out to breakfast the next morning, we took them to school. Megan remembers one friend in her kindergarten class asking why she was so late for school. She said, "someone burned my house last night." The friend replied, "Oh." And so life goes on.

Chuck and I returned to the house to see in the daylight how much damage had been done. The downstairs of the church was the worst. The interior was pretty well burned out. The flooring was destroyed and the library completely gone. The upstairs sanctuary remained intact but was smoke damaged. Overall, the structure of the church was still in good condition. This was encouraging, because more than anything, Chuck wanted to hold services in the church that Sunday. We felt that the sooner the church was functioning again, the sooner the message would go out to whomever had done this that "the gates of hell shall not prevail against the Church of Jesus Christ." The insurance company had contractors on the job fairly quickly, and the church was the first thing repaired. By Sunday, the sanctuary was clean, and except for the smell of newly-painted walls, one would not have guessed there had been a fire.

When we went into the house, it was cold from all the windows being left open the night before. It reeked of smoke, and everything was covered with a thin layer of black soot. Most of the walls would eventually have to be painted and all the furniture professionally cleaned. The firemen had saved our bedroom from being completely burned, but there was quite a bit of water damage. Chunks of glass and bits of burned material were all over the room. Our bed was completely destroyed. Our wedding album was still on the mantel, but some of the pictures had been destroyed.

I remember looking over at the window where the fire first came through. I was amazed at how the walls all around the window frame were scorched through, and yet, there were pieces of the curtains still hanging up at the top of the frame. The window seat had been burned halfway down and, of course, soaked with water. It contained a few "priceless" possessions. I opened it carefully and began to sift through several layers of burned items. A little wave of joy and comfort came over me when I lifted the last burned layer and underneath found the baby kimono and bonnet that I had made for Erin before she was born. All of the children had worn that kimono and bonnet home from the hospital as newborns. It was invaluable to me. It had suffered a bit of water damage, but otherwise it was completely intact. What a blessing. I now keep it in a frame on the wall of our dining room as a constant reminder of what happened that night. I also saved a piece of the glass from the window, to remember how powerful the fire was and just how marvelously the Lord delivered us.

Most of that first day I couldn't do much more than sit around in stunned silence. Church members came by, offering their love and concern as well as their help in cleaning up the mess. However, not much cleaning could be done; things had to be left as they were for the arson inspectors and insurance examiner. The insurance man finally came to assess the damage, and eventually a crew arrived to start cleaning up before reconstruction could begin.

The church's insurance policy covered the expense of a motel and meals until the house was habitable again. It was estimated that we could probably get back into the house in a few days and were told to find a motel for that time period. (However, what was supposed to be a few days, turned into a few weeks.) The electricity was turned back on fairly quickly, but some doors and windows had to be replaced before the house would be secure enough to stay in.

Later that afternoon, the kids were dropped off from school. We packed more clothes and a few of their favorite things, went to a restaurant for dinner, and checked into a motel downtown. We told the clerk we would probably be there for the rest of the week and paid him for the next four days.

The local news was beginning to run our story. Watching your house burning on T.V. is like reliving the trauma over and over again. I didn't want the kids to see it. At this point, they seemed to be doing very well emotionally. They certainly weren't as terrified as I was! They were still young enough to believe that if Mom and Dad were okay, they were okay. I didn't want that security taken away from them too.

Although the motel we had chosen was supposed to be in a "good part of town," it was a disaster! Some lights in the room didn't work, nor did the shower. However, the worst thing was the view we had. Directly across the parking lot from us was a house with shades open and lights on. There were two men in front of the window engaged in exactly that activity for which this city has become so well known. We closed the curtains and told the kids not to look out the window.

We left the motel early, in time to get the kids to school and me to work. After telling the clerk about the lights and shower, we told him that we had decided not to stay the remainder of the week and asked for our money back. On the T.V. behind the desk, he had the morning news on. They were just running our story, giving our name, the name of the church, etc. Of course, as always, it was the "anti-gay minister's church and house firebombed." The clerk looked at the T.V. and at our name in the register, and with a smirk on his face he said, "I would think that lights and showers that don't work would be the least of your problems right now." With that, we collected our money and left.

The routine of life becomes a security that you desperately need at a time like this. I went back to work at the law firm, and Chuck tried to resume his duties at the church. For the next few weeks, our normal routine was constantly interrupted by construction crews at the house, reporters calling all hours of the day and evening for interviews. The threatening calls continued; however, now they didn't speak. They just sat there on the line when we picked it up. We continued to stay at motels and also spent a few nights in friends' homes.

The week after the fire, school was out for summer vacation. It was clear that the house was not in shape for us to move back in, so we made arrangements to send the kids down to Long Beach to stay with relatives. That week the arson inspector in charge of our case came over to interview us about the events of that night, and also to make suggestions as to how we could make the house safer and more secure. He suggested we put an iron gate across the opening of the alleyway, get a guard dog, and have flood lights installed around the outside of the house. The idea that we had to take such steps to protect ourselves was such a foreign notion. When you're growing up, you never expect to be living in fear of your life!

One thing that the inspector said, however, became very real to me and was impossible for me to forget. He said that with the way the wind was blowing that night, if the person who started the fire had been smart, he would have set the fire at the other end of the house, right underneath our son's bedroom window. If that had happened, the inspector went on to explain, the whole house most likely would have been lost, and Ryan would never have gotten out alive! Things like that don't have to be said to a mother more than once to make an impression! The thought of something like this happening again was bad enough, but the thought of losing one of the children constantly played on my emotions, and that all-but-consuming fear stayed with me for years afterwards.

After the kids had been safely packed off to Southern California, and the doors and windows were repaired, Chuck and I returned home for the next phase: learning to sleep at night. It certainly was a learning as well as praying process. It's one thing to have a fire in your home, but quite another to know that it was deliberately set. Yes, sleeping at night was going to be tough from now on.

Part of the problem with feeling safe at night is the logistics of the house. Unlike most residential neighborhoods, there were no houses on the other side of the street from us. The Shriner's Crippled Children's Hospital occupies that entire block, and the grounds surrounding the hospital have trees and tall bushes—ideal for cover and get away. Many a night since that time, we have stood on the front porch, straining to see what sinister things those trees and bushes might be hiding across the street.

The first night back in the house was agonizing. The repairs on our bedroom were not finished, so we decided to sleep in the hallway by the front door. Two big doors separated us from the outside and also allowed us the freedom to flee if necessary. What a horrible thought! What a way to live! The creaking and settling of the 1907 structure of the house surely sounded like someone stealing down the long hallway to finish what they had started. (After all, they were still calling on the phone.) Every "bump in the night" sounded like an attempted break-in all over again. Any suspicious noise was a militant protestor ready to do us harm! The silence of the night was deafening . . . and I could not get out of my head, ". . . if they had set the fire on the other end of the house your son would have died. . . ."

For the next few weeks, until the house was completely finished (the children were still in Long Beach), we slept in the front hallway. A few times, just to get a good night's sleep, we slept in homes that had graciously been opened to us. I thought those first few nights were bad, but little did I realize how bad the nights would get for me when the kids came back. Those fears would surface in me even more when I felt the children were in jeopardy. For the next two years, except for nights when the whole family was away from the house, I could not sleep through the night. ". . . if they had set the fire on the other end of the house, your son would have died. . . ."

The Dog, the Lights, and the Fence

At this point, the congregation was more than willing to help pay for as much protection as they could. After repairs to the house and church were completed, we followed through with the suggestions of the arson inspector. An iron gate was installed at the alleyway entrance, floodlights were put up around the outside of the house, and we got a guard dog. Because I was most familiar with dogs, Chuck left the decision to me as to what kind of dog to get. I chose a boxer because 1) they're known for having great dispositions, especially with children, 2) they are protective of their own territory, and most importantly, 3) they have one of those faces that would scare anyone away. Casey, the boxer, has proved himself to be well-qualified in all those categories over the last ten years. The dog was taught that his primary domain was Ryan's bedroom. He was bought most specifically to be a protection for Ryan at night. (". . . if they had set the fire on the other end of the house, your son would have died . . . .") Pam, one of the tireless workers in our church, organized a work party to install a chain link fence around the side of the house, creating a run for the dog.

Now we were set: we had the dog, the floodlights, the iron gate, the fence . . . now it was time to bring the kids back from Southern California. Short of having a gun (which many suggested) we were living in an "armed camp." We had developed a "fortress mentality." We were secure . . . or were we? The psychology of terrorism is ingenious. No physical harm needs to be inflicted in an attack—just the constant threats, and one close call was enough! The demons of imagination plagued my mind at night and were far stronger than any gates, fences, or dogs. ("For our struggle is not against flesh and blood, but against the rulers, against the authorities, against the powers of this dark world and against the spiritual forces of evil in the heavenly realms" [Eph. 6:12, NIV].) ". . . if they had set the fire on the other end of the house, your son would have died . . . ."

The Anger Smolders

There are certain events in a person's life that leave an indelible mark. The fire was a definite turning point for me. I didn't realize how seriously it was affecting me. I was exhausted from sleepless nights spent checking on the children and patrolling the house. When I could sleep, it was fitful and full of nightmares. One night I awoke out of a dream and found myself paralyzed with fear. Not only was I unable to cry out, but my heart was pounding so loud in my ears I thought it would break; I was unable to move. I was fully awake and Chuck was just a few inches away from me, but I could neither call to him nor touch him to wake him up. I was paralyzed. I felt completely defenseless for those few moments, but God's promise never to leave me nor forsake me came to my mind. He alone was my defense on the right and on the left. I began to pray. What seemed to me to be a very long time in reality was only a few moments before this episode passed. It was a terribly out-of-control feeling.

Because of my fear, I became Chuck's worst enemy for the next few months. I blamed him for putting us through this ordeal. I was angry because he was not as terrified as I was. His stand against the homosexual community had nearly gotten us all killed. Why didn't he take us away? Why did he want to torture us by keeping us here? I wanted out—NOW.

I started arguments with him that degenerated into shouting matches. I would apologize, only to have my anger smolder again. I told him I couldn't take any more trouble, and I truly believed it. I have since learned that none of us knows just how much we can endure—only the Lord does; and He is faithful to preserve us in all our ways. But I was physically and emotionally exhausted. I was sick and tired of obscene phone calls, vandalism, and fearing for the lives of my children.

One night, in the middle of a heated argument, I said something that afterward I wished I had never said—but it had been preying on my mind for weeks. I told him ". . . if anything happens to my son, . . . if he dies, I don't think I'd ever be able to forgive you!" Without a pause, Chuck answered me in a very calm and quiet manner, and with confidence and sincerity he said, "I'd rather have my son die in a fire knowing that his father stood for Christ, than have him live a long life knowing that his father compromised the faith!"

His answer slapped me right across the face. It made me even more angry! . . . because I knew he was right. Christ said it in what seems to be an even harsher way: "If anyone comes to me and does not hate his father and mother, his wife and children, his brothers and sisters—yes, even his own life—he cannot be my disciple" (Luke 14:26, NIV). Christ wasn't telling us to hate our parents ("honor your mother and father"), or husbands to hate their wives ("husbands love your wives"), etc., but was warning us about idolizing any one or any thing in the place of Christ. It came down to a very blunt question: Donna, do you idolize your children more than you love Christ . . . do you love your children more than faithfulness to Christ and His Word . . . are you more afraid of the enemy, or do you really believe that Christ will "never leave you nor forsake you [or your children]"? Chuck's answer was right. I hated it, because it held a mirror up to my face, and I didn't like what I saw. "The fear of man [truly had me in] a snare."

We don't all have to be faced with situations as harsh as this one. (Perhaps it's only strong-minded, stubborn "Scots" like myself that need that kind of slap in the face.) However, we all face these dilemmas daily in more subtle ways. How about at our jobs when we're told to do or say something that clearly conflicts with Scripture? "Well, it's just a minor thing—just a little 'white lie' . . ." The temptation is to "go with the flow and don't make waves." Too often we rationalize our response (or lack of response), because we're afraid of losing that job. We offend Christ in order not to offend the boss. How about the Christian radio station we told you about who, out of vague fears of material loss that they fabricated in their own minds, lost an opportunity to give a faithful witness in San Francisco. They idolized that station in the place of Christ. Or, what about the Christian parent disciplining his child? The parent knows that the Bible forbids what that child might want to do, and, yet, that parent may fear saying "no," because he doesn't want the child to be angry with him or reject him. It's hard. We love our children, and we want them to love us. We might shy away from proper discipline out of fear of offending them, and in the process we offend the righteousness of Christ. We've idolized our children, and in fact, we end up not truly loving our children. The only way to truly love a child is to love him in Christ . . . to give him back to the Lord as Hannah did and

". . . entrust [our] souls to a faithful creator in doing what is right" (I Pet. 4:19, NASV).

Luke 14 makes it quite clear that loving Christ first applies to all our relationships. Now I had to scrutinize my loyalty to Chuck. I couldn't stay and see things through only out of love and loyalty to him. It had to be out of love and loyalty to Christ first, with faith in His promises to keep us, and satisfaction in the realization that He hasn't promised to keep us alive, but He has promised us eternal life.

In spite of all that had happened to us, I knew the Lord was working His will through every circumstance, whether good or bad. My comfort was in knowing that God is sovereign and that He has allowed whatever comes to pass; that "all things work together for good to those that love Him and are called according to His purpose"; and that which is done in faith and obedience to His Word He will bring about for our welfare and for His glory. Until God was finished with us here in San Francisco, our calling was to remain faithful and to continue an uncompromised witness to the gospel of Jesus Christ.

However, don't think for a minute that the fears are all gone. They are ongoing, and I constantly have to ask the Lord to "strengthen [my] weak knees." Recently, I told a close friend that I don't believe I have ever come back to "square one" (where I was before the fire), nor do I ever expect to. However, it is in our weaknesses that we become strong, and the Lord is glorified.

Throughout this ordeal, there were friends that deserted us, but there were also friends that stayed "closer than a brother." One friendship that I held most dearly fell apart because, in those months following the fire, I had "not been the friend to [her] that I used to be." She was right. I was not able to "rejoice" with her; and she wasn't able to "weep" with me.

However, among many friends that ministered to us in so many ways, one comes to mind for me: One Sunday afternoon there was an almost inaudible knock at my back door. Joyce poked her head in, and in her characteristic quiet manner, she said, "Donna, you seem a bit tense lately . . . do you think we could pray together about it?" (Joyce is not only known for her quiet spirit, but also for understating the facts! . . . "a bit tense . . ."!) She was such a wonderful and welcome relief. We read a passage of Scripture together, and then we both prayed for God to take away fears, to restore our souls, to "renew a right spirit within [us]." This effort on Joyce's part was the beginning of a women's prayer meeting, which has continued every Sunday since then, and has been a source of strength and encouragement for us all through the years.

As a result of the fire, I have developed a keen sympathy for those who are suffering from some sort of loss, whether it be home, friends, loved ones, etc. I also have a keener sense of the sacrifice Christian martyrs have made throughout the centuries, because I know (albeit on a small scale) the fears that by God's grace they had to overcome. We read books about such men and women and tend not to think of the fear associated with facing death—unless we ourselves have been so terrorized. I am more impressed now with the willingness of past saints to suffer for Christ and, what's more, to glory in that suffering. I recall reading about one incident in Fox's Book of Martyrs where a wife watched as her husband was burned at the stake for his profession of faith. As she stood there, she encouraged him in his love for Christ and faithfulness to the truth of God's Word. . . . I am in awe of such witnesses, . . . and am ashamed.

I still have fear: I still feel the dread of knowing there are people who hate us enough to kill us. They have continued to remind us of that over the years since the fire. I am concerned for the safety and welfare of the children, after all, they are a gift from the Lord. However, I have developed an even greater fear that overshadows all the others: the fear of denying Christ. He has so marvelously and graciously protected us over the years, even when city officials and officers appointed to such tasks have not. He has set His angels around and about us to guard us in all our ways. He has at all times been faithful. He has so clearly demonstrated the power of His keeping hand . . . by His grace, we dare not be faithless to Him.

We had the privilege of doing a radio program with Dr. James Dobson a couple of years ago. He and his entire organization have been continually supportive and encouraging, and we are grateful to them. During the interview, Dr. Dobson asked me how I would encourage other Christians who, because of the possible consequences, might be afraid to take an unpopular stand for Christ in their community. At that time, I gave an anemic answer. I said the greater the trial, the greater the blessing God has waiting for us on the other side of that trial if we persevere in faith. Although that may be true, I wish

I had remembered instead the words of the Apostle Peter: "And the God of all grace, who called you to His eternal glory in Christ, after you have suffered a little while, will himself restore you and make you strong, firm and steadfast. To Him be the power for ever and ever. Amen" (I Pet. 5:10-11, NIV).

The Pastors Unite: Chuck's Story

As a result of the fire and the harassment we continued to receive for those three years, twenty evangelical pastors from the city became so alarmed and outraged at what was happening to us that they rallied to our support. In fact, they all accompanied me to Mayor Feinstein's office to demand police protection for our family. I didn't want to go at first, but several of the ministers insisted not only for our sakes, but also for their own. They obviously didn't want to have what happened to us happen to their churches.

What the ministers basically told Mayor Feinstein was that they weren't going to put up with this kind of criminal behavior against any part of the Christian community. She forthrightly agreed and immediately assigned a police detective liaison to our family. We wanted assurances from her that if we had a pro-life rally or demonstration for traditional values that we could expect her to fulfil her God-given responsibility and protect our constitutional rights. She agreed. We proceeded to give her the gospel and pray with her. As I spoke, I told her that we appreciated her listening to our grievances but that it was the gay rights ordinance, which she sponsored as supervisor, that had gotten us into trouble. Churches were not exempted from the gay rights ordinance, and to date (1992), they still are not. I went on to explain to her that as Bible-believing Christians, and especially as pastors, we were conscience-bound to break such laws and would urge our people to do the same if they found themselves in a similar dilemma. Christian businessmen, for instance, are not exempt and are legally prohibited from denying employment to anyone on the basis of immoral lifestyles, are unable to fire employees for such behavior, and are not even allowed to advertise for employees with moral credentials. This law has, in effect, exempted morality from the business practices of this city. It is an unconscionable affront to God's law to penalize people for seeking to uphold His Word! As the civil magistrate, she, too, was bound by God's law to uphold morality and righteousness, whether it was politically popular or not.

We left her office relieved to know that she had at least been responsive and cordial. Her own administration had taken a turn toward more conservative positions as it had progressed. In 1982, when we protested the passage of "domestic partners" legislation, she responded by vetoing it and, she had also vetoed the Board of Supervisors' proposal for a resolution to officially support a liberal women's movement position on reproductive rights. We had various other contacts with her office during her administration, and she remained interested enough to listen to our concerns about the moral climate of the city. This could not be said for her successor, Art Agnos! As mayors change, times change also.

The ministers' involvement, however, didn't stop at the mayor's office. Eventually, a core group of these men formed, and whenever moral issues came before the Board of Supervisors, as was regularly the case, we would meet to strategize. We are still close friends and have worked together for the past nine years on confronting gay rights issues here and in Sacramento, abortion issues, school board issues, condom distribution, the ousting of the Boy Scouts of America from the public schools, etc. We have taken a public stand whenever our religious and moral freedoms were being threatened. It's not easy to do and it is time-consuming; however, we must ask ourselves, are we going to be salt and light in this wicked community or not? Is our salt and light going to shine at city hall, on the streets in front of abortion clinics, or at school board meetings where the lives of our children are at stake? Not every pastor has the time—every time—to speak before various committees on moral issues; but someone must, or wickedness will be forced upon all people. I like to send messages to the community by way of our church signboard. One message reads: DON'T KEEP CHRIST IN CHRISTMAS, HE BELONGS IN CITY HALL TOO.

Over the years, since this group of ministers has been meeting, each pastor has become an expert in a different field of knowledge. One pastor is well-versed on the medical dangers of sodomy, while another has become educated on the economic costs of immoral behavior, etc. But we all work together in harmony for a common cause: upholding Jesus Christ in our community and standing against evil.

It is tragic, however, that there aren't more pastors involved. In San Francisco there are approximately three hundred churches. There are about fifty pastors who would consider themselves evangelical. Of those fifty, there are only perhaps eight to ten pastors who can regularly be counted on to stand against various immoral issues. I'm certain that many of the ones who aren't involved are sympathetic, but they're simply too busy or perhaps too afraid to be involved. They've witnessed what our family has gone through and have openly said to us that they're not willing to risk the same for their families, their positions, or their properties.

The wicked have seized our city; and they remain in power through verbal intimidation, political scheming, and terrorist tactics. It may happen on the editorial page of the newspapers, or demonstrations at a church, or death threats over the phone in the middle of the night. The church, for the most part, has been silenced in San Francisco.

Today, the gay terrorists are more organized than ever before. With the advent of ACT UP and its even more violent offspring, Queer Nation, far too many church leaders seem paralyzed with fear. Their fears are certainly justified, but if they don't take a stand for righteousness, who will?

What has happened in San Francisco is going to be repeated all over the United States. In December 1991, Queer Nation of San Francisco announced that it was reorganizing and splintering into at least two new groups: Queer Nation and Outrage. According to an article in the *San Francisco Examiner*, Queer Nation is spreading out to the following cities: Atlanta, Georgia; Knoxville, Tennessee; Austin, Texas; Detroit, Michigan; Salt Lake City, Utah; Boise, Idaho; Santa Fe, New Mexico; Long Beach, California; and many other cities.

On vacation this past summer (1991), our family was visiting relatives in Brentwood, Tennessee, just outside Nashville. On the news there was a story about a restaurant chain called The Cracker Barrel. Demonstrations by Queer Nation were being held at several of the restaurants because of the company's employment policy regarding openly homosexual employees. As we understand it, this company is organized upon basic Christian moral principles. As we left Tennessee on our drive back to California, we stopped at a Cracker Barrel for breakfast. We mentioned the news item to one of the employees, and she recounted the crude and intimidating tactics of the Queer

Nation members who had demonstrated at that particular restaurant. We assured her that we knew all too well those tactics and that we appreciated the stand that the Cracker Barrel organization had taken.

In Hawaii, Christians are under serious threat by the homosexual community because of a state-wide gay rights ordinance. The 1991 law, passed by the legislature, signed by Governor John Waihee, and upheld by State Attorney General Warren Price III, prohibits employers from discriminating in the hiring and firing of employees based on sexual orientation. It also prohibits employers from printing anything that might be deemed discriminatory against homosexuals. The law allows for no exemptions for religious organizations or churches.

As a result of this threat, the Rutherford Institute of Hawaii is suing the governor and the state's attorney general. Rutherford attorney, Jim Hochberg, has analyzed the law and finds it seriously violates the religious freedoms of Christians and non-Christians alike. "Under this statute," says Hochberg, "churches, Christian schools and daycare centers could be sued for firing employees discovered to be practicing homosexuals. Religious groups could be forced to retain homosexual workers in violation of their religious teachings."

The section of this gay rights legislation that prohibits organizations from printing anything that is critical of homosexual behavior, is a clear violation of the First Amendment's protection of free speech. According to Hochberg, "The statute, as it stands now, even prohibits churches from having a Bible since it contains passages against homosexuality."

Technically, under this oppressive law, a militant gay could lodge a complaint against a pastor for preaching against homosexuality from the Bible. This, in effect, has happened in California. In the 10 February 1992 issue of *Christianity Today*, there is an article about Los Angeles Assistant Police Chief Robert Vernon who is suing L.A. city officials. The article reads in part:

> Los Angeles Assistant Policy Chief Robert Vernon will face off with city officials in March when a judge is scheduled to hear a $10 million lawsuit brought by Vernon. An elder in John MacArthur's Grace Church, Vernon claims he is being victimized by the city because of his religious beliefs. He filed the suit in November after the city council, under pressure by homosexual groups, called for an official inves-

tigation of him. Complaints center, in part, on a 1977 talk Vernon gave at Grace Community Church, in which he spoke against homosexuality and urged women to submit to their husbands.

Some city officials, while conceding that Vernon has a right to practice any religion, say he may be trying to impose his views throughout the police department. Vernon says certain city officials are on a "witch hunt."

So, what has happened to us in San Francisco is coming your way, sooner or later, unless pastors and lay leaders wake up to their calling and take a stand for righteousness in their own communities. You, your church, and your pastor will either become involved in the gay rights battle (whether you want to or not), or you will become like the Christ-less pastors and church members in the majority of the churches in San Francisco. The homosexual movement is coming after your right to free speech, to religious freedom, and, most importantly, after your public school children through homosexual recruitment programs disguised as "safe sex" and/or AIDS education classes, alternative lifestyle classes, or through counseling services for teens run exclusively by gays and lesbians. And, no, your private Christian school will not be spared if anti-discrimination/ sexual orientation ordinances are passed in your community. There will be no exceptions allowed in their bid for political rule over community after community—and why should there be? These are two mutually-exclusive moralities: one based on the Word of God, and the other based on the arbitrary will of men. There is no rapprochement between them. Both are totalitarian. Either we build our society on the principles of the gospel of Christ or the principles of the supposed autonomy of man. There is no bridge to span the gap between them. Neither should there be. Christ declares Himself and His saving work to be the bridge between alienated communities. He is, by his atonement, the only one that breaks down the middle wall that divides men and women, boys and girls. What our cities and communities need is not more morality for morality's sake, but more of the morality of the gospel of Jesus Christ. Possibly the only good thing that can be said for San Francisco, the gay community, and city government is that dividing line between morality and immorality is so very clear and blatant. That, however, does not necessarily make Christians come out and take a stand. In most cases it makes them go back into their closets, hiding in fear. Don't think you can wait until that moral line of demarcation is so blatantly clear in your community—by then, either you will be blinded to it by gay rights propaganda or, if you can still see the line clearly, the price you'll pay to make a stand will be very dear.

The big question is: what will your church do when the wicked attempt to seize your city? What will you do if your state passes a law that prohibits "discrimination" against homosexuals or any adulterer, and even includes a prohibition against speaking or writing anything critical of such immoral conduct? Will your church take a stand? Will your pastor take a stand? Will you support your pastor if he does take a stand, even though your reputation in the community may suffer? Or will you compromise and allow such legislated immorality to take over your community in the name of freedom? Will you allow your children to be recruited by such ungodliness in your tax-funded public schools and organizations? Only you can answer these questions, but they cannot be ignored.

The gay movement may cry freedom of expression and protest that their goal is not to force themselves on anybody, but you come to San Francisco and observe the lie of Satan for what it is. See how the citizens here are subjected to immorality even on bus stop posters on their way to work. Listen to safe-sex, not abstinence or holy matrimony, being propagated as the only reasonable approach to saving people from AIDS. See how promoting the gay agenda is the only politically correct way to get elected to public office. Listen to elected officials privately agree with you, and then watch your pleas for biblical morality go up in smoke. Don't wait until you're facing what we have in San Francisco. Time is shorter than you think. Use it wisely.

It is not in anger, but in the love of Christ, that we must oppose this insidious ungodliness. It is the love of Christ that constrains us to preach the gospel at city hall, as well as on the streets. The danger lesbians and gays are putting themselves in is awesome. We must be gripped by the impending judgment of God on them for their sin; but, we must also be gripped by the impending judgment on us if we do not warn them with tears to flee from the wrath to come. "Judgment begins with the House of God"—not the homosexual community.

EIGHT

Attacked Again!

22 March 1990: I was the first to wake up to the mysterious "ss sss ssss" sound and the smell of spray paint. Our bedroom window faces the street sidewalk, and underneath the window is the church signboard. As soon as I realized what was going on, I muttered to myself, "Oh, here we go again. They're graffitying the house and church again!" My reaction was more perfunctory than startled. It was the first part of the year, and it was about time they hit us again anyway! I thought more of the nuisance and the expense of clean up than anything else.

I got up, saw them from the window, and started down the creaking hallway toward the front porch. I had almost reached the girls' room, about fifteen feet away, when there came a loud "pop"—"bang," like a shotgun blast at their bedroom window. (Was it a gun? Had they gone that far? They'd been threatening to "blow [my] head off" all during this domestic partners campaign!)

Erin's bed was by the wall farthest away from that window, but the head of Megan's bed was directly underneath it. In panic, Megan let out an unearthly wail like I'd never heard before. I shouted to the girls, "Hit the floor and crawl out quickly!!!" Both girls fell to the floor and crawled out of their room into the hallway—trembling and terrified. At the same time, I ducked and ran for the front porch.

Donna had a cold and had been sleeping out in the living room so I could get a better night's rest. She dashed toward the girls' room shouting, "what's going on. . . ! ?" and called out for everyone. I shouted to her to call 9-1-1 while Ryan and I crouched by the giant bay windows on the front porch.

In those few terminally-long seconds that had passed, we had at least realized that the sound was not gunfire. When the

dispatcher answered the phone, Donna yelled at her that someone was smashing our windows with hammers or something and
that we needed police help NOW! The dispatcher was grossly
incompetent. The first thing she told Donna was "calm down,
lady. Just go to the front door and see if it's a friend knocking at
your door."

"Go to the door? Are you crazy?" screamed Donna incredu-
lously. "They're trying to break in, and I don't know if they have
guns or not!"

"Just look out the window to see who they are," was the
laconic reply of the dispatcher, "maybe it's someone you know."

The pounding at the windows was still going on, and Donna
held the phone out and screamed at me on the opposite side of
the house, "Chuck, this woman is insane! She won't send us any
help. Come and talk to her! . . ."

"Okay, okay, lady," was the response from the phone, "I'll
send a squad car over."

The banging went on for what seemed like an eternity.
(Actually, it was probably less than a minute.) We were frightened
out of our wits! Were these people armed with guns? Was their
intent to break the windows out completely and enter the house?
Would they really follow through with their death threats?

By the time the police finally arrived, the vandals had already
escaped in a couple of different directions into the night. Ryan
and I had watched four or five people running from the scene,
having left behind several cans of spray paint in front of the
church. The patrolman responding to the call immediately
phoned the sergeant on duty. When the sergeant arrived, he was
shocked to see what had really happened. He asked Donna what
she had reported to the 9-1-1 operator, and Donna repeated the
dialogue that she had had with the woman. Apologetically, the
sergeant told us that he had been only two blocks away dealing
with a couple of drunken teen-agers; however, the call that had
come over his radio from the 9-1-1 operator simply said that
"someone [was] ringing the doorbell and knocking on the door
at 1350 Lawton." She never said anything about our windows
being broken. The sergeant had thought it was a routine call, so
he took his time responding. When he saw how much danger we
had truly been in, he immediately called the dispatcher on our
phone and reprimanded her for failing to give them the proper
information and for neglecting to put out an immediate call for
help.

(Almost every officer that has responded to a call at our house has been familiar with our situation and our stand in the city. Most of them have expressed sympathy and concern. Some have even taken it upon themselves to make frequent "drive-bys" for weeks after we've been attacked. We have appreciated the response of the police at our local district station. If city hall had the same concern for our physical lives, I believe that by this time someone might at least have been questioned about the many felony crimes that have been committed against us over the years.)

After the vandals left, we were at least somewhat relieved to find that there had been no gunfire—only hammers smashing the windows. However, our fear of being killed was perfectly justified by the frequent death threats we were receiving by phone as well as mail. A letter with the ACT UP slogan, Silence = Death, and McIlhenny = S——, ended with "you'd better get out of town because you're dead." We let the answer machine handle our phone calls for a while. A few of them went like this:

> You're dead, mother ——, do you hear me? Bunch of Christians bashing gays! Well, you keep it up, mother ——. I'm going to come down there and strangle you with my bare hands!

> You're a dead man if this law [referendum against domestic partners] passes. You'd better stay out of gay rights, mother ——, because if this law passes you and your church are going to be blown up and you can let everyone else know that. Bye.

> Hello, my name is Satan. It is 2:05 and you mother —— —— in hell. May you burn in hell, and I'll be out watching for you. You'd better leave this city because you're gone!

We also received dozens of calls from people who would just remain silent on the other end of the line. We would hang up, and they would immediately call back—over and over and over again. One night Donna received such a call. She could tell from the sound on the phone that it was long distance. After several calls within seconds of each other, she decided to try something. When the phone rang again, she carefully lifted the receiver and covered it with her hand. She could hear someone breathing on the other end. After about thirty seconds she could hear him start pacing back and forth. Thinking that the long distance connection had not yet gone through, the caller became increasingly agitated. He started swearing and muttered to himself (or the phantom operator) that he was calling all the way from Los Angeles and that this was costing him money! Donna stayed on the phone until the caller hung up in anger and frustration. He didn't call back again, and what was even better, he had spent money on a call he never knew had gotten through!

Now we had to set about cleaning up the mess. I called my elder, Scott, and his wife Joyce, to tell them what had happened. Scott came to the house right away to help clean up. We took as many pictures as possible with our little camera. Then Ryan and I boarded up the windows. Joyce came the next day and took more "professional" photos. Over the years, Joyce has documented the destruction many times by taking pictures.

As we surveyed the damage, it was obvious that the vandals had spent a good deal of time spray painting the church and house before they used hammers to shatter our windows. Everywhere we looked there were spray painted slogans such as: My Body, My Choice; Dykes For Choice; Pro-Choice, Pro-Sex; Keep Your Bible Off My Body, Fake Abortion Clinic; No More Hangers; Not The State—Not The Church; We Will Decide Our Fate; F——Off Nazi Pigs; Pro-Life = Death for Lesbians (lesbian symbols used); etc. The F-word was used liberally—to enhance their message, I guess. Two window panes downstairs were completely gone. Upstairs by the front door, the girls' bedroom window (with old 1/4" thick glass) had a hole about the size of a softball right in the center of the pane. The whole thing would have been gone except that, because of past experiences and the constant threats, the house windows had been taped in a criss-cross fashion with heavy-duty, clear, protective tape. We hadn't anticipated this type of occurrence, but we would not have been surprised if rocks or beer cans had been thrown at the windows. The tape was there to keep broken glass from flying all over the place. When we checked the floor by the head of Megan's bed, we found some large chunks of glass, but for the most part, the broken pieces were hanging from the tape, still attached to the window frame.

All in all, the place was a MESS!

That morning, local radio began carrying the story. The word was out that the "out-spoken pastor" and his church were vandalized again. (This wasn't the first time we had been graffitied; in fact, it was the fourth time in nine months. However, this was the worst.) I personally gave the story to a Christian friend at one of the all-news stations, and thanks to her the item was well covered. As always, the local Christian station reported nothing.

As people drove by on their way to work, they slowed down to read the "writing on the walls." A truck pulled up and a couple of painters introduced themselves to me. They had heard a radio report about what had happened to us. They were Christians and had recently been praying that they would be able to use their business in a unique way for the Lord's work. As far as they were concerned, this was an answer to prayer; and they offered to help with the clean up. For the cost of materials, they would waterblast the front of the church building and repaint the defaced portions of both the house and church. What a blessing for us! We didn't know how we were going to afford to clean up this mess. There was still yellow paint splattered on the church from an attack years earlier that we couldn't afford to have removed. Finally, it was all going to be done. These men promised to be back the next morning to start, but still I was determined to contact the mayor about this to try to get the city to take at least some responsibility for the clean up.

Several of the ministers came by to offer condolences. Jim Robinson, who would later in the year run for the Board of Supervisors, suggested that we hold a rally here and invite the press to protest the violation of our rights. Grateful for his support, I politely refused any show or expression of retaliation. We're not in this for publicity, but for the Kingdom of God. Some suggested we leave the house and church a mess so the public could see the consequences of the tolerance San Francisco has for law-breakers and dissenters. However, our responsibility to the Crisis Pregnancy Center and its clientele was more important than wanting to advertise to the public. So, the next morning our painter friends went to work.

Donna and I were increasingly concerned about our immediate neighborhood. For the most part, it is made up of long-time conservative San Franciscans. They had seen our house and church burned, crowds of protestors, and ongoing vandalism over the years. Although they had been kind, things like this wear thin after a while. Even though they might agree with the religious/political stand we had taken, how long would they tolerate this kind of disturbance and defacing of their neighborhood? Many of them had lived here all their lives and were now retired—what were they thinking? We were soon to find out.

The rabbi from one of the local synagogues stopped by to

express his support for our stand, and the elderly head of the orthodox rabbis in San Francisco visited us to "pronounce a blessing on the house and a benediction for our safety." Several neighbors stopped by to express their concern.

One afternoon, an 87-year-old gentleman came to our door, while his "young, beautiful 77-year-old wife" waited in the car. She had driven him to the house as he was unable to either walk the distance or drive. He said that he had lived in this neighborhood for the past fifty years, and in all that time he had never seen anything occur such as had repeatedly happened to us over the years. He pressed ten dollars into my hand as a contribution toward the clean up effort. As he started to make his way back down the front stairs, he stopped, turned back to us and said, "We're glad you're here, and we don't want you to leave." Donna and I were very moved by this gesture, and heartened to know that there was that kind of support for us in the neighborhood.

Think about it for a minute. How many of us would want to live in a neighborhood that was constantly disrupted and defaced in this way? Even if we agreed in principle with the victim, would we feel that perhaps he was partially responsible for the disturbance in our peaceful neighborhood? Would we support such a person? The general populace of San Francisco, even non-Christians, keenly feel the oppression of the immorality of the city and feel powerless to do anything about it.

The greatest damage suffered that night, however, had not been to the house, the church, or the neighborhood. It had been done to our children, and particularly to 12-year-old Megan. She had been asleep with her head directly under that window when the first hammer blow hit! Awakened out of her sleep, her father's voice had told her to "hit the floor, it might be gunfire!" And she and Erin had obediently reacted to what they were told to do. She was alive, the family was okay—but was she okay?

Megan had been so terrorized that night that she couldn't sleep in her room. She tried, but could not do it. For a couple of months after the attack, she slept with me in the master bedroom. Erin, her older sister, had been quite brave, and even though she was obviously afraid, she went back into her bedroom to sleep with Donna sleeping in Megan's bed by the window. This arrangement, or course, could not last; and each night we tried to ease Megan back into her own room. At bedtime we would read Scripture to her and sing Psalms together. Erin offered to switch beds with Megan to get her away from the dreaded window. We would leave a night light on in the bedroom. Donna gave her a Walkman and played Christian music while she tried to go to sleep. And, Donna sat with her every night until she fell asleep and promised that she would check on Megan every five minutes after she was asleep. Through all of this, Erin slept in the same room and worked on overcoming her own fears while she patiently indulged Megan's.

Donna was faithful to her promise to check on Megan every five minutes. Sometimes she would find her asleep; however, more often than not, she would find Megan awake, listening to the music, and whimpering in fear. She was trying—but it was very hard. One night, Donna went in to check Megan and found her standing on her bed, pressed hard up against the wall, and staring at the window with her face grossly contorted in fear. She spoke to Megan, but she did not respond. She was so consumed with fear that she had momentarily lost reality and didn't even know Donna was there. Having been so paralyzed with fear herself, years before and after the fire, Donna could understand what was happening to Megan. She reached out and took Megan's hand that was clenched against the wall, and while repeating any Scripture that came to mind, gently pulled Megan down and held her until in a few short minutes she became herself again.

That night, Donna took Megan to our bed and put her to sleep as we had been doing for the last two months. She decided then and there that we would stop trying to get her back into her bedroom. She couldn't handle any more trauma at that time. We would simply continue to pray and ask the Lord to take Megan's fears away. (A righteous anger really began to well up in Donna that was soon to be vented!)

The dining room of the church's turn-of-the-century house in which we lived was a beautiful wood paneled, tapestried room situated in the very center of the house. It was the only room in the house that was surrounded by other rooms and therefore double-walled to the outside. It took some doing, and volunteer help from some of the men in the church and another local minister, but we eventually constructed a separate bedroom for Megan and Erin within the dining room area that kept them both away from the windows and walls of the outside of the house. Even though Megan is still up throughout the night checking out noises, etc., she feels safe enough to sleep there without panic.

We have taken even more safety measures. Special glass has

been placed on certain windows for added protection. Obviously, we are not telling anyone that reads this book specifically what protective measures have been taken for safety's sake. Ryan's room has also been appropriately secured.

As the days passed, we received a call from Police Chief Frank Jordan, expressing his sympathy, especially in regard to what happened to the kids. Chief Jordan, now Mayor Jordan, showed great kindness to us and promised to provide us with all the protection we needed and that everything possible was going to be done to investigate the case. Still, nothing came of the investigation, even though empty cans of spray paint were left in front of the church and in the bushes across the street. No finger prints—no eye witnesses from any of the neighbors, there was only silence. As we said before, of all the criminal acts committed against our church, home, and family, no suspect has ever been questioned nor prosecuted.

We received a call from Mayor Agnos' office. He had read about us in a newspaper article. The mayor expressed condolences and promised to help in the apprehension of those responsible. I asked for an appointment to meet with him personally and also asked that the city take care of the clean up of the sidewalk graffiti, since that was technically city property. He promised to have someone call to set up an appointment to meet with him, and he also promised to aid in the clean up effort.

Weeks passed and we heard nothing from the mayor. The church and house were back in shape thanks to the help of volunteers. However, due to the safety measures needed, the church once again had to bear a substantial financial burden. Finally, we received an innocuous letter from the mayor, expressing his sympathy, telling us what steps he had taken for our protection, and how the city had aided in the clean up. Mayor Agnos finished his letter by saying, "I know how you feel. . . ."

Whether the mayor's expression of sympathy was genuine or not; 1) we knew from local police that nothing had been done on the part of the mayor's office in regard to our safety; 2) after a couple of calls from us to his office, the only aid given toward the clean up had been one private painting contractor who came out and, in five minutes, simply painted over the graffiti on the sidewalk (those paint patches are still there today and are quite an "eye sore"), and; 3) there would be no meeting with the mayor as he had promised!

So, that's it from the mayor? No meeting as he had promised? How concerned was he for the safety and welfare of our family?

Donna was infuriated and immediately sat down at the computer to compose a letter to him. She stayed up until the early hours of the morning to get it done. She expressed her righteous outrage on behalf of our children. It wasn't just that we or our church suffered an attack; it was the children that suffered this time! In 1983, when we were firebombed, they were little children, not yet old enough to understand the danger. But now they were teen-agers, and they could fully comprehend the terror of being attacked in the dead of night. They understood what it meant to have the security of their home taken away. Was the mayor truly concerned about their right to life and liberty—let alone their pursuit of happiness!? Did anyone at city hall care about the trauma they had suffered?

Proverbs says: "Let a man meet a bear robbed of her cubs, rather than a fool in his folly." The mayor was about to meet the bear robbed of her cubs! Donna was about to confront the fool in his folly! Watch out!

In her letter to Mayor Agnos, Donna rehearsed a chronology of criminal acts committed against us in violation of our family's civil rights. Trained as a legal secretary, she put together a legal brief of sorts, with photographs, transcriptions of phone calls, copies of newspaper articles, etc., documenting events referenced in the letter. She brought to the mayor's attention the decade of harassment we had experienced by those who hate the gospel of Christ and His righteousness. According to Romans 13, she called upon the mayor as God's minister of righteousness to fulfill his responsibility and see that our children's "right" to safety be protected. All in all, the letter turned out to be forty-five pages long. She sent it to the mayor by messenger the following day.

Weeks passed, and we heard nothing from the mayor.

Then, one evening, there was a small article in the newspaper announcing a public meeting to be held at a high school nearby to discuss the mayor's proposed budget for the coming year. Pastor Will Holt had called me and asked if I would go and monitor the meeting especially in regard to domestic partners. I happened to mention the meeting to Donna as she was preparing supper that evening. She stopped. I stopped. Something was brewing in that pretty redhead. She said, "I want to go to the meeting and talk to the mayor. And I want the kids to go too."

It was one of the few times I wasn't really anxious to go, but I knew it was her time to "come out of the closet." I had protected her from the press all these years. Now, it was her turn to speak her mind. Just the evening before, we had had yet another depressing discussion on "how long are we going to stay in San Francisco?" How many more times were we going to just let them attack us? It had been going on for over ten years!

Now, it was Donna's time to express herself. She had a point to make in defense of the children—and it turned out to be the best thing possible.

We stopped dinner, found out at which school the mayor was to be, rounded up the kids, and took off. When we got to the school auditorium, Donna signed up to speak. The kids and I sat in the back row.

As the hours passed and speaker after speaker questioned the mayor, patted him on the back, or argued with him—still no time for Donna. As the close of the meeting drew near, the audience was told that only three more would be allowed to speak. Donna marched down the aisle and sat in the front row. The mayor's press secretary, Scott Schaeffer, asked her if she had signed up to speak. She told him that she had and that it was very important that she be allowed to address the mayor. He asked for her name—"Donna McIlhenny"—and for some reason, Schaeffer told her that she would be next. We were surprised at this since Scott knew me and my reputation in the city well—but he allowed Donna to speak next.

As she rose to address the mayor, I sat tensely in the back, wondering what she would say. The mayor didn't know who she was, but he was soon to find out! "That's Mom," I said to the kids. They responded, "Uh oh!"

The topic for the evening was limited to the mayor's real and proposed budget. Donna knew, however, exactly what she wanted to talk to him about, and while waiting to speak, she had figured out a way to weave her issue into a discussion of the budget. Among other things, the budget proposed funding increases for more police protection for victims of hate crimes. . . . THERE WAS THE ACHILLES HEEL! Donna began by telling the mayor that she very much supported increased funding in this area of hate crimes. (He still didn't know who she was!) Then, she suggested to him where he might find the extra funds needed to support such a proposal. Donna told him he should take the hundreds and thousands of dollars that he had been spending on the domestic partners program in the past fiscal year, which he had no legal right to do since the voters had said NO to domestic partners in the last election, and apply that revenue to increased protection for hate crimes victims. Then, she told the mayor that she personally knew of a family that was in need of just that kind of support.

Now, the mayor began to realize who Donna was! Ahhh . . . McIlhenny = TROUBLE. He lashed back at her, saying that she had a narrow view of what constitutes a "family" and that he did not agree with her bigoted Christian view! Donna argued back, "well, whatever your definition of 'family' might be, Mr. Mayor, it certainly includes the God-ordained nuclear family. Even you can't escape that, because that's how God created it! And, as mayor of this city, no matter how you redefine the family, you still have a responsibility to protect the human rights of my family. I wrote you a letter, Mr. Mayor, and asked what you could say to my children to convince them that their mayor is concerned about their physical safety. Well, we got no answer from you, so I brought my children with me tonight so you can answer them now." Donna pointed to where we were sitting. "They're sitting on the back row—tell them how their mayor cares for the preservation of their lives!" (As she pointed to where we were sitting, Ryan waved.)

Mayor Agnos was nonplussed. He sat there in a no-win situation—faced by the "bear robbed of her cubs!" In his typical back-alley, street-fighter, tough-guy image, he . . . hemmed and hawed . . . and called for the last speaker.

Donna thanked him for his time and started back to where we were sitting. The audience broke into applause. (That was amazing in itself. We didn't know who made up the audience. We didn't know whether we'd be chased to our car afterwards!) We all couldn't be prouder of our mom and wife. She needed to do it. The kids needed to hear her boldly defend them for Christ's sake. We left feeling that whether we'd ever get a personal meeting with the mayor or not, we had had one that night!

A few days later, I received a call from the mayor's office "confirming our Tuesday appointment with the Mayor." I said, "Confirming? We never had an appointment!" The aid assured me that we did and would we be there? I assured him that the whole family would be there.

We arrived at the mayor's office early that afternoon. Unfortunately, Ryan couldn't be with us because of a baseball game at school (after all, what really is more important—baseball or the mayor?!)

We waited for about thirty minutes. During that time the mayor's personal assistant "got our story" and expressed his concern for our continued safety. Police Chief Jordan also came into the office while we waited, and we had an opportunity to meet him for the first time and to thank him for his expression of concern for our family.

Finally, we were politely ushered into Agnos' office. He welcomed us in a rather business-like manner. The chairs were placed in a semi-circle so we all faced the mayor himself. For an awkward moment, we all sat there staring at one another. No smile on his face—or ours. We were there for business, the business of the Kingdom of God.

First, Donna spoke about the terror of the kids in the attack and especially Megan's fears and anxieties. I told him that though we disagreed politically and philosophically, we supported him in prayer regularly—both publicly and privately in family devotions. Without giving all the details of the meeting, we did have the opportunity to give him the gospel. As the discussion progressed, the mayor argued about the nature of good deeds and how God would somehow take them into account for salvation! I responded with the message of grace, not good works. He clearly disagreed with the biblical position on salvation and testified of his good deeds "that'll get him in—if there even is a heaven! And, if there is a heaven," he went on to say, "I'm going to have a lot of questions for God and by what right He allows the suffering that there is on earth. And, I'm going to ask Him just what He thought He was doing letting so many people die such awful deaths through AIDS?" ("But indeed, O man, who are you to reply against God? Will the thing formed say to him who formed it, 'Why did you make me like this?'" [Rom. 9:20].)

Before we left, I asked if I could pray. We told him we were praying for his salvation. He interrupted, "You mean, like born again? My mother's praying for me like that too!" In the prayer I again gave the gospel of Christ, prayed for his salvation, and for the redemption of the city. Then, we stood as awkwardly as we had sat down. He shook our hands, and we left.

Why the Attack?

Donna and I think there were two primary reasons for the violent assault on our home that night: 1) we had just helped defeat the domestic partners ordinance in the November election, and; 2) we had been pulled into a controversy that involved the Crisis Pregnancy Center (CPC) located next door in our church.

On 22 January 1990, the anniversary of the infamous Roe vs. Wade abortion decision, I received a brief phone call from a young man who identified himself as being part of a group of students from a local university. His group had managed to obtain a client list from Planned Parenthood and had been calling the women on the list to tell them their appointments had been canceled and to refer them to the CPC and to other pro-life counseling centers throughout the Bay Area. In effect, they had stolen the list and lied to these women.

When I heard what his group had done, I hit the roof. I told him that it was wrong to lie and steal—even if the intent was for the "greater good" of saving unborn children. Unfortunately, the "theft" made the newspapers, and pro-lifers were smeared in the press for having "stolen" from an abortion clinic. Our family had inadvertently become involved in the controversy because the CPC was located in our church.

Eventually, I had a meeting with some representatives of this group to explain our position on the matter. I explained to them that the CPC does not get involved with such protests; that we as Christians do not believe that stealing or lying or breaking the law of God is justified in the name of saving life. When Christians try to employ sinful tactics (lying, stealing, etc.) to accomplish their task, they not only will be discovered by the unbeliever, but they bring disrepute to the name of Christ. They must also realize that God will not condone such behavior from anyone—Christian or non-Christian. In defense of righteousness, Christians are bound by God's rule of warfare—the Bible. The ends DO NOT justify the means, no matter how sacred those ends are. Christians are faced with many serious moral issues these days, and in dealing with those issues, we must make sure that our actions are obedient to God's Word. There are already a number of just and legal ways to fight against abortion that have not been fully utilized. The CPC is not forced to break the law in order to save babies, or lie to expectant mothers, or scare clients, or to brow-beat anyone into agreement with our position. The Christian's method of protest against this greatest of injustices against children must follow the rule of the Word of God, no matter how slow or supposedly inefficient it may seem. We must not use the tactics of the world to try to further the cause of the Kingdom. Pro-life is our battle only because it is God's battle. Only His orders are guaranteed to succeed. As I told these students, I firmly believe that God will only bless honesty, integrity, and openness in the pro-life cause.

All of this occurred in January, and we're certain that the attack on the house and church was directly related to the "theft" at the abortion clinic. In this case, we'd been victimized by an over-zealousness to fight abortion. Zeal without knowledge is deadly and does not promote the righteousness of God.

Saving Babies and Souls

Even before our home was firebombed in mid-1983, we were ready to back off from our intense involvement in fighting the gay rights movement. We were emotionally exhausted and spiritually drained from the aftermath of the lawsuit and the trauma of pickets, hostile news reports, and death threats. It was time for a redirection of our activities into what we assumed would be a less controversial area—helping to set up a Crisis Pregnancy Center.

Let me make it clear, we did not set up a "clinic," as we've been accused. Our church, along with other churches, set up a center for counseling and any other tangible helps we could give people. We thought that becoming involved in pro-life activities would make us less likely to be targeted by angry homosexuals or protestors. Of course, we were wrong, because the gays and pro-abortionists are allied in their hatred of God's law in society. The goals and activities of the women's movement and the homosexuals' movement are inextricably linked, and they work together.

To get involved in the pro-life movement, a couple of us from church attended an organizational meeting of a new Center, which was to be established in our city. The meeting was spon-sored by the Christian Action Council, a group that set up CPCs around the country under strict ethical guidelines. We sat through a slide presentation and a speech by the CPC organizer and left the meeting determined we would do whatever we could to facilitate this outreach to pregnant women.

We began a series of meetings in various churches, discussing how the CPC would be structured, funded, and who would be chosen to be the first director. In fact, on the evening of the firebombing, I was at one of these organizational meetings.

The CPC was eventually set up. Joanne Georgeostathis was hired as director, and John Green, our deacon, became the president of the Board of Directors. About a year later, we offered our church facilities to them free of charge to help the CPC get going. Our members consider it an honor to be able to contribute in this small way for the cause of Christ in fighting abortion and supplying the needs of families.

The Center is a totally separate organization from our church, and we've made every effort to keep that distinction clear. We have also tried to maintain an obvious line of demarcation between what I do as pastor/public citizen and what the Center does to minister to men, women, and children.

However, our first involvement with the CPC was a bit strained. The CPC wanted to make clear that they were not part of my political activities. With this I could heartily agree. Nonetheless, on a few occasions, the director and I did clash on how to keep the two institutions distinct from one another. Since this was my church and home, the press would naturally come to interview me here. During one interview, I happened to be standing in front of the CPC sign right between the church and our house. The sign was picked up by the camera and momentarily that caused some friction. I made sure that no more interviews were done in front of the Center's sign. However, I pointed out to the director that because the CPC met in the church, and the church and house were attached, reciprocally, our family experienced the repercussions of any protests or attacks on the CPC. It was unavoidable. We eventually settled our differences and perhaps realized that we had a common cause—upholding God's standard of morality. We were all in this together.

Truth, Deception, and God's Way

Several years ago, a group of independent Catholics founded what they called the Free Pregnancy Center in San Francisco. The leaders of this center thought they'd be more effective if they disguised themselves as an abortion clinic to attract clients who intended to abort their children. When these girls came in, they would then seek to dissuade them from having an abortion. The pro-abortionists got wind of this and sued the center. They won, and the FPC was closed down.

The press had a field day with the story. Many bogus clients came to check out tactics used at the CPC, seeking to accuse them of so-called brain-washing and the use of intimidation to force their bigoted religious views on those who wanted abortions! It was interesting that, at the time the CPC was deciding whether or not to use our facilities, one primary objection was that the Center would be housed in a church building. The unofficial policy of Crisis Pregnancy Centers was not to be located in an obvious religious environment like a church. That might scare off potential clients. I argued, however, the reality was that the CPC of San Francisco had no money and couldn't spend over a thousand dollars a month on a one-room rental. In the providence of God, we were their best option. So, they moved in, with the understanding that as soon as financially able, they'd move to another location. (That was eight years ago.)

The up-shot was that, because the CPC did meet in a church building, it was manifestly clear that the Center could not be charged with deception, no matter how the papers described it. The CPC of San Francisco had never deceptively marketed itself as a kind of "clinic" or pro-abortion "clinic," and it met in a church building with a reputation for standing for pro-life causes. No undercover pro-abortionist could ever convince a judge that this CPC used deceit or subterfuge to lure girls into what they thought was an abortion facility. No undercover reporters or pro-abortionists have been able to accuse them of operating a fraudulent clinic, nor has any legal action ever been taken against the CPC. Any such actions or accusations would themselves be fraudulent. The fact that the CPC is located in a pro-life church provides it with legal protection not afforded centers or clinics operated in storefronts or in office buildings.

At present, there are only two pro-life centers in San Francisco. The CPC is the only one sponsoring full time staff, full service, self-administered free pregnancy tests, and distribution of clothing for those women and children in need. The new president of the Center, Ev Jones, is a retired Navy supply officer. He has brought his organizational and administrative skills to the

Center, and it has now expanded to another location in addition to our church. Also, Ev doesn't seem incumbered with a fear of association with me and the church.

In late 1991, pro-abortionists began a campaign to vilify Crisis Pregnancy Centers as "fake abortion clinics." The intent was to put them out of business, or at least to bring them under strict federal regulations (while abortion clinics remain relatively free of any government intrusion). As part of this propaganda attack on pro-life clinics, Diane Sawyer hosted a "Prime Time Live" program that unfairly linked legitimate, well-run CPCs with the very few clinics who had incompetent personnel running the operations, and with those that use deceptive or, at best, questionable methods.

As I've observed the operation of CPCs over the years, I've been struck by the integrity of the leadership behind these centers. One of the most important elements of the CPC strategy is the sharing of Jesus Christ with every girl who is facing a crisis pregnancy. In fact, Donna and I believe that is the most important function of the CPC. We don't believe a pro-life center is truly doing its job if its only emphasis is in saving the life of the unborn child. We don't believe it's wise to be pro-life just for the sake of saving the child, but center counselors should be clearly trained in sharing the gospel. We're interested in the life of the child and the life of the mother and father in a crisis pregnancy—for Christ's sake.

Politics, Preaching, and Picketing

Around the same time Donna and I started to get involved in the pro-life movement, I began work on my doctorate at Westminster Theological Seminary in Escondido, California. I chose as my doctoral thesis: Preaching to Politicians. As part of my research project, I had to organize San Francisco pastors to accompany me to preach before the Board of Supervisors and various other public committee hearings on issues of concern to the Christian community—whether educational, social, or medical, etc.

In addition, my elder and I began regular weekly picketing at three different abortion clinics in the city. We would rotate from one clinic to another over the weeks and would be there come rain or shine for two or three hours every Saturday morning. At these clinics we were continually subjected to verbal abuse from the volunteer escorts and passers-by. We found ourselves becoming just as hostile as the pro-abortionists and at times we ended up in shouting matches.

As the weeks passed, I began meeting these escorts in local supermarkets and stores, and suddenly it dawned on me that these were my neighbors. As much as I hated abortion and willing accomplices, I couldn't be screaming at them on Saturdays and then preaching the love of God on Sunday morning. What if one of these people from my neighborhood happened to come to the service?

Once that revelation hit me, Scott and I asked the Lord to forgive us and changed our whole demeanor at the clinics. Our strategy became simple: we would engage the escorts in as friendly a conversation as possible and attempt to share the gospel with them. We never did have enough time to talk to the clients rushing into the clinic, but we did begin to develop certain cautious relationships with some of the escorts. It was a difficult strategy to implement. On the one hand, we had to maintain our righteous anger against abortion, and at the same time make an attempt to befriend and convert them. I wouldn't say our strategy was a failure, but eventually the abortionists prohibited their escorts from engaging in conversation with us.

In addition to gathering the group of ministers to speak before the Board of Supervisors, picketing an abortion clinic each week, and helping with the CPC, I helped organize all-night candlelight prayer vigils at abortion clinics. Our church also spearheaded a Christian rally held on Mother's Day at Civic Center, commemorating the victims of abortion. For three years we held these rallies to pay tribute to the children who had died and to the women who had also suffered as victims of the abortion mentality. One year a protest against the war in El Salvador was held at the Civic Center the day before our rally. The El Salvador protest brought out over fifty thousand revelers. The next day, our pro-life rally, which called for a stop to the killing in the womb of millions and millions of innocent babies, could only muster about 150 faithful pro-lifers! The priorities of the Christian community in San Francisco are so skewed.

Gays and Pro-abortionists United

All that we've described about our involvement in the pro-life movement may seem to be totally unrelated to our opposition to the gay rights movement. However, as was said before, the abortion issue is inextricably linked to the promotion of homosexuality. If you recall, one of the slogans spray-painted on our house was Pro-Life = Death to Lesbians. How could the pro-life movement ever be considered deadly to lesbians? Initially, we had been puzzled as to why gays and lesbians would be so adamant in their defense of abortion rights, but then it dawned on us: both the pro-abortionists and gays are pro-death. Both of these movements are engaged in activities that never bring life, but always result in physical and spiritual death. And, there is a definite alignment of these two movements against biblical Christianity because, the promise of Christ is LIFE. The spiritual element to this alliance should be understood: Satan is the author of lies, of wrongful destruction and misery; and his ministers of death on earth do his bidding quite readily.

The Witches Appear

We saw a clear picture of the alliance of these pro-death forces against pro-life forces during the 1991 Life Chain in San Francisco. The Chain was held on a main thoroughfare that runs north-south through San Francisco, just a block away from our home.

Our whole family and several families in the church participate in this annual event. Our kids stood with school or church friends, and all our family members were stationed within one city block. On this particular Sunday afternoon, we noticed a curious phenomenon: there were three or four women who appeared to be lesbians walking back and forth in front of our portion of the Life Chain. One was beating a drum and chanting over and over again, "We do it for the goddess; we do it for the goddess." They taunted and teased the Christians in the Chain with screaming, hissing, and vulgar language. These women were not simply lesbians, they were witches, out to confront Christians who were taking a stand against the killing of the unborn.

As Donna watched these women march back and forth, she was immediately reminded of the story in I Kings where Israel began practicing the pagan custom of sacrificing their children to Molech. As the children were tossed into the fire of Molech, the "tophet" or "the beating of the drums" would start in order to drown out the screams of the children dying in the fire. It was fascinating to watch these witches still using the drum in an effort to drown out the "silent scream" of the dying, and the cries of God's people for mercy and justice.

These witches seemed to zero in on teen-age girls who were participating in the Life Chain that afternoon. Donna got involved in one incident involving Amber, one of Megan's friends from Christian school. A woman stood in front of this 14 year-old girl and repeatedly described graphic sexual activities to her. She asked Amber what her "daddy" would do when he discovered that his teen-age daughter was pregnant—which, of course, she assured Amber was inevitable. Then, she tried to taunt Amber further by telling her that her "white, middle-class, good-Christian daddy would buy his little daughter an abortion, of course."

Amber held up to the haranguing of this witch like a real pro, but Donna didn't want her to take any more abuse than necessary, so she moved between Amber and the witch. She kept her back to the witch as the woman continued to taunt Amber. Donna quietly encouraged Amber to begin reciting Scripture to keep her mind on the Lord. As the harassing continued, a young gay man came up to Donna just a few inches away from her face and yelled, "I hate you; I hate you. I hate you, Christians. You're sterile; you're sterile. You think sex is evil." Donna thought the boy was a bit silly considering our three children were standing nearby at the time. She wondered where his children might be standing.

While all the taunting, yelling, and beating of the drum was taking place, I was walking up and down the line, periodically standing in between young girls and the lesbian witches who were shouting obscenities at the girls. I overheard a "discussion" Ryan and his friend, Mark, had gotten into with a hostile young pro-abortionist. She kept hurling obscenities at them as they attempted to explain their pro-life position to her. She taunted these two Christian young men with "have you done 'it' yet? When was the first time you 'did it?' . . ." etc. Their attempts failed to convince her or to stop the flow of filthy language, but both Mark and Ryan gave a faithful witness for the Lord that day.

This whole event lasted only a couple of hours that Lord's

Day, but it seemed like a very long time indeed when confronting such wickedness. Our children had had a taste of the world in all its hatred of God, the gospel, and life in the womb as He created it. We had beer and wine thrown at us. We were spit on and subjected to a cacophony of whistles, drum beatings, and car honking. All of this hostility was generated because a group of Christians were standing silently in a line on a public thorough-fare holding up signs for life! Life in Christ! The signs read: Abortion Kills Children, Jesus Forgives Sin. We were not picket-ing an abortion clinic, or blockading the entrance to a killing center. We were there to publicly witness for Christ against the cruelest form of destruction: the living sacrifice of the unborn to the god of self-centeredness.

We later found out that of all the length of the Life Chain, it was only our particular block that was subjected to harassment from witches, because they knew who Donna and I were.

As we see this kind of venomous hatred from gays, lesbians, and witches, it becomes more and more obvious that this is not just a political issue, but a religious war. It is a clash between the forces of light and darkness. The homosexuals and witches obviously realize the spiritual nature of this war, or they would have simply ignored us that day. We must continue to pray that all God's people make a public stand against the double evils of homosexuality and child killing in this country. Christians must pray, fast, and act, if we are to prevail.

The Future

Frankly, we're not very optimistic about the future of the pro-life movement in San Francisco. The silence of the evangelical church leadership on the pro-life issue and the gay rights move-ment is deafening in a city that has been given over to the worship of freedom, license, and death.

As is the case with Christian opposition to the gay rights movement, there are literally only a dozen or so pro-life leaders in San Francisco willing to take a stand against the killing of babies in the abortion clinics here. For the most part, church leaders are apathetic. They fail to bring strong leadership to their own congregations or to impact the society around them. There seems to be an attitude implicit in San Francisco churches: Go through the motions of preaching and doing "churchly" activities, but never, never get involved in the society around you—outside the four walls of the church sanctuary. The problem with that kind of Christian isolationism is that these immoralities will not remain outside. They have already come inside the four walls of many churches and have destroyed the faith and witness of those churches; and most pastors and members don't realize it has happened. Apathy has become one of the primary tenets of faith and practice in so many churches. The end result is that they become as the majority of the mainline churches in this city. They have long since forsaken their "first love"—Christ.

Only fervent prayer and a revival of the Holy Spirit—a revival of holy indignation and a revival of jealousy for the cause of the Kingdom of God—will jolt churches from their fearful slumber here in San Francisco.

NINE

"I Now Pronounce You . . . Partners"

One of the main objectives of the gay rights movement is to have gay marriages legalized. Part of their step-by-step strategy is to work city by city, state by state to have so-called domestic partners laws passed. While not officially sanctioning homosexual marriages, these ordinances provide formal government protection for unmarried couples and homosexual lovers who have made "commitments" to each other. The domestic partners concept has provided homosexuals with a significant victory in their ultimate pursuit of legalized same-sex marriages.

A primary objective of a domestic partners ordinance is for homosexuals to obtain the same medical, legal, and social benefits that our society provides for the traditional family. An extremely important side effect of such legislation is to bring about a redefinition of what governments have traditionally considered a family.

By redefining the family, homosexuals hope to legalize all sorts of live-in arrangements. Even a commune could be considered a family, if goals are achieved. For example, the "stated" goals of the 1972 Gay Rights Platform say in part that an important objective is to: "Repeal all legislative provisions that restrict the sex or number of persons entering into a marriage unit; and the extension of legal benefits to all persons who cohabit regardless of sex or numbers" (Enrique Rueda, *The Homosexual Network* [Old Greenwich, Connecticut: Devin Adair 1982], 203.). Gays in San Francisco made their first serious attempt at passing a domestic partners ordinance back in 1982, not long after Dianne Feinstein took over as mayor. The author of the ordinance, Supervisor Harry Britt, had gained majority support on the Board of Supervisors, but Mayor Feinstein vetoed the ordinance.

Catholic Archbishop, John R. Quinn, had written a letter to Feinstein warning her of the potential ramifications of signing the ordinance. He immediately became embroiled in a media controversy and homosexuals blamed him for the veto. Of course, attorney John Wahl, who served on the Board of Directors of the liberal San Francisco Council of Churches, supported the domestic partners ordinance and attacked Quinn in the press. "He [Quinn] is trying to dictate the way non-Christian people live in the city," said Wahl. "We'll take him on, if necessary. His tax exemption will be seriously questioned. I question his Christian commitment. This kind of 'junk' drives people away from the church" ("Quick Reaction to Mayor's Veto by Church and Gay Advocates," *San Francisco Examiner* [9 Dec. 1982]).

In their anger against Feinstein's veto, several hundred gays organized a protest march from city hall to St. Mary's Cathedral and flooded the mayor's office with irate phone calls.

Harry Britt lambasted her in the press, saying that Feinstein was playing into the hands of Jerry Falwell and other anti-homosexual conservatives who wanted to oppress gays. "Jerry Falwell has charged that this law would lead to the moral collapse of our civilized society," said Britt. "By vetoing this law, Mayor Feinstein has shown that it is our nation's institutions which lack civility" (Harry Britt, "Live-in Lover Plan Vetoed," *San Francisco Chronicle* [10 Dec. 1982]).

The mayor also came under attack by Jo Daly. She and her lesbian lover were "married" in Feinstein's backyard while Feinstein was a member of the Board of Supervisors, and she became the mayor's first gay political appointee when Feinstein placed her on the police commission. Daly said that she and other gay commissioners "told the mayor we are unhappy and disappointed with her action. We believed she was going to sign it. If she had given us a warning that she was changing her mind, we could have done more work in the community" (Ibid.).

In addition, twenty-two local gay leaders sent a telegram to the Gay Rights National Lobby in Houston, asking the organization to "disinvite" Feinstein from a meeting at which they had asked her to speak.

They Try Again

In 1989, after a seven-year delay, the gays apparently felt confident about being able to pass a domestic partners ordinance and having the current mayor, Art Agnos, sign it. In the California Assembly, Agnos had been the grand patron for the gay political movement in California. Year after year he submitted "AB1" (now AB101) to the legislature for passage at the state level. Now that Agnos was mayor, they felt it possible to advance their agenda more than ever before.

Harry Britt again shepherded his pet project through the legislative process, and the Board of Supervisors approved the ordinance unanimously in May 1989. ORDINANCE NO. 176-89, File No. 216-89-1 (As Amended In Board 5/22/89), states in pertinent part:

SEC. 4001: DISCRIMINATION AGAINST DOMESTIC PARTNERS

"The City and County of San Francisco shall not discriminate against Domestic Partners or Domestic Partnerships in any way. This includes . . . using marital status as a factor in any decision, policy or practice unless it uses Domestic Partnership as a factor in the same way" (1:16-20).

SEC. 4002: DOMESTIC PARTNERSHIP: DEFINITIONS AND INFORMATIONAL MATERIALS

"Domestic Partnership Defined. Domestic Partners are two people who have chosen to share one another's lives in an intimate and committed relationship of mutual caring, who live together, and have signed a Declaration of Domestic Partnership in which they have agreed to be jointly responsible for basic living expenses incurred during the Domestic Partnership . . ." (1:23-28).

Any previous domestic partnerships "must have ended more than six months before the new Declaration of Domestic Partnership was signed . . ." (2:6-7). This requirement is waived if one of the partners dies.

"Live Together Defined. Live together means that two people share the same living quarters. It is not necessary that the right to possess the quarters be in both names. . . . Domestic Partners do not cease to live together if one leaves the shared living quarters but intends to return" (2:10-16).

"Basic Living Expenses Defined. Basic living expenses means the cost of basic food, shelter and any other expenses of a Domestic Partner which are paid at least in part by a program or benefit for which the partner qualified because of the Domestic Partnership" (2:17-21).

SEC. 4003: ENDING DOMESTIC PARTNERSHIPS

"A Domestic Partnership ends when: . . . (1) one partner sends the other a written notice that he or she has ended the partnership; or (2) one of the partners dies" (3:13-14,17-19). To end the partnership, "the partners must execute a notice of termination naming the partners and stating that the partnership has ended. . . . The Notice of Termination must be dated and signed . . . by at least one of the partners . . . [and] filed with the Clerk; . . . [or] notarized and a copy given to whomever witnessed the Declaration of Domestic Partnership" (3:22-4:2).

SEC. 4007: VISITATION IN HEALTH CARE FACILITIES

For domestic partners who meet "Patient Designation" standards as described by the Code, "the [health care] facility must allow the patient's Domestic Partner, the children of the patient's Domestic Partner, or the Domestic Partner of the patient's parent or child to visit . . ." (6:27-30).

As it reads, the domestic partnership law doesn't sound very threatening, but it was deliberately designed to sound innocuous. The truth is that the ordinance, if allowed to pass, would have allowed homosexuals to pursue a number of other objectives, which include gaining medical benefits for gay city employees and their live-in lovers. With those precedents in place, the next step was to mandate that San Francisco businesses recognize domestic partnerships and extend medical benefits as well. The ultimate goal, of course, is to influence the California legislature to recognize domestic partnerships as equal to married couples under the law.

One afternoon, Pastor Wil Holt from the Holy Spirit

Lutheran Church, called to say he was writing a letter to the mayor protesting the passage of this ordinance and wanted to know if I'd be willing to co-sign it. I said, "Of course," but then suggested that we demand a meeting with the mayor to confront him personally.

The same group of pastors that I've been working with over the years gathered outside the mayor's office, Room 200 of city hall. A few TV stations became aware of what was happening and were interviewing pastors here and there, asking for their opinion about the new legislation. I had come prepared to give the press a copy of my 1980 congressional subcommittee report, if any asked for it. I more or less stayed in the background waiting to go into the mayor's office. There were about twenty pastors gathered in the hall at the mayor's office door, but only ten of us were allowed into his chambers.

We had pretty much decided who would speak, for how long, and that I would close the meeting with prayer. As we filed into the office, we shook hands with Agnos and took our seats around a giant oval table. A Catholic priest and a Greek Orthodox priest had also joined the meeting. The mayor gave Pastor Holt the floor. As Will began to speak, a little Jewish rabbi scurried into the room and took the last remaining seat right beside the mayor. None of the ministers knew who this little man was. I had chosen to sit at the opposite end of the table to face the mayor head on. Agnos and I had formally debated his AB1 legislation years before when he was an assemblyman; that, along with my fundamentalist, "bigoted-Christian" reputation in San Francisco made for an antagonistic atmosphere between the two of us.

In his gracious way, Will decided to let the rabbi begin and then we'd go around the table, introduce ourselves, speak briefly about the ordinance, and then I would close the meeting in prayer.

In a slightly nasal tone, the rabbi spoke intensely about the immorality of the domestic partners issue and how it would completely change the definition of the family. He came across with a great sense of moral indignation. I was greatly impressed with his extemporaneous speech.

We proceeded around the table of somber-looking pastors, each one preaching his message to the mayor about the harmful effects of the ordinance. Periodically, the mayor would combatively interject his contrary opinion. He professed that, just like the rest of us, he, too, was a believer in God: "whoever he or she might be"! As far as he and his god were concerned, homosexuals "have a right to their relationships as much as heterosexuals." The conversation between the ministers and the mayor began to heat up, and I became heated as well. I hadn't anticipated talking; however, after hearing Agnos respond like that, I perked up. I interjected that he was the leader, the moral leader, of the city and that he couldn't just let any "Tom, Dick, or Harry" force their special interest legislation on everybody. "After all," I said, "it's up to you to set the moral tone for the whole life of the city." He obviously disagreed.

We continued around the table: one pastor spoke to the homosexual disease situation; another spoke to the psychological make up of homosexuals; and another simply gave him the five-fold plan of salvation—straightforward, no nonsense evangelism. For this last pastor, nothing else mattered until the mayor was first converted to Christ.

Periodically, the mayor's secretary would pop her head in the door, reminding him that he had other appointments. Finally, she came in and said that he'd better get moving as he was already late for his next appointment. With that, Agnos got up and made his way to the door of his inner office and away from us. We just sat right where we were! He turned and told us that he appreciated our coming but, as far as he was concerned, this issue was closed. Our arguments didn't make any difference to him. He intended to sign the legislation no matter what. We suggested that he put it to a vote of the people, to which he responded that, in his experience, any civil rights legislation put to the voters at large always loses. He believed that if put to a referendum, this ordinance would lose also.

We shook hands with the mayor as we left, half smiling and yet heart-sick at what we had heard for the last hour and a half.

As we gathered outside in the hallway, the rabbi was the first one to propose that we go for a referendum or an initiative. ("Referendum" in California law means that the passed legislation is *referred* back to the governing body to reconsider their action or put it on the ballot for the citizens to vote on; "Initiative" essentially means that we write a whole new law counter-acting the domestic partners law.) Most of us didn't quite know what to do, but the words of the rabbi struck a kind of exciting terror. "We're not politicians," I said to myself, "Not me, anyway." The rabbi turned to one pastor and said, "You be the chairman, and I'll be co-chairman." We decided to meet the following Monday for our first organizational meeting to decide what to do. The rabbi was to direct and dominate us as we plunged head long into the world of politics—like innocent lambs being lead to the slaughter!

The rabbi was to engineer the initial stages, and we rather naively followed his lead.

The Challenge

Our first challenge was that of TIME. We literally had no time to spare. In order to put the domestic partners ordinance to a vote of the people, we first had to decide whether to go for a referendum or an initiative. A referendum would be the harder but quicker of the two approaches. With a referendum we would have to gather twice the number of signatures in half the time allotted for an initiative. However, with an initiative, we would actually have to draft a law to replace the domestic partners ordinance. Since the domestic partners ordinance was not yet legally in effect, we decided to go for the referendum in order to stop the law before that happened. We had no money, no organization, and very little help when we began.

I immediately contacted Mick Imfeld, a friend and Rutherford Institute attorney at the time, for legal advice on how we should proceed. One word of caution Mick gave was that I, personally, not be too obviously involved, at least not publicly, because I would be a lightning rod, which could seriously jeopardize the success of the secret campaign. "Good advice," I concurred. I was not desirous of reliving past experiences. Mick told me to go to the Registrar of Voters and find out exactly how we were to word our petition. He warned me that if we didn't have the proper wording, spacing, type sizes, and everything done by code, the petition could be ruled invalid. We had to be precise, and above all, legal. All this work had to be done under the strain of our regular pastorates.

We all came in the following Monday afternoon and sat down to brainstorm. There we all sat, a bunch of novices, not knowing exactly what to do. The rabbi sat at one end of the table and immediately took control. It was as though he knew exactly what to do and just how we were to go about doing it.

My first concern was that we dedicate this awesome task to the Lord Jesus Christ. In my mind it was obvious that we must begin with prayer and ask the Lord to bless our endeavor. However, to my surprise, one of my fellow ministers objected. For him, this was a political, therefore secular, issue. Prayer at this meeting would be inappropriate. Christ had nothing to do with it. We could pray individually or at home before we came, but for him it was out of place in the secular-political arena. End of the discussion. (Perhaps there was silent concern about offending the rabbi. The rabbi didn't care about prayer; for him it was simply a matter of collecting signatures. Why pray? Especially to Jesus!) However, it wasn't so simple. At least two of us strenuously objected and gave our heated reasons. Ultimately, a majority of the pastors decided to move on without prayer!

This was shocking and upsetting to me. Here were Bible-believing pastors of evangelical churches who were strongly divided over whether we should bring prayer into the workings of the committee. Some said this was a matter of cold, hard politics—not a spiritual issue. For myself, it was a matter of dedicating the whole venture to the rule of King Jesus, and nothing less would do. The central issue in this entire endeavor was that Christ would get all the glory; and that we as Christian pastors would seize the opportunity to preach the gospel to a lost and dying San Francisco. I was a preacher, not a politician. My whole doctoral thesis was predicated upon the fact that preachers ought to remain preachers, even when addressing politicians.

As I said before, the rabbi seemed to know what he was doing, and even though he was not the chairman, we let him have his way. We knew very little about him personally, except that he had studied law and was familiar with the technicalities of drafting the petition for collecting signatures. As the meeting progressed, he autocratically assigned committee heads and introduced various things about which we had never thought.

The next item on the agenda was to decide how we were going to fight the ordinance: with a referendum or an initiative. The rabbi indicated that he would research the issue for a decision at the next meeting. He prided himself in knowing the law, whereas we ministers were there to inspire the people!

The committee agreed that our activities needed to be kept secret. We didn't want anything leaked to the press. The rabbi demanded that we not talk to the press at all, unless the public relations committee, of which he was the chairman, gave prior consent.

Suddenly, Will Holt apologetically rushed in toward the end of the two-hour meeting. Without realizing the opening discussion and heated exchange regarding prayer, as the meeting came to an end, Will rather nonchalantly closed in prayer. (Will has a habit of praying whenever and wherever. Thank God for that.) A few of us joined in quite enthusiastically. After the meeting broke up, some pastors relayed to Will the opening disagreement; I walked out with a couple of the men to talk to them about the need for public prayer. The committee's decision was reversed. From then on, we opened and closed our meetings in prayer.

Afterward, I also spoke to the rabbi and told him that I would like to learn how to research the law on this issue, and also extended my services to transport him wherever he needed to go. The rabbi was a no-nonsense businessman—free transportation was good! He agreed.

At the next meeting a few days later, the rabbi put the question to us: did we want to go for the long haul and go for an initiative, or a short gut-wrenching sprint with a referendum? As a committee we decided to go the fever pitch route: a referendum. The petitions must be in to the Registrar of Voters before the ordinance effectively became law. We had less than thirty days; however, the rabbi inspiringly pontificated about our ability to complete it. I must say that, although he lectured us as underlings, it was inspiring to sense his indignation against the sin of this ordinance. Would that Christ had been the essence of his message!

A few days after that second meeting, the rabbi called and told me to pick him up at a certain location. I didn't know if it was his home, office, or synagogue—he would not tell me. When I picked him up, he insisted on sitting in the back seat of the car, which would "give him more room to work" as we drove the two miles to city hall to file the application for the referendum. It seemed odd, because he talked to me all the way to city hall. I told the rabbi that earlier that week I had been contacted by the "700 Club" to participate in an interview in Los Angeles about domestic partners, but because of the committee's decision to keep this out of the press, I had decided against the interview. He agreed, and congratulated me for not "being enticed by the glory of the media."

When we got to the Registrar's office, he signed his name and address to a document. Then he turned to me and told me to fill in my address and sign my name: I did. We walked back to the parking lot, and he thanked me for being willing to add my name. Why? What was he thanking me for? What did I do?

A few days later the committee met again. At this point we were meeting three times a week for several hours. I came in late, and several of the pastors congratulated me on what I had done. But, what had I done? They explained to me that (without realizing it) I had agreed to be one of the official public sponsors, along with the rabbi, of the referendum to defeat domestic partners. (So, that's why he had thanked me for filling in my address and signing my name!) Our names were to be published in the local newspaper alerting the public at large of our intentions to gather signatures. (Signatures can be gathered secretly, but the intention to gather has to be made public.) What had I done? I smiled at them—dumb me.

In various publications around the country, the rabbi and I became known as the two "conservative clergymen," or "the rabbi and the presbyterian minister" who were leading the battle against domestic partners. "The rabbi and the presbyterian minister" . . . what a combination . . . what strange "bedfellows". . . and it was to get more strange as the days went on!

The Drive

We drafted the petition, had it professionally printed according to code, bought enough clipboards and pens, and all the other myriad details involved in putting together a referendum. We began recruiting people from both Roman Catholic and evangelical Protestant churches, to stand on street corners, at the various parishes, at grocery stores and shopping centers to gather signatures. The archbishop of the Roman Catholic diocese had come out against the ordinance years before, and still held that same position. This was a big help to us. Our Catholic friends from the pro-life movement were also willing to sacrifice time and effort to gather signatures. Jim Robinson at His Way Ministries agreed to be the collection point, and our church would be the storage place for the completed petitions. (Ours was the only church with a safe that could protect the "precious treasure.")

We told the signature collectors to go about this as quietly as possible. If the homosexual community knew what we were doing, they'd cause us a good deal of trouble. We did not want the press alerted under any circumstances—they'd have a field day with it![1]

At this point, Dave Gilmour, a marketing consultant and businessman, entered the picture and provided us with expertise in how to statistically determine where the best places in the city were to collect signatures, how many man hours would be involved, how many people were needed at each location, how often we should cover a particular site, and how much time should be spent at each location. Dave organized the petition drive like we never could have. This organization and statistical analysis in all areas was invaluable. However, it must be said that in the long run, it was only the grace of God that provided for us and protected us in the accomplishment of this arduous task. WE HAD TWO WEEKS LEFT TO COLLECT TWENTY-FIVE THOUSAND SIGNATURES!

We were under the gun. The intensity of the moment was the greatest pressure that I'd ever felt. I must give credit to my little church and especially my wife. We were all pushing to the limits of our ability. I was "brow-beating" my own congregation to gather signatures. I'd never applied so much pressure in such a short amount of time. Imposing guilt trips on my members was not beyond me at this point. Time was of the essence, and it was for righteousness' sake. Donna would work all day at the law firm downtown and then come home, eat quickly, and go out to the local supermarket for the rest of the evening

---

[1] In both signature gathering campaigns of 1989 and 1991, we were harassed by taunting, yelling, mocking, spitting, threatening homosexuals. Sometimes groups of homosexuals would surround one or two signature gatherers and "close in" on them in a most intimidating manner. In 1991, we listened to the Queer Nation "hot line" number which would detail daily events—where protests were to be held, etc. The hot line recording told their members how to disrupt and derail our signature gathering efforts and how to effectively interfere with our civil rights.

collecting signatures. She would spend all day on Saturdays at different locations. All the other signature gatherers from all the other churches did the same thing.

In addition to gathering signatures, the committee still met two to three times a week to discuss more strategy. We were growing weary of the incessant haranguing of the rabbi who was becoming more and more authoritative in his leadership.

After the first week of signature gathering, we counted 1200. We had a little over one week to get 23,500 more! When Jim Robinson dropped the completed petitions off at our home that Sunday night, he was so discouraged—and so were we. All of us were physically exhausted, and look what we had to show for our labors! Jim didn't see how we could possibly make it. But Donna said we had to be faithful for just one more week. We had to work as hard as we could. Then, if we were not successful, at least we could honestly say that we had given our best effort. We were doing this for Christ!

We prayed more and more at our committee meetings. The rabbi would either come late, or step out of the room as we prayed. We needed God's strength. The meetings were becoming unbearable. Something was sapping our strength!

Dave Gilmour pushed us harder and harder. The rabbi pushed us more and more. Several of the ministers dropped out in frustration. We asked him how many of the Jewish community were involving themselves in this campaign? He wouldn't answer our question. "I can't deal with that now. I'm too busy working on this," he would reply.

I began getting a few phone calls from the press, but nothing really came of them. I said nothing that would stir up their interest. They'd find out what was going on soon enough! For now, we needed anonymity so we could safely complete our task.

On 2 July about three days before the deadline, we got a phone call from the Registrar's office saying that according to the clerk of the Board of Supervisors, our petitions were due in by 5:00 that afternoon! How could this be? Could we have miscalculated our deadline? Was this really true, or was it another harassment tactic?

I immediately rushed home and began collating the petitions we had on hand. We put out a desperate call to those in the field to get their petitions in immediately! I called any of my church members that were available to come and organize the petitions. A few of the members came to do copying, boxing, or whatever needed to be done to get the petitions together. We tried to estimate how many signatures we had. (The petition drive had gone very well that week.) Knowing the political administration with which we were working, we knew that we should be able to validate each and every signature. We should have proof of how many signatures we had! We worked at a fever pitch! But, there was no time! Did we have enough? We didn't know for sure.

Then, in the midst of all this dashing back and forth, the rabbi, in his own way, had gotten on the phone with the Registrar's office and challenged their time calculations. By 4:00 p.m., the emergency was off. The clerk of the Board of Supervisors had "miscalculated." We still had the rest of that day, as well as July 3d, 4th, and part of July 5th to get more names. That Fourth of July certainly was one to remember—we gathered signatures from morning until night! We were literally exhausted.

This momentary scare, whether calculated on the part of the opposition or not, alerted us to verify every signature on every petition that we had. Donna stopped gathering signatures and, for the next couple of days and nights counted, tabulated, and put a reference number on each and every petition we had. Then, the petitions were xeroxed so that we had an exact copy of everything that was to be filed with the Registrar's office on 5 July 1989.

On the afternoon of 5 July, the committee met to begin the final tabulation of all the signatures we had collected. All petitions were called in. This was it. We sat around the table counting each new batch of petitions that arrived.

Everyone was tense. We had until 5:00 p.m. to have them at city hall. The clerk of the Board of Supervisors called one of the ministers to ask when the petitions could be expected. We didn't tell him. Strangely enough, the clerk insisted on personally receiving the petitions in the Board of Supervisors' chambers—not in the Registrar of Voters' office. We would not give him a definite time. We would meet the required deadline—not the Board of Supervisors' deadline!

We checked and counted every name. Some names had to be eliminated for various reasons. We tried to be exceptionally careful, in fear that someone might try to sabotage our efforts.

We counted—name after name. Finally, we reached 18,972. Technically that was the number of signatures officially needed; however, we had aimed for more to give margin for error (and, if necessary, argument.) 19,000 . . . 20,000 . . . 21,000 . . . 22 . . . 23 . . . 24 . . . 25 . . . 26 . . . 27 . . . 27,122 had been collected in two weeks time! 25,922 signatures in one week alone!

To this very day, I keep a small slip of paper in my pocket with the exact count on it—to constantly remind me how perfectly the Lord won this victory! Not one of us on the committee could ever claim responsibility for such impeccable timing. We all worked hard. We literally dragged ourselves through those two weeks, and God gloriously showed us how He is pleased to use "the weak things" of this world to "show forth His glory." It is a marvelous experience to be a weak vessel in the hands of the Almighty!

We quickly and carefully boxed up the petitions—taping the box in all directions to make sure they would remain sealed until the registrar opened them. We were ready to go to city hall.

The Drop Off

Several of us discussed how we were going to inconspicuously take the petitions downtown. We were all very excited! Three of the pastors, plus the rabbi, decided to go in two cars and meet in the Civic Center parking lot near city hall. Again, we didn't want the media alerted to anything.

The rabbi suggested that we all wear yamulkas ("skull caps") as he did—so that no one would know which one was the rabbi! Instead, we told him not to wear his yamulka.

We arrived about four o'clock at city hall. We stayed together—in close formation—watching warily. The newspapers had already run a few articles saying that we were running out of time and probably couldn't get enough signatures or get them in on time. The press had been calling the clerk's office to find out when we would be arriving. This was the stuff that movies are made of! We had begun this whole process only a month earlier knowing literally nothing about how to fight city hall, and here we were about ready to enter the battle of our lives! This was the first time that citizens not only objected to a gay rights ordinance but had actually done something to reverse the law!

Doug Robinson came with his video camera to document "the drop" and any activity of the press or any other acts of hostility. We walked into the clerk's office on the second floor almost at closing time. People were starting to leave for the day.

The four of us squeezed into the little atrium of the clerk's office. We asked to see the clerk of the Board of Supervisors. He came out. The press room down the hall came alive. Cameras and news reporters appeared to see what was going on. The rabbi did all the talking. He calmly and calculatingly asked for a clearly written receipt for the cache of petitions. The clerk responded with surprise. His thick bushy eye brows lifted high when he heard that we had collected 27,122 signatures in so short a period of time. This was the stuff that radio programs were made of—he looked as if he'd just heard that Martians had invaded San Francisco!

The press did their sworn "pressly" duty: hounding us as we left, demanding to know who we were, what we had done, and how we had done it! The four of us just smiled back and said the two most beautiful words that anyone can say to the press: "NO COMMENT!"

They followed us down the long flight of stairs in the middle of city hall's ornate rotunda. One newsman got so indignant, he shouted that we were as obstinate as Mayor Agnos' office on political matters, and then he cursed us. Having experienced the manipulation and sensationalism of the press many times, I really felt the JOY of not talking to them now. The frustration that they were obviously feeling seemed to be some sort of "divine justice" for the hurt and frustrations they had caused me over the years. The mainline San Francisco press, for the most part, had twisted and perverted every interview I had done with them, and through their misinformation, had at times brought harm to my church and family. One thing I have to say for the gay press as opposed to the mainline press: Although they do not hide their hatred for the message I give, in almost all of the personal interviews that I have had with them, they have most often reported what I said word for word—accurately and in context.

Doug lingered behind in the background with his camera to follow the secretary from the clerk's office to the Registrar's office as the valuable cargo was transported. We wanted to make sure it wasn't going to be bent, folded, spindled, mutilated, and/or somehow lost. We had done our civic duty for the cause of righteousness. Now it was time to hide.

We made it down to the underground garage, looked at each other, shook hands, and thanked one another for a job well done. We knew all hell was going to break loose now. We said our good-bys. It was time to hide until the fury of the storm blew over—and furious the storm was!

It had been a slow news day. The headlines of the *San Francisco Examiner* that evening touted the fact that domestic partners had become law. It read: "Partner sign-up begins in S.F.," by Elizabeth Hernandez. Above the article there was a picture of two lesbians, Cindy Bologna and Sidney Erskine, holding hands and showing their "commitment agreement" that they had drafted three years earlier. (I was to meet up with all three of these women again in the near future!)

On the news the following day, the city attorney had to announce that the ordinance would not go into effect because petitions for a referendum had been filed by an unknown citizens group. She said that until all the signatures were validated, the domestic partners legislation would be held in suspension. Even that in itself was a tremendous victory! If only for a moment, we had stopped a homosexual law!

On 7 July the *San Francisco Chronicle* ran an article headlined, "Referendum Petitions Block S.F. Domestic Partners Law." The first paragraph tells the story: "San Francisco's controversial domestic partners law was suspended yesterday, the same day it was to take effect." The homosexual community was infuriated.

The same day, the *San Francisco Examiner* headlines read, "S.F. puts partners law on the shelf:" "It feels like a vicious insult, a slap in the face—this is dirty pool," said Cynthia Goldstein, staff attorney at the National Gay Rights Advocates. Jean Harris told reporters, "To tell you the truth, I welcome the challenge: we have a very well-oiled machine. This is a highly intelligent community. I think we will have overwhelming support."

After the news hit the papers, I spent the next two weeks hiding out in my home and church. Donna still had to go downtown to work. There were some repercussions at the office, and she was concerned about that.

They Flock to the Church!

For the next few weeks things really heated up at the church. Picketers and reporters with T.V. crews plagued our Sunday morning services. The police were also there most of the time to keep order.

"Rent-a-mob" was there. This is a name we've given a group of people who attend every protest promoting immorality, whether it be for homosexuality, abortion, etc. They are people whose only conviction in life seems to be to attend any and all demonstrations, and to be as civilly disobedient as possible.

Demonstrators came inside during the service and attempted to disrupt my preaching. Some men were dressed in leathers, while others had dresses on, complete with bows in their hair. Some were quite "normal" looking (by San Francisco standards.) A few got up and walked around during the service. One man would open a window and then SLAM!! it shut—anything to generally disrupt the service. For the most part, the women were "butch"—masculine looking and tough.

Since the front doors and windows of the church are flush up against the sidewalk, the protesting outside got full play on the inside also. They performed mock same-sex marriages in front of the church. Some of the women lay down on the sidewalk, and chalk was used to outline them as though marking the spot where a dead body had fallen. They had red paint splattered on their clothing, referencing blood. They held coat hangers in their hands folded across their chests. This, of course, was to protest our stand against abortion. They sang raucous songs mocking the Christian faith, the church, and the family.

This was a real gay rights evangelistic meeting. They even came prepared with song sheets. One lesbian in particular who goes from protest to protest, made herself particularly obnoxious with her jeering, mocking songs. She lead "the congregation" in singing some of the following:

"It's my body and I'll choose an abortion
choose to have children
choose my own lovers
You would choose too, if your man would let you."

"Oh Suzanna, they lied to me again,
Went to Crisis Pregnancy Center,
The baby's name is Ben."

"Women loving women, men loving men,
Won't go in the closet again."

Copies of some of these songs were strewn around the neighborhood, and some were left in the sanctuary during the service. In the upper right hand corner of the sheet was a skeletal form, holding a cross in its left hand and a skull in its right hand. A picture of my head (taken from a local newspaper article) was superimposed on top of the skeletal form. Next to my face it said, "Rev. Charles McIlhenny" with "save this city from sin" coming out of my mouth.

During the service, policemen stood shoulder to shoulder across the front doorway, and a couple of officers stationed themselves on the landing of the stairs going up to the auditorium.

The next time you're tempted to complain that perhaps your worship service seems a little boring—don't!

As the people in our congregation left the church that morning, protestors stood at the entrance and/or followed the Christians to their cars, pointing their fingers and yelling in our faces "shame, shame, shame." Police officers in squad cars and on motorcycles lined the block; they were there to protect the protestors' right to harass. Donna overheard one officer say to another, "We're here to protect the right of these [protestors] against those [church people] inside? This is insane!"

For a while, news reporters lined the back rows of the service as well. (We had decided a few years earlier that we would not allow the use of TV or flash cameras during the worship. It wasn't for fear of public exposure, but to maintain the sacredness of the worship.) They sat with their cassette recorders on during the service, hoping for a slip of the tongue and thus a story "straight from the pulpit" about the campaign. I prudently refrained from mentioning anything about the campaign or domestic partners while preaching, although I continued to publicly pray for the salvation of the city, the mayor, and the Board of Supervisors. Those prayers did make the news. Reporters came up to me after the service, asking for a comment on the campaign: why we did it, what it would cost, who was involved, and just what we hoped to accomplish. With satisfaction I replied, "NO COMMENT!" I was asked to comment on why there was "no comment." I said, "No comment." Some reporters were polite and others were not—and their articles reflected the same. They went back to their typewriters and wrote all kinds of things about us. In obvious frustration (mixed with a great dislike for me) at not being able to get an interview, Elizabeth Hernandez (the *San Francisco Examiner* reporter who did the story about domestic partners becoming law the day we filed the petitions) did an article that was nothing more than a childish mock on what I wore while preaching—from my "horn-rimmed glasses" to my "polished loafers."

It is amazing what the press will invent about you whether you speak with them or not! I have since become an advocate for Christian journalism. Not only do we need integrity in the news, we need God-fearing Christians who will determine to tell the truth, and nothing but the truth, so help them God.

Though the reporters were angry and frustrated about not getting interviews, little did they know that the very real story they were missing was just how scared I was . . . how scared we all were!

We continued to receive hate calls and mail during this time. Sometimes, before a Sunday morning service, I'd get a phone call saying, "My name is Satan. I'm going to kill you . . ." or "We're coming over to get you!" This really makes for a calm, worshipful attitude!

Once, the police arrived before the service even started to warn us that protestors had already disrupted the worship service at St. Mary's Cathedral. One demonstrator had been arrested, and they were coming to do the same here. Inside, I was terrified; however, I reassured the sergeant (and myself) by telling him "the Lord will fight our battles for us." I proceeded upstairs to the auditorium to warn the congregation that protestors were on their way to disrupt the service, but not to be afraid because the Lord would defend us. As afraid as I was, a paradoxical calm overwhelmed my shaking voice as I spoke those words.

I must candidly admit that for the next few months I was literally scared to death. I had not understood the fear that Donna had experienced after the fire of 1983. Now, it was my turn. I spent many hours alone in my office just praying that God would have mercy on my soul, and asking Him to deliver me from death. I read and reread the Psalms where David himself was surrounded and about to be crushed by his enemies. The terrorist tactics of the callers and protestors had effectively worked all kinds of fears and anxieties in my mind. Every ring of the telephone frightened me! My heart had never pounded so hard and for so long as it did through those L-O-N-G months of the summer of 1989.

I remember one time taking the kids out to the suburbs to drop Ryan off at the Osterhaus' home. (Jim and Marcy were dear friends from our Moody days.) As I drove, waves of panic rolled over me. I stared straight ahead, not wanting the kids to see the tears in my eyes. I never felt such a fear of death than at that time. What if my time really was up, that the end is near, that I'd never see my family again, that the stories of the martyred missionaries would be my story, too?

But it wasn't only the fear of unrelenting harassment that had gripped me. It was also the realization that I was completely in the Lord's hands, to do with me as He pleased. I had no protection or defense other than the Lord—and there was no greater protection or defense. The "peace that passes understanding"—that's what I needed: God's comfort amidst the confusion and dread of the moment. The Lord cutting me down to size. I had been too arrogant through the years. Now, it was my turn to cry to the Lord in the very words of the Psalmist:

O LORD, how my adversaries have increased! Many are rising up against me . . . O LORD my God, in Thee have I taken refuge; Save me from all those who pursue me, and deliver me, lest he tear my soul like a lion, dragging me away, while there is none to deliver. . . . In pride the wicked hotly pursues the afflicted; let them be caught in the plots which they have devised. For the wicked boasts of his heart's desire, and the greedy man curses and spurns the LORD. (Pss. 3, 7 and 10)

The reality of the Psalmist hit me harder than ever before. I cried to the Lord. I had never before felt my own sinfulness or mortality so keenly. Would I survive the summer? Would I survive this battle?

Months before all this began, I had agreed to speak to our presbytery youth camp. The kids were going as campers, and

Donna was to be the cook. It was a welcome deliverance from the city for a few days. What a relief to be away from the fight: but then, I had to preach to those kids about boldness and "fighting the good fight of faith"—when I was so tired and afraid!

While we were there, I read San Francisco newspapers to keep up with what was going on. Every day there were articles about domestic partners. One criticized the "two conservative homophobic clergymen" who sponsored the referendum, and made it quite clear that we were not welcome in tolerant San Francisco. "Take your bigotry elsewhere," it said. At a distance of 140 miles, tucked away in the Sierra Mountains, it was easy to be brave; however, it would soon be time to come down from the mountain and back to reality.

Many times over the years, Donna has said to me, "I can't take anymore, Chuck—not one more thing!" And then, something else would happen—and, by God's grace, she'd take it. Just when we think that we have endured all that we can, the Lord gives us one more thing and says, "My grace is sufficient for you . . ." We arrived home from the mountains to find ourselves embroiled in another controversy!

A lesbian minister named Lynn Griffis claimed that in late July she had been assaulted at her home by an anti-gay attacker. She said that she had heard a noise in her garage. She went to investigate. She came to the bottom of the stairs leading into the garage, and a man jumped out and hit her in the face with a shovel. Anti-gay, white supremacist graffiti had been sprayed all over the inside of the garage. She appeared on the news several times for days on end, with her face stitched and swollen. In her interviews, Griffis immediately linked this attack to the campaign against domestic partners. She claimed that there was a "climate of hatred" in San Francisco against gays and that the right wing, ultra-conservative, fundamentalist Christians who were sponsoring the drive against the partners law were to blame. Griffis became the "cause celeb," and she showed her scars to the public on all the local news and talk show programs.

My heart sunk! This was a terrible thing that had happened to this woman, and I knew we'd be blamed. Since the rabbi and I were the only public sponsors of the referendum, and since no one knew where the rabbi lived, I was the obvious villain—and my church and family were the logical targets for backlash.

That next Sunday, we were picketed again by angry demonstrators carrying signs demanding to know, "WHO HIT LYNN GRIFFIS WITH A SHOVEL: WE WON'T FORGET!" A photo of this demonstration appeared on the front page of one of our newspapers with a caption under the picture which read: "Gay activitists and supporters demonstrated Sunday in front of a . . . church where a petition drive against the Domestic Partners ordinance was organized by an anti-gay reverend" ("Sunset Church Protested: Protestors Target Anti-Gay Minister," *San Francisco Independent* [19 July 1989].). There was no stopping the association of the attack with the referendum drive as fabricated by the press! Members of our congregation were jeered as they entered and left the service. One of our elderly ladies, Mrs. Bain—Scottish and proud of her presbyterian heritage—stood in front of the narrow doors of the church cross-armed, defying the marauders.

Donna confided in me that she didn't believe the assault story. It was obvious that Lynn Griffis had been injured, but how and by whom? In Donna's mind this was all too convenient and timely. She just didn't buy it. I didn't agree with Donna, and I told her not to even think that way. It was too fantastic to even imagine that this was a hoax!

A few days later, the evening news reported that Lynn Griffis had been attacked yet a second time! (Just when you think you've had all you can take!) This time she said that she had been dragged into a car by a couple of "skin heads," assaulted, and thrown out of the car. This was just too much! Would this never end?

Now Donna was really suspicious—and vocally so. She didn't believe it for a moment! The whole thing was a fabrication! (Maybe I was beginning to waiver in my belief, too.)

Two weeks after the report of the initial attack, I received a phone call from a sympathizer who alerted me that Griffis had made up the whole story—BOTH attacks. It was her own church, a branch of the Metropolitan Community Church, which had uncovered her lies and exposed her story to the press. Within twelve hours of this exposure, Griffis left the city (in the middle of the night.) For the next two weeks, the press analyzed "what drove Griffis" to do such a thing, which brought such embarrassment to the gay community! (Of course, there was no mention in the press of regrets or sympathy on the part

of anyone for the demonstrations and threats that we had
suffered as a result of these lies.)

For us, there was no analyzing, there was no asking WHY:
it was yet another example of God's divine intervention and
protecting Hand—that "He keeps us in all our ways."

There were no more violent protests or demonstrations
against us for the remainder of 1989.

Sued Again!

Although we received a respite from that kind of harassment for a while, the onslaught of the enemy continued. This
time, in the form of legal action. Late that same month, July
1989, I found out that a petition for writ of mandate had been
filed against me, the rabbi, and the Registrar of Voters' office,
alleging fraud in our referendum petition drive. The suit was
brought by the two lesbians, Cindy Bologna and Sydney Erskine,
who had been pictured in the San Francisco Examiner article the
day we filed the petitions at city hall. The argument from their
legal papers was that the voters were not fully informed on our
petition about the nature of the domestic partners ordinance.

The hearing was short but interesting—for several reasons:
We appeared before the judge assigned to hear our summary
judgment motion in the Walker lawsuit ten years earlier. (The
judge who left town to go to cooking school at the last minute.)
Bologna and Erskine were represented by three attorneys from
the Gay Rights Advocates office. (The same organization that
sued us ten years ago, and the office that shut down in 1991
due to infighting.) A deputy city attorney represented the
Registrar's office, Mick Imfeld represented me, and, to no
one's surprise, the rabbi represented HIMSELF!

Donna attended the hearing with me. When she entered
the courtroom, she sat down next to one of the ministers from
our committee, a row or two behind Bologna and Erskine. She
greeted our minister friend. Without looking at her, he bowed
his head slightly and quietly said, "Don't talk to me here." He
whispered, "If they [whomever "they" might be] know that we
know one another, they may try to track me down and perhaps
they'll find out who I am!" A tiny spark of anger flared in
Donna for a moment, but it gave way to a feeling of hurt. We
have understood over the years why many Christian friends
have not wanted to be publicly associated with us; nonetheless,

it has been a painful experience. Donna acquiesced to our friend's request and even moved away from where he was sitting. Privately, in Christian surroundings, we still maintain a good relationship with this man.

Fortunately, the deputy city attorney argued that our petition campaign had been conducted properly, and the suit was dismissed in the Superior Court, and also in the appellate court.

Be Still My Soul

The pressure of working on the committee, collecting signatures, death threats, newspaper articles, demonstrators, the Lynn Griffis affair, and this legal challenge to the referendum had taken its toll on the family. Plus, I was really doing battle with my own fears now. So, we decided to take a short trip down to Southern California to visit my family.

Donna understood my fears all too well, and while we were on vacation, she suggested that both of us visit Dr. Jay Adams at Westminster Seminary. In his own nonchalant way, Dr. Adams agreed that we were definitely in danger living in San Francisco. He said that I had a clear decision to make: to leave San Francisco and remove myself and my family from danger, or to stay and continue the fight. If I chose to stay, he likened the reality of the situation to that of a soldier on the battlefield—the possibility of dying was very real. What I had to do was to face that fact and make my decision. He called Dr. Robert Godfrey into his office, and together the four of us prayed for wisdom and confidence to do what the Lord had for us to do. Before Donna and I left that day, both Dr. Adams and Dr. Godfrey graciously offered to help raise funds on our behalf, if we decided to move out of San Francisco.

Dr. Adams was very supportive and, if I could criticize my friend and teacher in any way, it would be that he was almost too sympathetic. But, the decision was mine! Even Donna understood that. What I needed was a swift kick in the pants and someone to say, "Wake up, McIlhenny! This is what you were called to! What did you expect? Are you willing to die for your faith? It's happened many times before . . . you wouldn't be the first . . . nor the last. So, stop belly-aching! You do have a savior who went through this and much more. Now He's in charge."

Again, I was reminded that the Lord is our protection from

harm. One Sunday night shortly after our Southern California visit, Donna and I were listening to Christian music. An old hymn came on that we had both known all our lives, and the words became even more real and remain much more dear to us now:

> Be still, my soul: The Lord is on thy side:
> Bear patiently the cross of grief or pain;
> Leave to thy God to order and provide;
> In every change He faithful will remain.
> Be still, my soul: Thy best, thy heavenly friend
> Through thorny ways leads to a joyful end.
>
> Be still, my soul: Thy God doth undertake
> To guide the future as He has the past!
> Thy hope, thy confidence let nothing shake;
> All now mysterious shall be bright at last.
> Be still, my soul: The waves and winds still know
> His voice who ruled them while He dwelt below.
>
> Be still, my soul: The hour is hastening on
> When we shall be forever with the Lord,
> When disappointment, grief, and fear are gone,
> Sorrow forgot, love's purest joys restored.
> Be still, my soul: When change and tears are past,
> All safe and blessed we shall meet at last.

The Battle Had Just Begun

The lawsuit and the Griffis controversy had slowed us down a bit in our referendum efforts to overturn the domestic partners ordinance. However, as quickly as Griffis' name disappeared from the papers, San Franciscans for Common Sense (the new name our committee had taken on) was ready to launch into a full-scale educational and marketing campaign to convince San Francisco voters that they should repeal the ordinance.

Dave Gilmour took a prominent role throughout this next phase of the battle. With Dave's expertise in using marketing polls and his current political wisdom, he would show us how to appeal to the voters on the basis of economics and common sense.

I wasn't altogether happy with the "Common Sense" approach. My concern was that we keep our Christian witness clear and distinct and not merge it into some pragmatic methodology whose goal was simply to win votes. The rabbi had drummed into us that the main thing was getting signatures—our philosophy did not matter. For me, it was our Christian testimony that was most important. The typical American approach is to win votes; and if that be your goal, then everything must be dedicated to the "winning of votes." It was my Christian understanding that "winning votes" was not the first goal, but rather "winning Christ "—even in a political campaign. "Ah . . . but Chuck, you're so naive! It's such an impractical idea!" Nonetheless, even in politics, our witness for Christ comes first—whether we win elections or not! That's not only an impractical idea, but political heresy in this day and age!

With the success of the petition drive, our referendum was placed on the November ballot as Proposition S. Gilmour, and his associates immediately went to work, drafting printed materials and radio announcements denouncing the domestic partners law as too costly to the taxpayers of San Francisco. The cover of the one flyer we mailed out had a simple and colorful design. The headline at the top read, "The Domestic Partners Law." Directly beneath it in a white box were two men silhouetted in black, holding hands. One of the men had a white dollar sign on his chest. Beneath them were the words, "Proposition S—It isn't FREE . . . and it isn't fair! One section entitled, "IT INVITES ABUSE," read:

> The definition of a domestic partnership is so broad and permissive that it would be impossible for the city to draw a distinction between real live-in relationships and "partnerships of convenience" aimed at qualifying friends for benefits. Randy Smith, the veteran executive director of the health services agency, warned long ago city workers might be pressured into claiming partnerships as a means of helping friends suffering from AIDS and other chronic diseases to obtain insurance.

Another section said:

> Don't be misled by emotional rhetoric. The real purpose of Proposition S is to allow unmarried city employees to qualify their live-in lovers for fringe benefits—a well-established goal of Supervisor Harry Britt and the gay lobby.

The flyer also featured a panel that had a brief history of the Domestic Partners law. This part cleverly used quotes from Dianne Feinstein in 1982 when she was explaining why she vetoed the ordinance.

In the meantime, the gay and mainline papers were doing everything they could to assure our defeat on election day. In the August 1989 issue of the gay publication, *San Francisco Bay Times*, an article appeared entitled, "Revenge of Neanderthal Men: The Religious Right Marshalls Their Forces To Stop Domestic Partners Legislation." The author, Tim Kingston, gave this description of our campaign: "It was McIlhenny's petition, but all sorts of people jumped on the bandwagon to get it circulated, signed and delivered. Add them all together and you get an evil brew of homophobia and right wing bigotry which threatens to toss domestic partnership legislation back to the Dianne Feinstein dark ages." In the article, Tim also referred to me as "the iron fist of orthodoxy"—a title which I have worn proudly ever since. His article put a bit of iron back into my all-too-trembling fist!

As has been mentioned before, in the 2 August 1989 issue of the *San Francisco Bay Guardian*, Harry Britt declared: "This campaign is a spiritual war . . . our enemies are saying they want the authoritarian, man-on-top, woman-on-bottom world." In keeping with its statement of faith, the *San Francisco Examiner* whole-heartedly supported the domestic partners ordinance. One of its 2 November 1989 editorials said: "Society bestows benefits to assist a husband and wife to stay together and raise children. The extension of rights to support stable relationships among gay men and lesbians, the offering of this small degree of dignity, is the humanitarian thing to do."

Another mainline paper reported that by their own poll they found that "gay and lesbian voters support the measure by an overwhelming 87 percent to 7 percent, . . ." The article goes on to describe the election strategy of the pro domestic partners forces: "For strategists seeking to pass the law, the prime concern has been voter turnout. 'Our strategy is not to convince (voters) that the legislation is OK,' said Jean Harris, an aide to Supervisor Harry Britt, author of the partners law. 'We're trying to get people out to vote'" ("Voter turnout crucial for Domestic Partners," *San Francisco Chronicle* [6 Sept. 1989]). Though the point of this statement is to win this particular election, an underlying "statement of faith" is present: The morality—rightness or wrongness—of an issue is not important in the gay political philosophy. Whether the general public agrees or disagrees with proposed legislation, or how offensive it may be, is of no consequence. There is no dialogue, no consideration of another point of view, no scruples, and no "live and let live." Winning the election by organizing and getting out the gay vote is the order of the day. Nothing else matters. This philosophy is consistently employed in their lobbying and intimidation tactics and is clearly seen in the activities of groups such as ACT UP and Queer Nation.

> Woe to those who call evil good, and good evil; who substitute darkness for light and light for darkness; who substitute bitter for sweet, and sweet for bitter! Woe to those who are wise in their own eyes, and clever in their own sight! . . . who justify the wicked for a bribe, and take away the rights of the ones who are in the right! (Isa. 5:20-23 NASV)

The Rabbi and the Preacher Are Ousted!

A curious thing happened on the way to the election. An article appeared in the 18 September 1989 edition of the *San Francisco Chronicle* which announced the rabbi and I had both withdrawn from the campaign. Chronicle Religion Writer, Don Lattin, observed,

> The Rev. Charles McIlhenny, pastor of the First Orthodox Presbyterian Church, and Rabbi Feldman, who has no congregation, are described as having "withdrawn" from the shadowy campaign against Proposition S. Their departure— blamed on death threats and arson attacks against McIlhenny—has brought forward a new group of religious opponents . . . executive director of the Roman Catholic archdiocese's Justice and Peace Office, and P. T. Mammen, . . . president of the San Francisco Association of Evangelicals. . . . are meeting with other church leaders in an attempt to broaden church opposition to the ordinance.

Mr. Lattin reported that the representative from the archdioceses "has met with both McIlhenny and David Gilmour, coordinator of San Franciscans for Common Sense, . . . and vice president of the San Francisco Association of Evangelicals."

This article came as a shock to Donna and me. I had not withdrawn from the campaign, nor did I have any intention of doing so, nor had any member of the committee approached me. Also, I had not met with Dave Gilmour and the representative of the archdiocese. Lattin went on in the article to detail the new group of religious people who had picked up the campaign and were going forward with it. It certainly was "news to me."

Donna and I have our own theories about where Lattin came up with this story containing so much inside information. From the beginning, the committee agreed that there would be no talking to the press. This decision had been particularly difficult for me, as I was the only one of the ministers with an ongoing reputation known to the press. Don Lattin had come to my Sunday morning worship service and sat on the back row. When he asked me for an interview, I said, "No comment," as I had said to every other member of the press that came to my door during this campaign. Then, to open up the paper one morning and find a picture of myself (that had been taken at one of our services without permission) with my head bowed (as I was in the process of reading Scripture from the pulpit), looking quite "defeated," and with a caption underneath that read, "The Rev. Charles McIlhenny: He withdrew from campaign," was very discouraging. Especially so, since right next to my picture was a photo of Supervisor Harry Britt, with head erect, and a confident smile on his face.

Suffice it to say, we felt used and abused by individuals we trusted. Donna particularly felt it was like "adding insult to injury" since our church and family had been taking the brunt of demonstrations, vandalism, and death threats as a result of the campaign. Perhaps one reason the article was written was because of my incessant exhorting of the members of our committee to take a clear stand for Jesus Christ in fighting domestic partners. Interestingly, the article went on to report that Supervisor "Britt, however, said the new campaigners cannot so easily disassociate themselves from McIlhenny and Feldman. . . . For years, Rev. McIlhenny has been trying to create the kind of born- again Christian religious right here that we see in other parts of the country." Establishing a "religious right" I don't care about; but "born-again Christian"— YES. That character statement I accept. Thank you, Harry Britt.

Don't be afraid of the religious issue or fearful of being called "fundamentalists." Don't be afraid to bring Christ into every area of your life. "Every one therefore who shall confess Me before men, I will also confess him before My Father who is in heaven" (Matt. 10:32 NASV). The cause of Christ will only be positively maintained by members of the Kingdom of God. The world does not look kindly on Christians; and the unbelieving press is not sympathetic to His cause. However, Scripture assures us that ". . . at the name of Jesus every knee should bow, . . . and *every* tongue confess that Christ is Lord, to the glory of God the Father" (Phil. 2:10-11 NIV).

The Earthquake

That hot October afternoon, the San Francisco Giants were just about to face off with the Oakland A's in the fourth game of the 1989 World Series. The atmosphere was very still and silent. At 5:04 p.m., God's creation spoke!

A small group of us, including our kids, were folding flyers for Dave Gilmour in our downstairs basement. Donna had just gotten home from work and was upstairs preparing dinner. Suddenly the earth began to shake. It shook . . . but we were used to that . . . but it kept shaking . . . and it started rolling under our feet . . . For a moment I thought, *This was the big one!* It seemed to go on and on. We ran for the door posts; some got under the tables we had been working on. Things were flying off the walls and shelves, especially in our home upstairs. Terror struck! The electricity was gone, and all communication facilities were shut down. SOMEBODY else was protesting!

Everything stopped! Fires broke out throughout the city. Black smoke billowed into the sky from the Marina District to the north. We grabbed our portable radios and dashed outside to survey any damage. The Crisis Pregnancy volunteers dashed out of the downstairs portion of the church. We listened. The news came in slowly. We heard that the Bay Bridge had collapsed! It was rush hour! How many people could have been killed? In the next few days we got *accurate* reports that, miraculously, only one man had been killed on the bridge, and that only one section had fallen. However, a portion of an on-ramp linking another freeway with the Bay Bridge had collapsed killing approximately forty people. (Thankfully, because of the World Series game, many workers had left their jobs early to watch the game; consequently, fewer people were on the freeway at a time when it would normally be packed.)

What was peculiarly interesting about the earthquake was that it struck one month before the election, and had a profound affect on the outcome of the vote. Mayor Agnos was campaigning for a new ballpark. He was also adamantly supporting domestic partners. In what he thought to be a shrewd political move, he teamed the two ballot issues together in order to get both of them passed in November. He elicited support from the gay community for the ballpark, in exchange for support from the "new ballpark advocates" for the domestic partners law. One issue would support the other—and vice-versa. The owner of the Giants had publicly contributed to the domestic partners campaign. However, the proposed site of the new ballpark was to be on a patch of landfill in the Marina District where the greatest damage was done by the quake. Not only did the ballpark initiative fail on the November ballot, but its piggy-back cousin, domestic partners, also failed at virtually the same percentage rate! The mayor had thought that in teaming the two issues together he could achieve the best possible result, at the least amount of cost, and in the shortest period of time. What he got was defeat for both issues.

The earthquake stopped the World Series. It stopped all campaigning in order to help with the victims of the tragedy. It stopped talk of a new ballpark on that site. It quieted the volatile rhetoric about Proposition S. The creation groaned! . . . The mayor was defeated, the homosexuals were defeated, the owner of the Giants was defeated.

Our Common Sense committee tried to keep the momentum going—but at a reduced level. Gilmour organized a phone bank operation to be used for the remainder of the campaign, alerting voters to what domestic partners was really all about. The campaign FOR domestic partners really couldn't get back on track.

On 7 November 1989 by the grace of God alone, PROPOSITION "S" WON! We surprised all the pollsters and political pundits. We even surprised ourselves! We were a rag-tag bunch of ministers with no political experience and no political machinery; we utilized very little public advertising and engaged in very little debating; we were out-spent two to one by the opposition; we had every community leader—senators, assemblymen, congressmen, mayor, supervisors, and all the newspapers, TV and radio media—against us—but WE WON. It truly was an act of God in His mercy, showing what a few faithful timid folks could accomplish in His Name.

With a 50.5 percent to 49.5 percent margin, we narrowly won the referendum and defeated domestic partners . . . for this year! It was a victory that caught the gay community off guard and surprised everyone. After the election, Harry Britt was quoted as saying the "fight was far from over." He wasn't sure what the next step would be, but "believe me, it's not over. I haven't found my husband yet" (Philip Matier, "Prop. S defeat a setback for gays," *San Francisco Examiner* 8 [November 1989]). Interestingly, the plethora of postmortems on the election concentrated on the defeat of the homosexual lobby, not on how our side won. After all, we'd have to give God the glory, and why would the press want to give us the chance?

A few days after the election, I received the following letter:
"Dear Rev. McIlhenny,

"Please allow me to introduce myself. My name is Keith ——. I am 26 years old, gay, and have been a resident of San Francisco along with my lover (domestic partner), —— , since 1984.

"With that introduction I would like to mention that I am aware of your role in overturning the Domestic Partners proposition, Proposition S. Although I am most confident that the Domestic Partners proposition will return again next year, and every year after that until it ultimately passes, my lover, ——,who is a bit younger than I am, woke up this morning to the news that Proposition S lost in a city-wide vote by a margin of 3,000 votes. I will never forget how he sat down on the floor of our bedroom and cried. I don't think he really fully composed himself until I mentioned to him that we both will probably outlive you. [He] finally broke into tears of laughter when I told him that as a symbol of our feelings for your self-appointed mission in life to persecute homosexuals, we as a couple plan to pour a cup of our urine on your grave after you die.

"[He] probably thinks that I'm joking, but I can't think of a better way to pay tribute to your life.

"Incidentally, Reverend, are your parents still alive? Of course, it would be easy enough to find out where they rest without your help. Have a nice day. Signed, Keith ——."

How do you react to a letter like that? I could only reflect with sadness that this young man probably will not live to be older than thirty-five or forty, if that long. He might die of AIDS as thousands of others like him have died, without knowing Jesus Christ as Lord and Savior—without knowing the cleanness of forgiveness of sins—without knowing that we love him for Christ's sake. Our home always remains open to anyone in the homosexual community who wants to know the way of escape from such bondage. We live to see men like him come to Christ.

The Domestic Partners Ordinance Returns

Keith was right. In 1990, the Board of Supervisors, backed by the gay political machine, placed Proposition K back on the ballot. Prop K was a reworded domestic partners bill.

To help gain public acceptance of the original domestic partners law, Art Agnos had established a Mayor's Task Force on Family Policy to "study" the issue of the diversity of families in the city. They were supposed to report just before the 1989 election but didn't, and their activities continued in spite of the defeat that year. The mayor had appointed attorney Roberta Achtenberg, one of the lesbian members of the Board of Supervisors, to head up this project.

Her report, "Approaching 2000: Meeting the Challenges to San Francisco's Families," was issued on 13 June 1990. What did Achtenberg's task force discover about family life in San Francisco? Take a wild guess. They revealed that "Lesbians and gay men are subject to prejudice and discrimination in all walks of life, ranging from employment to education; judicial remedies for this bigotry are limited. The prejudice and discrimination suffered by this community, sometimes erupting into violence, has persisted throughout most of history. The effects are particularly felt by lesbian and gay male families" (p. 16).

The report concludes that ". . . the diversity of San Francisco, coupled with economic and societal changes, demands that the term family be given a flexible meaning. It is clear that in America today a family is not just a heterosexual married couple and their children. There are other families, such as multigenerational and extended families, single parent families, gay male or lesbian families with or without children, families where children are raised by grandparents or other relatives, and immigrant families which reflect both the immigrant experience and different cultures" (p. 16).

The Task Force proposed that the city adopt a redefinition of the family as provided by a Los Angeles group called the Task Force on the Family Diversity (run by homosexuals). According to Achtenberg's report, the family should be defined as

> a unit of interdependent and interacting persons, related together over time by strong social and emotional bonds and/or by ties of marriage, birth and adoption, whose central purpose is to create, maintain, and promote the social, mental, physical and emotional development and well being of each of its members (p. 17).

The Achtenberg report went well beyond the boundaries of the domestic partners ordinance we'd defeated in 1989 and effectively prepared the way for the 1990 effort to reinstate it and to establish this redefinition of family.

Earlier in 1990, the ministers of San Franciscans for Common Sense attended the *only* public hearing on this report. The Task Force had had other meetings throughout 1989, but none open to the public at large. We addressed the issue of the family from a biblical perspective. We complained that the evangelical Christian community (certainly a minority community in the city) had not been consulted for input on the report as every other minority community group had been. We argued that the voters had rejected domestic partners in November; however, that didn't make any difference to the Task Force. It was amazing to us that this appointed public commission summarily rejected the vote of the people, refused input from our community group, and were about to carelessly tamper with God's creation ordinance of the family.

It is one thing to argue that the family concept included extended family members like grandparents, aunts, uncles, and cousins; it is quite another thing to draw from that conclusion that homosexual lovers are therefore part of the "extended family" idea. The original domestic partners *did not* extend to grandparents, parents, cousins, or any blood-related person. Domestic Partners is specifically a special interest legislation designed for homosexuals, bisexuals, and heterosexual fornicators. All the talk about grandparents as members of the family was bogus.

The hearing ended with the original decision of the Commission unchanged.

The "Benefits" of the New Ordinance

With the help of Task Force Commission member Matthew Coles, gay staff attorney with the American Civil Liberties Union of Northern California, Harry Britt's domestic partners ordinance was reworded to take out all references to benefits. Now the ordinance was presented without financial obligations on the city and county and only as an "affirmation of gay relationships." It would simply be a symbolic gesture of support for the gay, bisexual, and lesbian community. A "yes" vote from four of the eleven members of the Board of Supervisors was all that was required to put it back on the November ballot. Board members voting for it didn't even have to agree with it. (Two of the supervisors who did so, were themselves leaving the Board that election year anyway.) Although *we* had to gather over eighteen thousand signatures, the Board rules allowed only a minority of four to refer the ordinance to the ballot.

In the 23 August 1990 issue of the *Bay Area Reporter*, Matthew Coles described the importance of domestic partners law. He claimed that straight society had oppressed gays by forcing them out of the mainstream with the ". . . myth that we are emotionally shallow, incapable of serious, abiding commitments to each other.

"One of the most effective tools the lesbian and gay rights movement has for destroying that myth is bringing our relationships into the open.

"Harry Britt's domestic partnership law . . . makes our relationship undeniable. That alone makes the law well worth the right to pass it" (Matthew Coles, "An Important Beginning," *Bay Area Reporter*, [23 Aug. 1990]: 6.]). To date, one year later, there have only been 1069 domestics that have signed up to do what Matthew Coles argued would be worth while: to make their relationships undeniable! Apparently a very small percentage of the homosexual community wants to bother with such "undeniable relationships."

In October, a month before the vote on the new domestic partners law, the San Francisco Civil Service Commission approved a new definition of unpaid family leave to include city workers who cared for children, ailing relatives, or unmarried domestic partners. According to a report in the 16 October 1990 edition of the *San Francisco Chronicle*, the Civil Service Commission had used Roberta Achtenberg's redefinition of the family as the basis for changing the laws on unpaid leave. With the stroke of a pen, our faceless, nameless city bureaucrats had redefined the family to include unmarried heterosexual and homosexual couples, i.e., fornicators, adulterers, and whatever other sexual deviancies that will assuredly become decriminalized in the coming years: pedophiles, necrophiles, incest-philes.

We Lost

We were worn out after our exhaustive effort in the 1989 campaign, but we decided to resurrect the San Franciscans for Common Sense for one more battle. We were thousands of dollars in debt from '89 and had to pay that off before incurring any more debts. However, the call to fight one more battle was too strong to resist.

Again, the ministers, including our manager Dave Gilmour, forged ahead with a new campaign against Proposition K. Dave streamlined the operation. We weren't going to be as secretive. We didn't have to collect signatures this time since the Board of Supervisors put Prop K on the ballot themselves. Mark and Kris Poggioli took on the duties of press coordinator and phone bank director, respectively, for this campaign.

This time I was allowed (and quite willing I might add) to speak to the press. But, the homosexuals had learned a lesson from us: don't talk—just do the job. Whatever publicity they got, we would get—so the best tactic for them was to remain silent. Mark Poggioli wrote some news articles and did a few interviews, but our side wasn't "chomping at the bit" for publicity either. More businessmen were willing to come out against domestic partners this time, although the whole political establishment still opposed us. I must admit, for such a volatile issue, this was a quiet, low-key campaign.

A provocative editorial in the 30 September 1990 edition of the *San Francisco Examiner*, entitled, "Yes on domestic partners: Proposition K will help undo the fabric of oppression that gays and lesbians live with every day," came out in support of the 1990s domestic partners by attacking the Christian faith. The editorial states in pertinent part: "Even in enlightened San

Francisco, gay men and lesbian women are second-class citizens. . . . Partners as loving and caring and committed to each other as any man and wife are not recognized by the law.

"In a subtle and insidious way, this structural inequality fosters discrimination against gays and lesbians and prevents them from achieving the full equality that is their due. That's why it is important for San Francisco voters to pass Proposition K, the domestic partners measure on the November [1990] ballot. Unlike the domestic partners measure that was narrowly defeated last year, this one carries no health benefits to partners of city employees. In one sense, it is purely symbolic. But, it is a symbol of great importance.

"Proposition K set up a city registry that would enable committed, unmarried couples to legitimate their relationships in the eyes of the law. They would have to pay a fee, so it wouldn't cost the public a dime. The couples would get no monetary benefits, but the psychological benefits would be enormous."

ON THE CONTRARY

• 12/12/90: *San Francisco Chronicle*, "Dramatic Panel Vote on Partner Benefits: San Francisco board President Harry Brit appoints himself at last minute to break tie." The article reported: "San Francisco took a key step toward offering health benefits to domestic partners yesterday, minutes after Board of Supervisors President Harry Britt appointed himself to a city panel in order to cast the deciding vote.

"Britt, . . . replaced Supervisor Nancy Walker on the city's Health Services Board in the middle of the meeting, after it became apparent that his vote was needed.

". . . The panel's attorney scrambled to determine whether such a substitution was legal. Before he could come up with an answer, Britt strode in and announced that he was not sitting in for Walker, but had instead accepted her resignation from the panel.

"*I have appointed myself,*" he said.

"Minutes later, the board, including Britt, voted 4 to 3 to move on the rapid schedule" (emphasis added).

• 4/11/91: *San Francisco Sentinel*, "Board Approves Insurance for Partners of City Employees" (AP Report). The article states in part: "The San Francisco Health Services Board has approved a medical insurance plan that would cover companions of unmarried city employees, a benefit long sought by the gay community.

"The vote Thursday came two months after the city began registration of unmarried gay and straight couples as domestic partners.

• 5/7/91: San Francisco Chronicle, "Domestic Partners Benefits OKd: Supervisors vote to widen insurance for city workers." The article states in part:

"'This has been a very long road,' said Supervisor Roberta Achtenberg, who chaired a mayoral task force on the family that recommended the new benefit package.

"'Today is the first step toward doing justice to gay and lesbian families.'"

• 5/8/91: And yet another editorial from the *San Francisco Examiner*, entitled "An Important Step," published just eight months after the 30 September editorial, which says in part:

"San Francisco has taken an important step in the march to social justice by making the domestic partners of city workers eligible for health insurance benefits. This action recognizes the broad changes that have occurred in society's view of relationships.

"This recognition has been long in coming. . . . The voters narrowly rejected a local ballot measure in 1989. But, they adopted a no-frills domestic partners measure last November, and the city has now extended the benefits that go with it. Social change sometimes comes slowly, which makes it sweeter when it arrives."

• 5/14/91: *San Francisco Chronicle*, "Next Step for Partners' Benefits." The article states in part:

"It came as little surprise last week when San Francisco, known for its liberal politics, extended health benefits to the domestic partners of its municipal employees.

"In the more conservative corporate world, however, executives are just starting to consider health benefits for unmarried partners of both gay and straight workers.

"But benefits analysts say clear signs are emerging of a quiet evolution in the private sector's definition of 'family:' . . . Hundreds of firms, . . . have taken what some of them acknowledge is a first step in offering unmarried partners full benefits . . . ."

• 2/14/91: *San Francisco Chronicle*, "Domestic Partners Celebrate: Anniversary of S.F. law benefiting unmarried gay, straight couples." The article states:

"[Supervisor Harry] Britt said that in the coming year he wants to push for domestic partners recognition in private business."

Another paragraph in the 30 September 1990 editorial in the *San Francisco Examiner* states:

> Last year's opposition focused on the potential cost of the health benefits, but that was just a smokescreen for what was really at stake. As this year's measure contains no such benefits, the opponents will have to come out of their closet and say what is really on their minds. They will have to argue from outdated, narrow-minded, self-serving views of morality. They will call themselves religious, but theirs is a religion of hate. We were always taught that religion is about love.

The editorial is right: In the long-run, economics is not the issue, nor can it be! As seen in the articles quoted above, the gay political machine will not allow economic arguments to stand in their way. Do not expect economics to be a "common ground" of discussion. That is a smokescreen. The lesbian and gay movement conducts their politics and economics as they do their sex lives—in total defiance of biblical morality. There is no "general standard" of fairness or honesty. Theirs is a "self-serving" ethic whose standard of righteousness allows for anything that will effectively establish the gay political agenda, and thus the gay lifestyle. Theirs is a "narrow-minded" ethic whose standard of "wrong" is anything, any opinion, any person, any organization, or any religion that stands in the way of the gay agenda. Theirs is an ethic of "hate," whose standard ultimately justifies any tactic, whether it be lying, cheating, violence, etc., if it is effective in establishing the gay agenda.

Economic arguments may be right and good, but are ultimately ineffective in stopping such immorality. In the final analysis, it is standing for the righteousness of Christ that alone will turn the tide.

As if the spreading of obvious (purposeful?) "misinformation," which the press uses to form the opinions of the general public, is not enough, here is a major newspaper that not only endorses homosexuality and homosexual "marital" relationships, but calls those (and their faith) that oppose it "outdated, narrow-minded, self-serving" and their religion a religion of "hate."

Once again, the "faithful few" (and they were getting fewer and fewer now) decided to confront the president and publisher, William Randolph Hearst III (grandson of William Randolph Hearst). About nine ministers met with him in his office. Each pastor, in his own way, challenged the editorial and Hearst himself for promoting hatred against the Christian faith. This apparently was the first time a major newspaper had attacked Christianity as "the hateful religion."

Since I had called the meeting, I remained the last one to speak. In a low voice, shaking with a combination of fear and anxiety, I slowly told Hearst that what he was really doing was making war on the Lord Jesus Christ by his attacks on Christian morality. Down through the centuries, many others had done the same, and no one making such an assault on the gospel has escaped the righteous judgment of God's law. History is strewn with the toppled empires of those that have rejected the Son and sought to do harm to his Kingdom. I called on him to repent and to retract the editorial. He politely acknowledged my sincerity, but refused to retract the editorial.

Interestingly, two generations before, William R. Hearst had not only supported, but promoted the ministry of America's most famous Bible-believing evangelist, Billy Graham. Now, over 40 years later, his namesake was openly declaring war on the morality his grandfather had publicly endorsed.

This campaign by the San Franciscans for Common Sense, although less officially Christian in its operation, was more laden with prayer than the previous one. The committee had decided not to fight the issue on an openly moral basis this time (which was what I wanted to do); but, at least we recognized that it was in the Lord's strength alone that we could carry on. There were fewer of us this time, but we met weekly (and towards the end, daily) for corporate beseeching of the Lord in his mercy to intercede for San Francisco. Donna had taken it upon herself to assemble the wives and friends of the pastors for weekly prayer through that fall of 1990. She felt that her best contribution to this campaign would be prayer not only for election success, but also for Christ-centerness of the committee members. She knew that the wives of the pastors needed to uphold their husband's efforts in prayer.

We spent half as much money on this campaign; we had half as many ministers as before; we had fewer parishioners willing to help; and we had no earthquake or "miracles" to bolster our flagging efforts. We were tired! Dave Gilmour was able to raise enough money to end this campaign without debt, but we still had 1989 debts to pay! The election vote was close—but we lost.

The law went into effect on Valentine's Day 1991 with a big celebration at city hall and in the War Memorial Opera House down the street. The rotunda at city hall was filled with couples (yes, and some triplets, too!) getting "partnered"—some by judges, some by clergy, and some by "affirming friends." The San Francisco Gay Men's Chorus sang in the rotunda. Prominent political leaders and activists, including members of the Board of Supervisors and the Board of Education attended. Jean Harris, Supervisor Britt's aide, and her lesbian lover affirmed their commitment to one another by getting "partnered" that day. (They would be "unpartnered" less than a year later: so much for commitment!) More than 274 couples registered. TV and radio stations had a field day with it as you can imagine.

Ironically, on that very same day, 14 February 1991, San Francisco reached another milestone in its history: Health Department officials announced that the 10,000th case of AIDS had been diagnosed on that day. According to the city epidemiologist George Lemp, it is estimated that 20,000 to 24,000 San Franciscans are infected with HIV. "We have at least two-thirds of the epidemic left to go," he said. An estimated 20 percent of the city's gay men between ages sixteen and twenty four might be infected. According to Lemp, "It's possible AIDS could become one of those persistent, endemic disasters in San Francisco, around for decades" (Jayne Garrison, "Sad S.F. Milestone: 10,000th AIDS Case," *San Francisco Examiner* [7 March, 1990]).

Happy Valentine's Day, San Francisco . . .

Do It Again? Are You Crazy?!

In the spring of 1991, a group of the tired ol' San Franciscans for Common Sense pastors were brainstorming about how to pay off the 1989 debts, when an enthusiastic young man introduced himself to us and presented a plan to put domestic partners on the ballot AGAIN. This old, worn-out pride of lions sat around the table, half-heartedly listening to this zealous but naive young cub! The battle-weary veterans of the by-gone wars did not enthusiastically receive his idea of another long campaign. Our "scars" of the last two years were evident, as we picked apart his "half-baked" scheme.

However, Joseph was undaunted by our smugness, and several of us "old-timers" decided to encourage his efforts in starting San Franciscans for Responsible Government. We became advisors of sorts, without being directly involved in the operation. I spent time with him personally, showing him the serious persecution that our family and church had undergone due to our efforts and warned him to be prepared for the worst! The devil doesn't give up territory without a demonic fight, but the Lord will honor those that put Him first.

I decided not to get involved publicly, because I felt it was time to re-group and evaluate where we were in this on-going battle in San Francisco.

The San Franciscans for Responsible Government hastily put together a mixed group of lay persons (predominantly evangelicals and Catholics) to gather nine thousand signatures to get domestic partners back on the ballot one more time. Their budget was even more limited than ours had been a year before: no mailer went out this time, and there was no phone bank. Again, the signatures were in on time, and it was on the ballot in November. This wasn't going to be an easy year for fighting such laws. It was a very important election year, with the mayoral race and other key issues, but it proved to be a very difficult year to again bring up this ordinance.

The domestic partners law passed handily—this time with 60 percent of the vote. Each year the gap between the votes grew greater and greater. The law was still promoted as simply a way for unmarried couples to officially "affirm" their commitments to each other. Again, the gay politic said that there was no price tag attached to it, and we were unsuccessful in convincing the voters otherwise.

TEN

Homosexualizing The Public Schools

As I walked toward the elementary school where the San Francisco Unified School Board meeting was going to be held, my heart raced and my nerves grew frail. I uttered a prayer without showing emotion, "Oh Lord, have mercy. Give me wisdom and protect us tonight." Over and over I uttered these words for my own solace. We were about to enter into the "valley of the shadow of death."

With me that evening was Don, a friend and co-worker on our Christian AIDS Council. This 12 June 1990 hearing was the last in a series of school board meetings called to debate the merits of establishing a pro-homosexual counseling program in the junior and senior high schools. Because of parental concern, more than two hundred individuals had signed up to speak. The school board, headed by Superintendent Ramone Cortines, decided to limit the comments to four speakers for each side, with fifteen minutes allotted to each side. Don and I were there to provide moral support for those people who were scheduled to speak against the proposal.

As we drew closer and closer to the school, we could see a demonstration was being held outside. The crowd of mostly young men, and a few masculine looking women, huddled to hear the next speaker tirade against the fundamentalist right and against their hate-mongering blocking of the proposed "Project 10"—type counseling program. There were approximately two to three hundred in the group, milling in and out of the building during the demonstration.

After watching the demonstration outside for a while, we went in to find seats. We thought we would arrive an hour early

192

to find good places, but were surprised to find that the gays had already nearly packed the auditorium. There were probably two to three hundred gays already seated. Those of us against the proposal numbered around fifty.

Don and I immediately spotted Jean Harris, the tough-looking lesbian assistant to Harry Britt, one of the openly gay city supervisors. She stood facing the audience, dressed as usual in pants, shirt and tie, and a vest. With bullhorn in hand, it was clear that Jean was in charge of the demonstration inside and outside the auditorium. Whatever she yelled through her bullhorn, the militants would obey—although reluctantly at times.

The room was packed. The aisles were full of men with men, hugging and handling one another. A few police officers circulated through the crowd, hobnobbing with friends. Posters representing both sides waved, blocking the view of those of us that sat through the whole event. Some posters glorified homosexual sex, others mocked the Bible, and some threatened anyone that might oppose them. A few brave Christians stood with their posters too, simply saying "NO TO PROJECT 10." We looked around at the screaming, taunting crowd, afraid to actually stare too long at any one person. Fierce-faced muscular homosexual men jeered and spit obscenities in our faces and sent chills up and down our spines. As I sat and watched this crowd of gays and lesbians paralyze the school board with their bullying tactics, I wondered why they should care what is taught in the public schools. Most of them didn't have children. What was the reason behind this adamant demonstration for a school program that would only affect other people's children?

The board was impaneled and the president made an effort to call the meeting to order. What can only be described as demonic mocking and ridicule of the Bible and the Christian faith went on continuously for approximately forty-five minutes. One tactic homosexual activists use is to blow whistles in their opponents ears. There was a full fifteen minutes of nonstop whistle-blowing. The board tried repeatedly to call the meeting to order but was unsuccessful. Finally, Jean Harris got up on a chair and, shouting through the bullhorn, quieted the mob down, and the meeting was then called to order. It was clear to everyone in the room, including the school board, that Harris was in charge of this meeting.

As the meeting began, the ritual of saluting the American flag became a divided protest. When we uttered the part that

says, ". . . one nation UNDER GOD . . ." the anti-counseling
forces shouted; and when the phrase, ". . . WITH LIBERTY
AND JUSTICE FOR ALL" was uttered, the pro-gay forces
screamed back. The pledge of allegiance cannot even be said
without feeling the repercussions of the division between homosexual activists and Christian activists.

The fear-producing tactics used by the gays that evening
were pure fascism. Their goal was to disrupt and stifle free
speech. There was no willingness to allow the anti-counseling
speakers to have their say in a civilized forum. Whenever someone opposing the program would stand to speak, he would be
subjected to cat-calls, boos, whistles, and obscene gestures. Or,
the homosexuals would climb on their chairs and silently stand
with their backs to the speaker, giving the Nazi salute.

Four men spoke in opposition to the gay counseling program. Among them was Dr. Paul Cameron, the founder of the
Family Research Institute in Washington, D.C. Cameron is
continually under attack by the homosexual community because of the research he has conducted on gay lifestyles, including studies on gays and child molestation.

Another opposition speaker was Dr. Joseph Nicolosi, director of the Thomas Aquinas Psychological Clinic in Encino,
California. Nicolosi has treated more than a hundred homosexuals for sexual orientation disorders and in 1991 published
Reparative Therapy of Male Homosexuality, a counseling book for
therapists.

Dr. Nicolosi attempted to present his views on gay counseling programs, but was largely unsuccessful due to the shouting
and whistle-blowing tactics used to silence him.

Earlier in the year, he had written an article criticizing a gay
counseling program known as "Project 10," used in the Los
Angeles public school system since 1984. His observations not
only apply to Project 10, but to any pro-gay teen counseling
program. His article states in pertinent part:

> Gay vs. Homosexual: to understand the potential hazards of
> Project 10, we must clarify first of all the distinction between
> 'gay' and 'homosexual'. Homosexuality is a psychological
> condition which affects a small percentage of the popula-
> tion, while "gay" denotes a particular subcultural ideology.
> While gay-activist ideology has received a great deal of me-
> dia attention, it does not represent all homosexuals.

****

Gay activists attain political power by claiming to be the only legitimate spokesmen for persons of a homosexual orientation. With the same rationale, they would have the adolescent believe that because of his homosexual thoughts, feelings, or behavior, he is by definition a member of the gay counter-culture.

When a gay-identified therapist or counselor speaks to the teenager, the teenager may be seen as precious booty in a cultural war. For we must make no mistake about it—this is a cultural war. When the young man expresses hesitancy about adopting a gay identity, the gay-affirmative counselor is likely to tell him that his hesitancy is due to an internalization of what they call society's 'homophobia,' or its irrational fear of homosexuality.

****

Not a Decision for Adolescence: When a young boy or girl with homosexual feelings comes to a Project 10 counseling office, it will be determined that he is gay. In contrast, many therapists believe that adults who come in with a homosexual issue should be in therapy for four or five months before they determine whether or not they are of a homosexual orientation.

Adolescence is a particularly vulnerable time when self-concept is still fragile and accessible to outside influences. Self-labeling—the labels that we apply to ourselves—determines our behavior and the way we interact in the world. This is true for all people, but it is particularly true for the adolescent, for whom self-definition in relationship to society is a key developmental issue.

It is an injustice to direct a youngster into a gay identity with life-long emotional, social, and health consequences which he is still too young to understand.

****

The potential damage of Project 10 is all the more significant when we realize that the younger the client is when he seeks change, the better. The longer the person stays in a gay identity, the more difficult it is to change that identity. Many studies have shown that for both homosexuals and heterosexuals, sexual behaviors are established in adolescence. Once a sexual pattern becomes established, it becomes a dynamic in and of itself.

When the behavior is set in motion during adolescence, it takes on a life of its own. And, adolescence is exactly the time when Project 10 will have its influence. I have had clients in their late 40s who have come into therapy complaining of unhappiness with the lifestyle, complaining of their inability to control a homosexual behavior pattern; but by that time there is a resignation and loss of hope. Interestingly enough, they characteristically say that what they once thought was disgusting or repulsive behavior when they were young, now they do much more frequently and do not seem to mind it.

A Done Deal

The school board members, of course, had already made up their minds. (Or should we say the gay community had already made up their minds for them.) Our core group of ministers had personally visited with each member of the board prior to this meeting. From these private meetings, we knew the board was split 4 to 3 in favor of the project. But, when the final vote came, all board members voted unanimously, and without deliberation, to institute the gay counseling program. The gays had won through intimidation. After two hours of raucous campaigning—shouts, cat-calls, screaming whistles, anti-Christian chanting and sloganing, songs mocking the Christian faith; after constant berating of anyone in the audience who opposed Project 10, after repeated obscene shouts and gestures—the board had "no other alternative" but to pass the resolution if they wanted to get out alive. Who on the board would dare object to the homosexual agenda after feeling the insults and intimidation of "mob rule."

This had been a demonstration of Nazi tactics fully implemented. I literally feared what they might do to us. I feared for those that spoke out on our side. I prayed that the gospel would be proclaimed to this crowd. Sadly, however, none of the speakers brought up the gospel. The only message that could truly deliver the "death blow" to such behavior was not mentioned by any speaker on our side. It seemed as though the only tactic thought to be effective against Project 10 was to point out the psychological trauma of homosexuality and to leave out the healing message of deliverance in Christ. We had again failed to seize the moment for Christ. I greatly regretted this secularizing of our opposition to Project 10.

Over the years I have attended meetings with, and/or testified before various civic leaders and groups such as this. In that time, I have been impressed with one thing: Biblical Christianity is most often raised by the gay community, and hidden by the Christian community. The gay community hates the things of the Bible because they recognize it as the only thing that can stop their movement. They believe in the power of the gospel to destroy their "culture." Even gay Supervisor Harry Britt said during the domestic partners campaign, "This campaign is a spiritual war . . ." For whatever reason, however, Christians tend to shy away from bringing up the claims of the gospel, somehow thinking it an ineffective argument against such politicized immorality. (It certainly was effective against the politics of Rome, Babylon, etc.)

I had flown up from the meetings of our General Assembly of the Orthodox Presbyterian Church in San Diego just to be at the final meeting of the board. Afterwards, I thought perhaps it wasn't such a hot idea. The gay militant community had rallied their forces successfully to stomp out any opposition to their cause. "When the wicked rule, the people go into hiding," says Proverbs. If only the "outside world" could see this mad mob acting like spoiled children wanting their own way. The outside world would not believe what they saw!

After the vote, Ramone Cortines spoke briefly on how the program would be funded. He made it clear that this was not Project 10, but it was a program he'd developed. The plan was to hire a homosexual school counselor who would be available to help those "self-identified homosexual" teens. (In a 2 June 1990 radio interview on Focus on the Family's Family News in Focus, Mario Chakon, a Cortines aide, said that the school board had decided to fund the gay counseling program by shifting money from the Drug Education program.)

After the meeting broke up, Don and I went up to the board and spoke directly to Ramon Cortines. We showed him two thousand signatures on a petition against the gay counseling program that a group of churches had collected in just one weekend. He refused to consider them as valid. We also had copies of legal statutes in hand, pointing out to him that since sodomy laws were still on the books in California, it would be a criminal act to direct minor children into such a lifestyle through this counseling program. In a very arrogant and angry manner, he summarily dismissed us, telling us that he knew the law and that we didn't know what we were talking about!

A couple of mothers approached Cortines and, with tears in their eyes, appealed to him not to implement this program. They argued that Cortines was virtually giving their children over to the gay community. One mother said, "they're our children, they belong to us. You can't give our children over to them, . . ." as she pointed at the gay mob still milling around. Without a word, Cortines turned around and walked away from these distraught mothers!

As we left the auditorium, we saw various groups of Christians outside praying about the fateful decision. Some of those gathered were devilishly taunted by persons who actually attempted to fondle and manhandle them. It truly was a satanic spectacle: the culmination of months of protesting by Bible-believers against a tidal wave of immorality that had swept over the public school system. It had been the most forceful the Christian community at large had ever been against the homosexual movement in San Francisco.

Donna Takes On ACT UP

At one of the first full school board meetings convened to hear testimony on Project 10, the Christians far outnumbered the gays, but the board hesitated to take a vote at that point in time. The gay community was surprised at this show of strength by the Christians and, so they made sure that they were fully organized and in control of that final school board meeting.

Donna and Ryan had accompanied me to one of those earlier meetings. Ryan sat down toward the front in a row with me. Donna sat in the back toward the middle of the auditorium between the homosexual contingent and the Christians. Since at this time the gay community didn't know who Donna was, she could sit nearby and listen to their comments during my testimony, sometimes being able to pick up on the "mood" of the community and maybe determine whether our family needed to be a little more safety-conscious for a while.

One speaker, identifying himself as a representative of ACT UP, took the microphone to speak. During the course of his tirade, this man used almost every slogan and foul phrase that had been spray-painted on our house and church on 22 March when the windows had been smashed with hammers. One slogan that is particularly associated with ACT UP is "Silence = Death." That had been painted on the house, and we had received a letter shortly before the attack which simply said "Silence = Death" and "McIlhenny = s——." (It is frustrating that we not only have this information, but we have pictures of demonstrators outside the church on a Sunday morning before that 22 March attack with "Member of ACT UP" on their T-shirts and "Silence = Death" signs; and yet, somehow the police "have no clues" sufficient enough to question anyone as to who might have attacked the house!)

After the man finished speaking, he returned to his seat—right behind where Ryan was sitting. Donna's frustration got the best of her! She came down from the back of the auditorium, into the row where Ryan was in front of this ACT UP member. Much to Ryan's chagrin, Donna told him to turn around and look the man directly in the face. After a bit of persuasion, Ryan did turn around. The man was incensed. He threw his hands up in the air and said, "Whadda ya want, lady!?" To which Donna replied, "I want my son to look one of you in the face for a change, instead of only seeing your backs as you run away from our house after trashing us again!"

"You probably painted that stuff all over your house yourself, you b——, just so you could blame us!" he said. "And you probably took the hammers to your own windows, too."

"You know," Donna retorted, "I never mentioned who I was, nor anything about what was done to our house, but you seem to know everything about it!" It was obvious that he had personal knowledge of what had happened to us in March of 1990.

During this time, I was milling around in the back of the auditorium and could only see the conversation from a distance. I was thinking to myself, "Isn't that marvelous how Donna is able to witness to this guy! Boy, has she got courage!" I laughed later when I found out what she was actually saying to him.

Unknown to everyone else in the room, except the school board, the PTA board was seated in the row directly in front of Donna and Ryan. The vice president of the PTA had called me earlier in the week to complain about the impact Project 10 would have and asked if I would organize as many people as I could to speak out against it and write letters of protest. When I suggested that the PTA board itself speak out against it, they deferred to others "more courageous than themselves." They feared retaliation if they openly opposed any part of the pro-gay agenda in the public schools. The homosexual mystique had created such fear in their minds that they were unwilling and/or unable to do anything about it. Real or imagined, such fears overwhelm even the most conscientious parents, and they feel powerless to fight the immorality promulgated in the public school system.

Organizing the Troops

Prior to these meetings, early that Spring, a courageous man named Mark Poggioli had become concerned about the gay influence on the school board and had alerted many of us to what was happening.

He attended the first meeting of the subcommittee that had been charged with gathering facts on gay counseling programs, and spoke in opposition to such programs. As he and his wife, Kris, left the meeting that night, a group of men chased them all the way back to their parked car. They were terrified!

Mark got wise real fast! He took friends with him to the next meeting for mutual protection. With episodes like the one Mark and Kris experienced, you tend not to want to speak up for fear of retaliation; or some people are tempted to give pseudonyms out of fear of some sort of harassment. Gay militants work at city hall and can "report" your activities to their political leaders. It gets quite uncomfortable speaking for righteousness in San Francisco.

Since that time, Mark and Kris have not desired to take on any more such protesting—not so much out of fear as of exhaustion. Mark is a businessman, and such renowned activity can hurt his business, too. He and Kris had to sacrifice time, money, and reputation to stand for righteousness.

Gay Textbooks Next?

On 18 July within weeks of the school board's approval of the gay counseling program, a group called Bay Area Network of Gay and Lesbian Educators (BANGLE) made headlines in the *San Francisco Chronicle*. They announced the launching of a campaign called "Project 21," organized to lobby the state legislature for new school textbooks that would show gays and lesbians in a positive light.

According to BANGLE spokesman Rob Birle, a teacher in Antioch, California, "There's tremendous ignorance about homosexuality, and we think it's time to break down the myths and stereotypes of who gays and lesbians are." Birle wants textbooks to include information on the modern gay rights movement, on the Nazi persecution of homosexuals, and on the sexual orientations of famous people.

If successful, the BANGLE campaign could mean serious trouble for other state educational systems. California and Texas both purchase the majority of textbooks. If publishers are pressured into introducing positive themes involving homosexuals, it is unlikely they will tailor-make pro-gay textbooks for California. They will introduce these themes in all of the textbooks they sell to other states.

Virginia Uribe and Project 10

Although the San Francisco school board has not adopted the actual Project 10 program developed for the Los Angeles school system by Fairfax High School teacher Virginia Uribe, our program is most certainly patterned after that system. A look at the origins and purposes of Project 10 is essential if you're to effectively counter such a program when it comes to your public school system.

Virginia Uribe, an openly-declared lesbian, has been teaching in the Los Angeles school system for more than thirty years. In 1984, Project 10 was started by Uribe as an informal lunchtime "rap" session for teens who felt they were "gay." The impetus for Project 10 came after a sexually troubled youth came to Fairfax from another school and was harassed by other students. He eventually dropped out of school.

According to Uribe, "When this happened, I didn't know what to do. I talked to another kid who was gay to set up an informal rap at lunchtime. This kid and other kids looked at me like I was crazy. No one had ever talked to them about this" (Manley Witten, "Project 10: What schools teach children about gay sex," *Valley Magazine* [Aug. 1988]: 30.).

With the approval of Fairfax principal Warren Steinberg, Uribe eventually set up a gay and lesbian center in the school with a complete library of pro-gay materials, including "One Teenager in 10," *Changing Bodies, Changing Lives*, and gay fiction. When the explicit and pornographic contents of these books became public knowledge, Uribe was forced to stop handing out "One Teenager in 10" to her counselees, but she still maintained both texts in her library.

"One Teenager in 10," has an introduction written by Rita Mae Brown, a self-confessed bisexual, who thinks that switching back and forth from males to females is totally appropriate. It contains a series of short testimonials by teen-agers who have chosen to become homosexuals—either after being molested, or by choosing to have sexual relations with others. The following is the testimony of one 16-year-old girl who was seduced by her teacher on a dance recital trip:

> I am a sixteen-year-old lesbian. I have been a lesbian since I was twelve. I had known my dance teacher for three years before I was asked to give a special dance presentation in another city . . . "I want to make love to you. Let's go to bed," (my dance teacher said) . . . We continued that night, all weekend and for almost three years until I had to move with my family. I became a lesbian and a woman that weekend! (Ibid, 26.)

Changing Bodies, Changing Lives is another textbook designed to promote the homosexual lifestyle. Written by Ruth Bell, and published by Vintage Books, a division of Random House, *Changing Bodies*, freely discusses heterosexual intercourse between teen-agers in a "nonjudgmental" way and then devotes several pages to "Exploring Sex with Someone of Your Own Sex (Homosexuality)."

One bit of advice given is this: "You don't want to deny your feelings and attractions, even if they happen to be toward people of your own sex. Yet you have to be aware that there are people who will consider you bad or sick because you have them" (Ruth Bell, *Changing Bodies, Changing Lives* [New York: Random House, 1988], 119.).

In a Project 10 brochure, Uribe describes the purpose of her outreach to homosexual teen-agers this way:

"Project 10 IS COMMITTED TO THE FOLLOWING GOALS:

"1. Preventing drop-out before graduation among lesbian and gay youth.

"2. Providing campuses that are free of physical violence and verbal abuse toward sexual minorities."

"3. Providing intervention in alcohol and substance abuse among lesbian and gay teenagers.

"4. Increasing self-esteem among lesbian and gay teenagers by presenting educational images and role models that are positive in nature.

"5. Having accurate information on lesbians and gays included throughout the curriculum.

"6. Seeing that information on AIDS and other sexually transmitted diseases reaches all students, teachers, parents and administrators.

"7. Reducing discrimination against lesbians and gay men by providing information and demystifying homosexuality.

"8. Bring issues of lesbian and gay youth to the attention of educators and the general public." (Virginia Uribe, "Project 10—An Outreach to Lesbian and Gay Youth." [Undated material.])

How is Uribe to accomplish these goals? Through the training of educators to accept homosexual behavior as normal—to change curricula to reflect a pro-gay bias—and to funnel "gay" teens into the Gay and Lesbian Community Services Center where they will be exposed to "positive" gay role models.

Another goal listed is to expand the "school library in both fictional and non-fictional areas . . . removal of pejorative material on homosexuality." That last sentence is significant and can easily be missed. Uribe is suggesting that all books considered to be anti-gay be removed from public school libraries. If fundamentalists suggested that pro-gay materials be removed from libraries, there would be an incredible shriek of horror from the ACLU and the liberal press. However, to our knowledge, there has been no such alarm at Uribe's suggestion of censorship.

Pro-Gay Counseling Recommendations

In a packet of Project 10 materials distributed to school counselors in California, Uribe included a list of recommendations for changing society's view of homosexuality. The author of this list was Paul Gibson, a San Francisco-based therapist. Among his recommendations are the following:

1. Society: "Enact legislation that guarantees equal rights to homosexuals in all areas of life. Repeal of laws that discriminate against homosexual relationships."

2. Society: "Reduce stigmatization of homosexuals by promoting a positive image of homosexuality at all levels of society. Promote positive adult gay male and lesbian role models for gay youth. Take personal responsibility for revising negative attitudes and conduct towards homosexuals."

3. Religion: "Assess the extent to which condemnation of homosexuality impacts on gay youth suicide and conflicts between gay youth and their families. Promote a positive image of homosexuality with families and church members. Accept gay and lesbian youth, and make a place for them within the church that provides them with the roles and activities of other youth."

4. School: "Develop curriculum that provides students in junior high and high school with accurate and positive information about homosexuality relevant to all areas of life (i.e., sexuality, health, literature, history). Provide students with a diversity of adult lesbian and gay male role models. Provide gay and lesbian youth with a safe educational environment that protects them from abuse by peers. Rebut homophobic remarks and enforce serious consequences for students who victimize gay youth."

Youth Suicide Report

Paul Gibson's influence in promoting homosexuality extends far beyond Virginia Uribe's program. Gibson was one of the authors of the January 1989 U.S. Department of Health and Human Services study, "Report of the Secretary's Task Force on Youth Suicide," edited by Marcia R. Feinleib.

The report generated considerable controversy after it was published—primarily because of Gibson's undocumented assertions and blanket condemnation of religion and parents.

In his section of the report, Gibson makes these assertions:

• "Homosexuality is not mental illness or disease. It is a natural and healthy expression of human sexuality" (p. 3-115).

• "Family problems are probably the most significant factor in youth suicide. Youths derive their core sense of being cared about and belonging from their families. Gay youth may make suicide attempts after being rejected by their families" (p. 3-127).

• "Religion presents another risk factor in gay youth suicide because of the depiction of homosexuality as a sin and the reliance of families on the church for understanding homosexuality. Many traditional (e.g., Catholic and fundamentalist, e.g., Baptist) faiths still portray homosexuality as morally wrong or evil. Family religious beliefs can be a primary reason for parents forcing youth to leave home if a homosexual orientation is seen as incompatible with church teachings. These beliefs can also create unresolvable internal conflicts for gay youth who adhere to their faith but believe they will not change their sexual orientation. They may feel wicked and condemned to hell and attempt suicide in despair of ever obtaining redemption" (pp.3-127-128).

• "The failure of schools to educate youth about homosexuality presents another risk factor to gay and lesbian adolescents. By ignoring the subject in all curricula, including family life classes, the schools deny access to positive information about homosexuality that could improve the self esteem of gay youth" (p. 3-128).

• "Encouraging these youths to change can cause regression in the development of a healthy gay identity and reinforce traditional stereotypes of homosexuals as sick and self-destructive. This, in turn, further weakens the youths' self-esteem, and ability to cope with problems" (p. 3-130).

The Pro-Gay Education Establishment

Through the influence of men like Paul Gibson and women like Virginia Uribe, a pro-gay influence is being felt throughout the educational establishment in the U.S. In fact, several years ago, the National Education Association (NEA), a radical, left-wing lobbying organization, favorably endorsed the concept of having gay counselors available in every school. The NEA has even commissioned educators to develop a pro-gay training course to help teachers discuss homosexuality in a positive light (Gary Putka, "Effort to Teach Teens About Homosexuality Advances in Schools," *The Wall Street Journal* [12 June 1990]: 1.).

The Myth of Gay Teens

Homosexuals have long promoted the notion that 10 percent of the population is gay. In fact, that's why Virginia Uribe named her outreach "Project 10," on the erroneous assumption that 10 percent of the teen population is homosexual. Gay militants continue to repeat the 10 percent figure until it has been widely accepted in the news media. If you repeat a lie long enough, and loud enough, people will believe you.

Why do they continue to cling to the 10 percent figure? Simple: if this propaganda is accepted, their cause is provided with a greater measure of respectability and political clout. When asking for funds to set up a Project 10 program, for example, the 10 percent figure helps them get more money for their pro-gay causes. One of their favorite slogans is, "We are Everywhere." The 10 percent helps them maintain that false image.

But, what is the truth about the 10 percent figure? Where did it originate?

The gays pulled the 10 percent figure from Alfred Kinsey's 1948 book, *Sexual Behavior in the Human Male*. Kinsey's research methods have been thoroughly exposed as fraudulent by researchers Dr. Judith Reisman and Edward Eichel in *Kinsey, Sex, and Fraud* (published by Huntington House).

At one point in his book, Kinsey made the comment, "10 percent of the men are more or less exclusively homosexual for at least three years between the ages of 16 and 55." The gays have continued to use the 10 percent figure even though on the same page, Kinsey notes, "4 percent of the white males are exclusively homosexual throughout their lives after adolescence."

From these two quotes, it is clear that Kinsey did not intend to say that 10 percent of the population is homosexual. And, because of his shoddy research techniques and pro-gay biases, it is unlikely that the gay population is even at 4 percent— although they're quite a vocal minority.

A recent scientific survey casts new light on the fraudulent 10 percent claim. In 1989, the National Opinion Research Center (NORC) at the University of Chicago conducted an extensive study on sexual behaviors.

The survey revealed the following facts:

1. Of the sexually active adults surveyed, 98.5 percent have been exclusively heterosexual during the past year.

2. Although some inferences had to be made by the authors of the report, their best estimate of the sexual orientation of the respondents during adulthood was 5.5 percent are homosexual or bisexual.

3. Less than 1 percent were exclusively homosexual.

According to ex-gay Alan Medinger, in his May 1990 issue of *Regeneration News*, these results are consistent with those from a 1970 Kinsey Institute—NORC survey, which was studied and reanalyzed by Robert E. Fay, et al, and reported in the 20 January 1989 edition of *Science Magazine* ("Prevalence and Patterns of Same-Gender Sexual Contact Among Men," pp. 338-348). The article states in pertinent part:

> That study reported that 6.7 percent of the male respondents had sexual contact (to orgasm) with another man after age 19 and between 1.6 percent and 2 percent had had such contact during the past year. In the 1970 survey, 1.4 percent said they had adult homosexual contacts "fairly often" and 1.9 percent characterized their frequency as "occasionally," a total that we would presume reflects most active male homosexuals of 3.3 percent.
>
> If it is true that homosexuality among women is less common than among men, then the average for the entire population would certainly seem to be something less than 5 percent." (Alan Medinger, *Regeneration News* [May 1990]: 3.)

These lowered figures have also been confirmed by Dr. James Moore, a senior psychologist with the Seattle Public School system. Moore, in his study, "Perpetuating Homosexual Myths," has stated, "In my 27 years as a psychologist, I can say without reservation that far less than 1% of the students may have homosexual conflicts." (Dr. James Moore, "Perpetuating Homosexual Myths," *The Public Education Committee on Children and Youth* [1989]: 2.)

So the statistics indicate that the 10 percent figure is a myth. The truth is that only around 2-3 percent of the general population is exclusively practicing homosexuals and the figure for teen-agers is closer to 1 percent.

Reaching the One Percent

The question logically arises: Then what do you do about the one percent who think they are struggling with homosexual feelings in junior and senior high schools?

One of the things you don't do is establish pro-gay counseling programs to recruit young men and women into a lifestyle that will almost inevitably lead them to death or infect them with seriously debilitating venereal diseases.

Dr. George Rekers, an expert on childhood sexual disorders wrote a book in 1982 entitled *Growing Up Straight*. He advises parents on how to help their children develop healthy sexual lifestyles. He is particularly alarmed by the growth of pro-gay counseling programs. "To refer a child or a teenager to a gay counseling center will seriously interfere with that child's capacity for choice in the future . . . Gay counseling centers encourage a destructive lifestyle that will interfere with personal psychological well-being" (p. 82).

Rekers has treated literally hundreds of children for sexual identity disorders and has flatly stated, "If a child ever starts giving himself a label like 'queer' or 'homosexual', the parents should immediately correct him by telling him that the words homosexual and queer do not even apply to children. These are words for adults. There is no such thing as a homosexual child" (George Rekers, *Growing Up Straight* [Chicago: Moody Press, 1982]: 78.).

Speaking as a theologian and not a psychologist, I would concur with Dr. Rekers' statement that there is no such thing as a homosexual child. If, however, the definition of a homosexual is one who commits homosexual acts, we have no warrant from Scripture to say that a child cannot commit a homosexual act. Homosexual acts are sin, first and foremost. Anyone is capable of committing sin, even children. They're born with a sin nature.

It seems to me that Rekers thinks of homosexuality exclusively as a psychological disorder, not sin. A two-fold problem then arises: 1) what to do with the biblical proscription against homosexuality—that it is a sin, and 2) the absence of certain deliverance from a "psychological" disorder, for the Bible clearly promises deliverance from sin—including the sin of homosexuality—through faith and repentance in Jesus Christ.

Dr. Rekers goes on to explain the danger of children "labeling" themselves as homosexuals, because a label can often result in a self-fulfilling prophecy. He notes that there is ". . . no such thing as a 'natural' inclination toward homosexual involvement. Instead, there are adverse situations in a child's life that can lead to homosexual temptations" (p. 81).

Although these statements are true, and I would agree that children should not be labeled homosexual as an orientation, again, one very important thing is left out: the question of sin and its consequences (precisely the question that the gay movement wants us to leave out of the discussion). Is Reker saying that a child cannot be a sinner? If homosexual acts are sin, then is a child capable of committing such sin? The Bible clearly says that the child—whether he labels himself or not—is included in the class of sinners because of the sin nature with which he was born. When he sins, whether it is homosexual acts, lying, stealing, etc., he must be counseled to repent, to find forgiveness in Christ, and put away sin by the power of God. Unless we see homosexual acts as sin—transgression of the law of God—whatever else we may call them, e.g., "psychological" destructive disorders, etc., we have no standard by which to consider them destructive! At bottom, we think of such acts as destructive, because they are spiritually immoral, not "psychologically" destructive. Homosexuality is harmful and destructive precisely because it is a transgression of God's Law.

There are a series of adverse conditions that can predispose a child to get involved in homosexual behavior. Homosexuals are made, not born. A child may be influenced by any number of circumstances, including home life, negative father role models, domineering mother role models, peer pressure and seduction by older homosexuals. The gay community recognizes this far more readily than does the straight community. In fact, it is the gay agenda that spoon-feeds the straight community into accepting statistical reports and psychological studies to legitimize what is nothing more nor less than sin. The gay community knows that survival is dependent upon recruitment. If they can make the general populous accept the proposition that one person out of every ten is constitutionally homosexual, the institution of programs such as Project 10 in the public schools becomes that much easier. The general populous will accept it as a necessary program for "an ignored and suffering minority." The way is thus paved for the gay community, under the guise of a respectable and legitimate minority, to freely recruit children to their cause. They know that a child who is seduced in his early years begins to think of himself as a homosexual, especially if he is repeatedly told that he is homosexual, and continues to engage in the behavior as he grows up.

Jerry Arterburn is a victim of homosexual child molestation. He tells his story in *How Will I Tell My Mother?*, published by Oliver Nelson Books. Arterburn was molested as a young boy at a church camp and entered into the homosexual lifestyle as a result. From years of experience as a homosexual, Jerry wrote, "Early experiences with older persons are a key to the development of homosexual behavior. I place this factor as one link between normal and abnormal development" (Jerry Arterburn, *How Will I Tell My Mother* [Nashville: Oliver Nelson Books, 1988], 45.).

Although Jerry eventually repented of his sinful lifestyle, he later discovered he was HIV positive and died of AIDS several years ago. His tragic life and death should be a lesson to all who advocate the "gay" lifestyle. It inevitably ends up in despair and death because homosexuality is abnormal and is a sin against God and man.

Studies have indicated that a high percentage of current homosexuals were sodomized by older men when they were in their early teens.

According to Dr. Brad Hayton, in his exhaustively footnoted book, *The Homosexual Agenda*, "Although homosexuals represent 1-4 percent of the total population, they perpetrate between a third to a half of all recorded child molestations.

"Homosexual teachers have committed between a quarter and 4/5 of all molestations of pupils. Thus, they are at least 12 times more apt to molest children than heterosexuals are, and homosexual teachers are at least seven times more likely to molest a pupil. In surveying the literature on pupil-child molestation, one investigator found that teachers who practice homosexual acts are between 90 to 100 times more apt to involve themselves sexually with pupils than teachers who confine themselves to heterosexual acts. New York homosexual teachers agreed that homosexual relationships with their students were improper, but reserved the right to have relations with children outside the classroom.

"Homosexuals are about 18 times more apt to incorporate minors into their sexual practices than heterosexuals are. In fact, 31 percent of those claiming molestation by men before they had reached age 13 were homosexually assaulted.

"One survey by two homosexual authors found that 73 percent of homosexuals had at some time had sex with boys 16-19 years old or younger" (Dr. Brad Hayton, "The Homosexual Agenda," *Focus On the Family* [1990]: 15.).

Here again, I would be careful in presenting comparative statistics. There seems to be an incongruous mixing of categories that we miss here. The category of homosexual is compared to the category of heterosexual. Biblically, homosexuals are heterosexuals. Heterosexuality is not a sinful condition. It is the natural sexually-constructed condition all humans are born into. Homosexuality is wrong because it is a perversion of the original condition into which one is born. **Homosexuals are heterosexuals who have twisted God's original intent for them.** An adulterer is a heterosexual. A pedophile is a heterosexual by birth. Necrophiliacs are heterosexual. The Bible describes homosexual acts as those acts between persons of the same sex acting like they're having sex with the opposite sex partner. "You shall not lie with a man as you do a women . . ." (Lev. 18:22). The homosexual sex act is described as performing a heterosexual act with someone of the same sex!

To say that more homosexuals commit crimes of child molestation than heterosexuals is to compare two disparate categories. Heterosexuals range from pedophiles, necrophiles, etc. Yet, each of these sex acts are perversions of the original heterosexual condition for which God created us. For example, adult men having sex with male children is called pedophilia, not homosexuality! In fact, the gay community considers it a heterosexual deviance!

Recently, on our local San Francisco T.V. news, a member of NAMBLA (North America Man/Boy Love Association) attempted to defend pedophilia as "not harmful" to minor boys. He disclosed that his first sexual encounter was with his grandfather when he was a minor child. His point was that he was fine, and it didn't harm him one bit! My question is: was that incest, homosexuality, pedophilia, or fornication? The answer is: All of the above. And the reason it is harmful—whatever category you want to put it into—is that it is sin.

What's Next?

In closing this chapter, I thought it appropriate to quote from a Boston newspaper, the *Gay Community News* 15-21 Feb. 1987 as reprinted in the *American Family Association Journal*. See what self-described gay revolutionary Michael Swift has to say about our children and of the gay agenda. I call this the gay rights movement's Statement of Faith:

> We shall sodomize your sons, emblems of your feeble masculinity, of your shallow dreams and vulgar lies. We shall seduce them in your schools, in your dormitories, in your gymnasiums, in your locker rooms, in your sports arenas, in your seminaries, in your youth groups, in your movie theater bathrooms, in your army bunkhouses, in your truck stops, in your all-male clubs, in your houses of Congress, wherever men are with men together. Your sons shall become our minions and do our bidding. They will be recast in our image. They will come to crave and adore us.
>
> Women, you cry for freedom. You say you no longer are satisfied with men; they make you unhappy. We, connoisseurs of the masculine face, the masculine physique, shall take your men from you then. We will amuse them; we will instruct them; we will embrace them when they weep. Women, you say you wish to live with each other instead of with men. Then go and be with each other. We shall give your men pleasures they have never known because we are foremost men too and only one man knows how to truly please another man; only one man can understand with depth and feeling the mind and body of another man.
>
> All laws banning homosexual activity will be revoked. Instead, legislation shall be passed which engenders love between men.
>
> All homosexuals must stand together as brothers; we must be united artistically, philosophically, socially, politically and financially. We will triumph only when we present a common face to the vicious heterosexual enemy.

If you dare to cry faggot, fairy, queer, at us, we will stab you in your cowardly hearts and defile your dead, puny bodies.

We shall write poems of the love between men; we shall stage plays in which man openly caresses man; we shall make films about the love between heroic men which will replace the cheap, superficial, sentimental, insipid, juvenile, heterosexual infatuations presently dominating your cinema screens. We shall sculpt statues of beautiful young men, of bold athletes which will be placed in your parks, your squares, your plazas. The museums of the world will be filled only with paintings of graceful, naked lads.

Our writers and artists will make love between men fashionable and derigeur [sic], and we will succeed because we are adept at setting styles. We will eliminate heterosexual liaisons through usage of the devices of wit and ridicule, devices which we are skilled in employing.

We will unmask the powerful homosexuals who masquerade as heterosexuals. You will be shocked and frightened when you find that your presidents and their sons, your industrialists, your senators, your mayors, your generals, your athletes, your film stars, your television personalities, your civic leaders, your priests are not the safe, familiar bourgeois, heterosexual figures you assumed them to be. We are everywhere; we have infiltrated your ranks. Be careful when you speak of homosexuals because we are always among you; we may be sitting across the desk from you; we may be sleeping in the same bed with you.

There will be no compromises. We are not middle-class weaklings. Highly intelligent, we're the natural aristocrats of the human race, and steely-minded aristocrats never settle for less. Those who oppose us will be exiled.

We shall raise vast, private armies, as Mishima did, to defeat you. We shall conquer the world because warriors inspired by and banded together by homosexual love and honor are invincible as were the ancient Greek soldiers.

The family unit—spawning ground of lies, betrayals, mediocrity, hypocrisy and violence—will be abolished. The family unit, which only dampens imagination and curbs free will, must be eliminated. Perfect boys will be conceived and grown in the genetic laboratory. They will be bonded together in communal setting, under the control and instruction of homosexual savants.

All churches who condemn us will be closed. Our holy gods are handsome young men. We adhere to a cult of beauty, moral and esthetics. All that is ugly and vulgar and banal will be annihilated. Since we are alienated from middle-class heterosexual conventions, we are free to live our lives according to the dictates of the pure imagination. For us too much is not enough.

The exquisite society to emerge will be governed by an elite comprised of gay poets. One of the major requirements for a position of power in the new society of homoeroticism will be an indulgence in the Greek passion. Any man contaminated with heterosexual lust will be automatically barred from a position of influence. All males who insist on remaining stupidly heterosexual will be tried in homosexual courts of justice and will become invisible men.

We shall rewrite history, history filled and debased with your heterosexual lies and distortions. We shall portray the homosexuality of the great leaders and thinkers who have shaped the world. We will demonstrate that homosexuality and intelligence and imagination are inextricably linked, and that homosexuality is a requirement for true nobility, true beauty in a man.

We shall be victorious because we are fueled with the ferocious bitterness of the oppressed who have been forced to play seemingly bit parts in our dumb, heterosexual shows through out [sic] the ages. We too are capable of firing guns and manning barricades of the ultimate revolution.

Such are the words of one possessed by the spirit of this world that rejects God's law. Though sinful man tries over and over again to flaunt God's laws and reject the lifesaving gospel of Jesus Christ, no one survives that hatred against the church of Jesus Christ—not because the church is so great in and of itself, nor because the members are so faithful, but because this world belongs to the Lord Jesus Christ and He rules over all things for the sake of His Body, the Church. He has been exalted as Lord and Messiah over all the nations. All authority has been given to him in heaven and earth. Whoever touches the Body of Christ, touches the "apple of His eye" (I Cor. 3:16, 17).

These have been the words of any and every sinner—whether gay or straight makes no difference. It is the ultimate challenge that ends up as empty words in the end.

". . . the body they may kill, God's truth abides still; His Kingdom is forever . . ."

ELEVEN

Gay Rights Or Gay Riots?

Five thousand angry protestors surged through San Francisco streets on the evening of 30 September 1991 to protest Governor Pete Wilson's veto of AB101, a gay rights bill, which had passed the Senate and Assembly.

The gay community was expecting to win a major victory with Wilson's anticipated signing of this legislation, but he had received so much pressure from concerned citizens that he vetoed the bill in the end. News stories indicated that his office had received one hundred thousand letters and phone calls asking him not to sign the legislation.

With the governor's veto, gay rage was immediately evident in San Francisco. The five thousand protesters gathered in the Castro district for speeches denouncing Wilson. One of the keynote speakers at the protest was Eric Rofes, executive director of Shanti Project, an AIDS outreach. He told the crowd, "We will win. If it's not this year, then maybe next year, or in 10 years. They will hurt us. They will attack us. But we will win" (Elaine Hersher, Dan Levy, "Gay Rights Protest Turns Violent," *San Francisco Chronicle* [1 October 1991]). Then the angry mob marched from the Castro district to the Civic Center.

Ironically, the pro-gay, former police chief, then candidate for mayor, Frank Jordan, tried to join the demonstration in an attempt to identify himself with the homosexual community and their causes. One of the gay newspapers reported that "Jordan was literally chased out of the Castro district during the first hour of the demonstration. It was almost three blocks before he received [police] help" ("New Chief, New Policies," *San Francisco Sentinel* [7 October 1991]). The screaming, whistle-blowing militants yelled, "Go home, basher!" as they drove him out of the Castro district.

As the protestors reached the old state building where Pete Wilson maintains an office, "[a] break-away group of about 400 people suddenly ran toward the building, which was being protected by fewer than 20 San Francisco and State Police officers. Grabbing metal barricades, news racks and other objects, some among the 400 began smashing the $60,000, multi-colored, leaded-glass entrance doors. . . . Others hurled missiles that shattered windows, then tossed large wads of paper and ignited flares inside. The resulting fires destroyed office equipment, including costly computers, before the blazes were extinguished" ("Eight face arrest in riot over rights veto," *San Francisco Examiner* [10 October 1991]).

As the fires blazed, the militants stood outside jeering and screaming, "Gays bash back!" Inside the building, however, were dozens of frightened state and local police, as well as California state employees who'd been trapped by the mob outside and the fires inside. The greatly outnumbered police had first fought the gays with mace and fire hoses, but had retreated to the safety of the building to avoid being violently harmed. The same 10 October 1991 *San Francisco Examiner* article reported that "[f]our State Police officers and two San Francisco police officers were injured before reinforcements arrived and cleared the street."

After order was restored, the police officers who had been inside the building complained to the press that the "higher ups" in the police department had ignored their calls for help. However, the *San Francisco Examiner* reported that Police Chief Casey ". . . disputed the story that police on the scene at the old State Building were told that no back-up was available, saying 'A review of tapes has shown that operators told them that help was on the way'" ("S.F. Chief defends gay riot handling," [8 October 1991].). Chief Casey also criticized them for taking their case to the public without going through proper channels.

In spite of the fact that the gays had set fire to a government office building, graffitied the new state office building one block away, threatened the lives of dozens of police and state employees, and caused $250,000 in damages, no arrests were made that evening.

City officials basically approved of the Police Chief's handling of the riot. The Board of Supervisors called him in to review the demonstration and how it was handled. One article reported: "Casey restated his assertions that police handled the incident 'in accordance with crowd control measures established two years ago,' and downplayed the fact that no arrest had been made. . . .

"The chief's appearance was met with little hostility . . . although Supervisor Harry Britt grilled him about how police are supposed to respond to injured protestors.

"'I saw nothing in the papers about injuries, but a member of my staff saw a severely bloody person being laid on the ground and attended to by bystanders,' Britt said. . . . Britt said it took 25 minutes for the ambulance to arrive, and no effort was made by officers to help stop the flow of blood. Britt said he would pursue the matter through the Police Commission. . . .

". . . Supervisor Kevin Shelley said, 'While certainly no one condones violence, I would like to commend you, Chief, for following crowd control measures" ("S. F. Chief defends gay riot handling," *San Francisco Examiner* [8 October 1991]).

Mayor Agnos, in reaction to the rioting, did the politically correct thing in denouncing it; "The attack on the state building," said Agnos, "harmed people who are blameless and is unacceptable. It's wrong, and it's a mistake to divert attention away from the governor's veto, and that's what last night's violence did" ("Riot Sparked by Gay Rights Veto Caught S.F. Police by Surprise," *San Francisco Chronicle* [2 Oct. 1991]).

As expected, Agnos and the Board of Supervisors were quick to pass a resolution denouncing Governor Wilson for vetoing AB101.

The news media also reported that arrest warrants would be issued as protestors were identified with the aid of TV news footage, newspaper photos, and "with help from the gay community" in identifying the perpetrators.

The day after the state building demonstration in San Francisco, at least three hundred angry protestors harassed Governor Wilson as he spoke at Stanford University's centennial celebration. Shouting "Shame, shame, shame!" a number of gays rushed the platform where he was standing and threw oranges and eggs at him. "I will give you some advice—this is not the time or the place for fascist tactics," he told them ("Noisy Attack Over Veto of Gay-Rights Bill," *San Francisco Chronicle* [2 Oct. 1991]).

Over forty police in riot gear had to keep demonstrators from assaulting the speakers on the platform, and secret service agents were also in abundance to protect Wilson from harm. At the conclusion of the speech, a number of gays chased three unmarked cars down the street—thinking Wilson was leaving under escort. Police used tear gas on them to keep them at bay.

A few days later, militant gays closed down public street intersections in the city to protest the governor's presence at a Republican fund-raiser in the city.

Gays and lesbians also rioted and/or protested in Sacramento and in Los Angeles over Wilson's veto of the gay rights bill. In Sacramento, on 11 October 1991 approximately seven thousand marched on the state capitol. The rally was held on "National Coming Out Day"—a day set aside to encourage "closeted" homosexuals to openly and proudly declare their homosexuality or others would do it for them. The 17 October 1991 edition of the *San Francisco Sentinel*, in a front page article entitled "AB101 PROTEST," described the day in part as follows:

> Carrying an inspired array of signs and blowing whistles and airhorns, the angry but mostly non-violent crowd sent a deafening message to Wilson, . . .Gay and lesbian elected officials, who were not invited to speak at the noon rally, began the day by holding their own press conference. Among those present were Santa Monica Mayor Judy Abdo, San Mateo County Board of Supervisors President Tom Nolan, San Francisco Supervisor Roberta Achtenberg, Laguna Beach councilmember John Heilman, who organized the gathering.
>
> San Francisco mayoral candidates Angela Alioto and Dick Hongisto both made the trek to Sacramento to lend support to demonstrators and perhaps sway a few voters.
>
> Protest organizers passed out "Promote Non-Violence" buttons and small plastic whistles to busloads of demonstrators arriving from every corner of the state. Whenever demonstrators began engaging in confrontations or advocating violence, they were summarily shouted down by event organizers with bullhorns.
>
> However, not everyone was advocating non-violence. Crystal Mason of ACT UP/San Francisco told the crowd, "Let vio-

lence speak. Why should we allow straight society to jam their justice down our throats."

The tensest moment of the day came when activists knocked down police barricades and charged the east steps of the Capitol where they were greeted by stunned State Patrol officers.

One lesbian protestor broke past the officers before encountering a locked Capitol door where she was thrown to the ground and dragged away by four officers. An incited crowd began a thunderous cry of, "Shame! Shame! Shame!"

To the left of the Capitol steps the Governor's windows were covered with closed curtains, which offered a sharp contrast to Lt. Governor Leo McCarthy's windows on the right side which were decorated with rainbow colored bows in commemoration of National Coming Out Day.

After leaving the Capitol, the protestors marched to the headquarters of the Traditional Values Coalition, home of Rev. Lou Sheldon who spearheaded the effort to defeat AB101. Lance Fortin, a legislative assistant for the TVC said, "They kicked the door so hard that the windows were shaking." Shouts and whistles at the TVC reached a deafening crescendo as marchers waved to on-lookers peering down from the windows of adjoining buildings.

San Francisco Board of Supervisors member, Roberta Achtenberg, was at the protest: "The whole goal is to make sure that if Gov. Wilson seeks reelection, he will not be reelected," she said ("Thousands protest governor's veto of California gay-rights bill," *The Denver Post* [12 Oct. 1991]).

In Los Angeles, the reaction of the gay militants was the same. Over one thousand protestors disrupted businesses on Rodeo Drive and Westwood Village on Saturday, 5 October to protest Wilson's veto. Chanting "gay rights now," and blowing whistles and horns, they marched through posh Beverly Hills, Century City, and Westwood and brought traffic to a stand still.

All of this violence, vandalism and rage is to be expected from the gay community. One protester's placard said it well, "Gay Rights or Gay Riots." They have shown time and time again that if they don't get their way, they will resort to any kind of civil disobedience that they consider necessary to achieve their goals. The gay political movement is not kind and gentle;

if you oppose them, you can expect to have your life and family threatened, your job security threatened, your property vandalized, and your character vilified.

When the law of God, which is the only standard of protection for society, is discarded, then by what standard do you maintain decency and order in that society? When a father rejects God's law with respect to the care of his family, what's to keep him from abandoning them? Even if he doesn't abandon them—for whatever reason—surely the next generation will act out the logical consequences of his doctrine. The second generation becomes "twice the sons of hell." It's not a matter of rejecting "absolutes" versus accepting "relativity"; it is the rejection of God's absolute standard that makes the difference. As Christians, we do not advocate "absolutes," as such, as the ground of our behavior, but rather the absolutes of God's law, clearly found in the Word of God, as the basis of society. Even the relativity of the unbeliever is his absolute—absolutely not God's!

A History Lesson

It's important to understand the history of AB101 because if your state has not already passed a similar law, it undoubtedly will be considering one in the months and years ahead. AB101 was introduced by Assemblyman Terry Friedman, a liberal Democrat from West Hollywood. If you're unfamiliar with West Hollywood, it's a town dominated by homosexual activists. West Hollywood, in essence, is a miniature version of San Francisco.

AB101 would have banned employment and housing discrimination against homosexuals and bisexuals. The bill would have added the words "sexual orientation" to a list of categories protected by the state Fair Employment and Housing Act. Those categories include race, religion, creed, color, national origin, ancestry, physical handicap, medical condition, marital status, sex, and age. Thus, sexual perversion would have been given the same legal protections as one's race or religion.

Friedman introduced AB101 in December of 1990 and managed to get it through the Senate and Assembly, and on to Governor Pete Wilson for signature. Wilson, a moderate Republican, has a long-time reputation of being pro-homosexual and pro-abortion. The gays thought they had a winner when AB101 went to Wilson for approval.

In order to get Wilson's signature, the bill was altered to delete "sexual orientation" from the housing section of the Act. Also, in order to lull Christians and other religious opposition into a false sense of security, the legislation also included a "religious" exemption. However, a close reading of AB101 revealed that it still threatened the religious freedoms of nonchurch-related ministries such as TV and radio ministries, Christian schools, bookstores, book publishers, and other parachurch organizations.

The supporters of AB101 claimed that its passage would help stop "discrimination" against homosexuals resulting from their sexual orientation. Homosexuals continue to claim—in spite of the lack of scientific evidence—that being a homosexual is just like being left-handed instead of right-handed, or having blue eyes as opposed to brown. They would have us believe that homosexuality is biologically determined and that we should never discriminate against people because of something that is genetic or inborn. Homosexuality, of course, is a sin, a sexual perversion, and a very destructive habit that can be effectively treated through the gospel of Jesus Christ.

Dr. James Dobson, founder of Focus on the Family, a radio ministry based in Colorado Springs, Colorado, took a major part in helping alert Christians to the dangers of AB101. In a letter written to several thousand California pastors before the housing provision was removed, Dr. Dobson noted:

> . . . AB101 will force employers and landlords to employ or rent to people whose actions they consider to be immoral. As repugnant as all of this is to me, I simply cannot sit by and watch it happen without trying to stop it.

> As I have thought this issue through, the question comes to mind : Should Christians ever "discriminate"? . . . I have concluded this: the issue is not discrimination. The issue is the forced legitimization of an unhealthy, destructive lifestyle. I believe there is not a single homosexual man dying of AIDS who would not readily work to rid himself of his sexual habits in order to have another chance at life. The most compassionate act I can think of right now is to stand strongly against any attempt to portray homosexual acts as normal. AB101 will do just that. Too many have already died. Too many families have already suffered horribly at the tragic loss of their loved ones. Will you not stand against this immorality?

Included with his letter to these pastors, was a video tape of the 1990 gay pride parade in San Francisco showing gays and lesbians strutting half naked—publicly flaunting their immoral behavior. Whether seen on that video tape or not, prominent politicians, both local and state, proudly participated in the parade as if just another member of one big happy family.

A Lawyer Analyzes AB101

In reading through AB101—or any gay rights legislation for that matter—it's often difficult to read between the lines to see what such a law will actually do to restrict the freedom of individuals who "discriminate" against a perverted sexual behavior. Fortunately, as AB101 was working its way through the legislature, David Llewellyn, president of the Western Center of Law and Religious Freedom, took the time to analyze the bill for California Christians. He discovered a number of very frightening phrases in the bill, which directly assaulted freedom of speech, freedom of association, and freedom of religion.

In another mailing to pastors, Dr. Dobson quoted much of Llewellyn's analysis of AB101. I am quoting his analysis here, because the oppressive restrictions that appear in AB101 will undoubtedly appear in other state's "anti-discrimination" laws:

> While the bill exempts employers of non-profit, religious organizations, it covers all for-profit businesses employing five people or more. This includes Christian bookstores, Christian radio and television stations, day-care centers, for profit Christian schools and churches that have chosen, out of spiritual conviction, not to organize formally.

> Although the bill exempts certain "employers," it becomes illegal for any **person** to, "aid, abet, incite, compel, or coerce the doing of any of the acts forbidden under this [law], or to attempt to do so." This section presumably includes even the employers exempted by the section I mentioned earlier. According to Llewellyn's analysis, "anyone who takes a stand against this law as a matter of religious conviction of moral conscience, including any pastor, is at risk of attempting to incite people not to obey the law. For example, if a pastor were to tell his congregation not to become unequally yoked with unbelievers, and as a result a member of the church declined to accept a homosexual for employment or for an

apprenticeship program, the pastor would be liable along with the employer or other person."

Since the bill would ban any discrimination related to sexual orientation, Christian businessmen will find it risky to exclude sexually promiscuous employees of any sort. Nor could Christians who rent rooms in their homes or other housing to more than one person even legally ask about renter's sexual orientation! In other words, anything goes sexually, with the official protection of the state. Typical rental housing owned by churches is not exempt. No exemption would allow Christians to refuse homosexual roommates.

The bill includes money to pay for government programs and publications that would explain why it is wrong to discriminate on the basis of sexual orientation. This material would be paid for by your tax dollars and would seem to run directly counter to the plain teaching of Christian moral principles.

Portions of the bill cover all people (regardless of religious conviction) who hire even one person, as baby sitters, tutors, maids, day care workers, etc. Can you imagine discovering that your baby sitter has unusual sexual desires, perhaps toward children, and then being accused of sexual orientation discrimination when you tried to dismiss the sitter? It becomes illegal to "harass any employee or applicant" over his or her sexual beliefs, and "harassment" isn't defined. Presumably, any applicant who believes he was denied a job because of sexual orientation could legitimately feel "harassed" and could sue. I can practically guarantee you that should this bill become law, Christians churches and schools, and individual Christians, will be hauled into court when they try to obey the clear commands of Scripture by living and teaching according to traditional moral principles. In fact, no one really knows what devastating impact this bill will have until the liberal court system gets through the lawsuits that will come by the truckload.

Well, Dr. Dobson and thousands of Christians felt very much relieved when Wilson vetoed AB101 in September 1991. Our relief is short-lived.

Sodomy: A Constitutional Right?

On 25 October just three weeks after the Wilson veto, we were shocked to learn that the California Court of Appeal in San Francisco had determined that homosexuality was a "right" protected under the California Constitution's "right of privacy" provision.

In his November/December 1991 newsletter, attorney David Llewellyn described this terrible decision in these words, "The California Court of Appeal in San Francisco has elevated homosexuality to a state constitutional right! If allowed to stand, the October 25 decision in **Soroka v. Dayton Hudson Corp.** will subject every California employer to potential criminal prosecution for discrimination against homosexual employees or applicants.

"This ruling advances the gay rights agenda further than AB101 ever could have. Small businesses with fewer than five employees would have been exempt under AB101 but not under this ruling."

****

Under this court's decision, there would be no religious exemptions. Consequently, any ministry could potentially be liable for prosecution if allegedly "discriminating" against homosexuals in hiring. However, the Supreme Court of the State of California has suspended implementation of the decision until it makes its own ruling. According to a *San Francisco Examiner* article on 1 February 1992: "A court ruling declaring that California law prohibits job discrimination against gays was set aside Friday by the state Supreme Court until the justices decide the scope of the right to privacy . . . The court's action automatically removes the appellate ruling from the books and leaves the issues in the case unresolved." So, we're not out of the woods yet.

Decisions of this high court are themselves reviewed by the Ultimate Court of Appeals: God's judgment. As the Psalmist says, "God takes his stand in the congregation of the gods [i.e., judges]; He judges in the midst of the gods . . ." (Ps. 82). Our job as ordinary Christians is to "storm" the gates of heaven with intercessory prayer for our judges and leaders—that they turn

to the Lord Jesus Christ for the wisdom necessary to protect
and defend true justice.

Gay Rights Laws – A Long History

How did we come to this point? I think much of the credit
for our present predicament in California must be given to Art
Agnos and his performance as an assemblyman in the 1970s
and 1980s. It was Agnos who every year introduced AB1 (now
AB101) to the California Assembly. When he became mayor of
San Francisco, other pro-homosexual secularists like Terry
Friedman took up his cause and began pushing for AB101.

As described in an earlier chapter, I testified before a 1980
Congressional Subcommittee regarding a gay rights amendment to the Civil Rights Act of 1979. At that same hearing, Art
Agnos testified in favor of the gay rights amendment. The
following is a portion of what Agnos said. (As you read it,
remember this testimony was given before the discovery of
AIDS.):

> Homosexuality is not taught—it is felt. The idea that children
> or adults will become homosexuals by having gay teachers or
> by associating with gay people is as silly as suggesting chil-
> dren will become Catholic by having teachers who are Catho-
> lic or by associating with people who are Catholic.
>
> No one proposes that we solve the problems of racism by
> making everyone white. We will not solve the problem of job
> discrimination for the homosexual by making them hetero-
> sexual.
>
> Gay people are neither evangelists for their sexuality—nor
> are they rapists.
>
> Sexual orientation does not comprise one's character, it only
> states one's sexual relationship with members of one sex or
> the other.
>
> This antidiscrimination legislation will not license bad con-
> duct in the classroom, the office, squad car, hospital, or
> anywhere else.
>
> Gay people—like straight people—are just as capable of sepa-
> rating their private lives from their public behavior.
>
> Wherever gay rights legislation has been passed at the state,
> county, or city level, there have been no after effects—on
> adults or children.

These are the views of the man who has fought for the

cause of legalized immorality harder than anyone else in recent California history. He also advocates same-sex marriages in the whole package . . . and why not? "If the foundations be destroyed,". . . what else can the unrighteous do? As the book of Proverbs teaches, "Where there is no vision [i.e., revelation from God], the people perish," literally, "cast off restraint." With the help of politicians such as Art Agnos, this is how San Francisco has become.

Legalize Gay Marriages?

In fighting gay rights legislation since the 1980s, a half dozen San Francisco pastors have journeyed to Sacramento year after year to testify against legislation such as AB101. During the fight to defeat AB101, we were also faced with another bill, AB167, which would have changed the California Civil Code regarding marriage to delete the terms "man" and "woman" as marriage partners to "persons"—thus making way for all kinds of "marriages": homosexual, bisexual, fornication and incestuous. Polygamy would not be far behind. Bizarre sounding, perhaps—but not in San Francisco. The "bizarre" of 30 years ago is the "norm" of today.

The proposed legislation had been introduced by Assemblyman John Burton (D-San Francisco). The day public testimony was to be heard, I wasn't very interested in going. I thought I'd done enough for a while; just this once, let me stay home! However, on the urging of a couple of Christian brothers, I decided to go along and see what could be done—or said.

I learned from my experience with those hostile legislators on the 1980 congressional subcommittee panel that quoting statistics about homosexuality as a dangerous health hazard or as a sexual dysfunction was of little effect. I learned that it is the presentation of the gospel of Christ alone that ultimately changes the lives of the legislators, and, thus, changes the laws they generate.

Now, having the opportunity to speak against AB167 and not being "statistically" prepared, I simply read Romans, chapter 1 to the legislators. This passage is a clear and penetrating picture of a society that has exchanged the truth of God for a lie and now worships and serves the creature rather than the Creator. It describes homosexual and lesbian relationships as the epitome of a society consumed with self-gratification. The

text comes through loud and clear to convict of sin, righteousness, and judgment. And, so, I read the passage to the lawmakers. If anything is finally to get through to the hard hearts of
men, it is the Word of God. Whether that Word penetrates,
leading to conversion (change of mind and heart), is God's
business. Being a faithful witness of that Word is our calling.

Years ago believers stopped being distinctively Christian
witnesses to the civil magistrate out of fear of being foolish and
offensive! But, fools we are called to be—for Christ's sake! (I
Cor. 4:10). Speaking at one of our fund-raising banquets, our
good friend Cal Thomas reminded us that being a fool for
Christ does not give Christians license to be "boorish" in their
behavior—if they are, they deserve the just criticism of the
world. However, being a fool for Christ's sake means at all
times faithfully speaking the truth of God's Word—not concerning ourselves about appearing unenlightened to the non-Christian. Let's face it, since they "are wise in their own eyes" and
have "substituted [God's] truth for a lie," we will only appear
foolish to them. In light of their blatant and unabashed rebellion against God's righteous standard, what level of sophistica-
tion or intelligence can we hope to achieve in their eyes?

Don't be foolish . . . be a fool for Christ.

TWELVE

A Look Into The Future

Wisconsin:

In 1989, Ann Hacklander and Maureen Rowe advertised for a roommate to share their apartment in Madison, Wisconsin. When Cari Sprague answered their newspaper advertisement, she promptly informed them that she was a lesbian. They both politely refused to accept her as a roommate. Sprague then contacted the Madison Equal Opportunities Commission and charged Hacklander and Rowe with sexual orientation discrimination under a city ordinance.

When Hacklander and Rowe met at the office of the MEOC, they were pressured into agreeing to the following: They would pay Sprague fifteen hundred dollars in damages; they would attend a two-hour pro-gay training class conducted by a homosexual group; they would have their housing situation "monitored" for two years; and they would write a letter of apology to Sprague for "discriminating" against her (Katherine Dalton, "Live With Lesbian Or Else . . . ," *Human Events* [25 November 1989]: 9.).

Washington State:

Members of ACT UP are distributing a so-called "safe sex" pamphlet on high-school campuses in the state of Washington. The pamphlet, "How To F— Safely," provides high-school students with graphic photographs of lesbian, gay, and straight sexual intercourse, a drawing showing how to put on a condom, plus instructions on how to create a "dental dam" out of a condom in order to prevent the ingestion of bodily fluids. ACT

UP also offers a free clean needle service to teen drug addicts, supposedly to help stop the spread of AIDS.

California:

In 1991, an irate parent from California called the office of Concerned Women for America to ask for legal counsel on a problem she was facing at her son's school. Her son's sixth grade teacher was a militant gay activist who repeatedly discussed his sexuality in the English class. She went to the teacher in private to discuss her concerns, but he made it obvious that her view didn't matter to him. He would continue promoting homosexuality in spite of her objections. She then went to the principal to complain. And what did the principal tell her? He said that she was violating a Hate Crimes Act, which prohibited her from saying negative things about gays. When she said she would then have her child excused from the class, the principal warned her against taking such an action because her son would then be expelled from school (Tim LaHaye, "Christian Discrimination in Public Education," *Education Report* [January 1992]: 2.).

In Los Angeles, Connie Norman, a transsexual and ACT UP militant has her own radio talk show on station XEK-AM. Norman, 42, has also tested positive for HIV. She was once a 14-year-old boy who ran away from home in Texas and became a street hustler and drug addict in Los Angeles. Norman eventually kicked her drug habit and then decided to have a sex change operation in 1976.

Since that time, Norman has been involved in gay rights activism and not long ago became a member of the Los Angeles School Board's AIDS Task Force, which has recommended explicit pro-gay AIDS education and the distribution of condoms on high-school campuses.

****

I have mentioned these seemingly unconnected items because they should provide you with some idea of where the gay rights movement is headed if unchecked. Edmund Burke said, "The only thing necessary for the triumph of evil is for good men to do nothing." The gay political movement is not going to go away on its own. It is not going to respect church/state boundaries. The gay rights movement is as totalitarian in its belief as is Christianity. They will accept no peaceful coexistence between themselves and Christians that take seriously the commandments of God's Word. They know that in order to survive, they must silence the bible-believing, gospel-preaching church, and those individual Christians who dare to criticize them. They are aggressively promoting their agenda on junior high and high-school campuses through explicit sex education, AIDS education, Project 10-type programs, and off-campus "rap" groups.

In San Francisco, we have seen first hand what happens when the wicked seize the reins of power—starting in the individual human heart and spreading through all the community and culminating in the legislative halls of our cities and counties. The clear-headed Christian, one who is well taught in the Scriptures, is our only hope to slow down, halt, and reverse such a demonic trend. These two conflicting belief systems cannot remain within the same community. One has got to go; one will prevail. For the Christian, it is the law of God that must, and ultimately will, prevail in our society.

One moral system or another will always be imposed. The question is not whether to impose it, but which morality will be imposed: either God's law or man's law. We have clearly seen that "the wages of sin is death," and it's costing millions of dollars in a very practical sense. As I said to one reporter, "Keeping God's commandments doesn't cost any money!" And, what's more important, it saves LIVES.

The Christian must take this responsibility seriously. The gay community isn't playing games. If you oppose them, they will try to silence you any way they can. If you remain passive, they will leave you alone, but will not refrain from evangelizing your children to make them over into their image.

It is absolutely essential that Christians become informed on the issue of homosexuality, AIDS, the gay/lesbian "rights" agenda—and that through their churches, they begin at the local level to actively apply the gospel in word and in deeds to every sphere of the community. It's more than just witnessing on a personal level; it also must include practicing the compassion of Christ publicly as well as privately, individually and corporately, personally and politically. As Abraham Kuyper (early 20th Century Prime Minister of the Netherlands) said about the reaches of Christ's reign and rule, "There is not a plot of ground where Christ cannot say, 'It is Mine.'"

Christians need to oversee city hall meetings, school board meetings, human relations committee hearings, AIDS task force groups—in short, any area of government that the gay movement has targeted to gain political power in the community at large.

"But, wait a minute, McIlhenny! It sounds like you think that the gay political agenda is the one GIANT conspiracy poised to take over the world!" That is not my thinking—let me clarify. We see the gay agenda as symbolic of the all-encompassing plan of the kingdom of darkness as a whole. This particular movement is simply one late 20th century event in a long history of little conspiracies down through the ages. We do believe in the grand over all conspiracy of Satan's attempt to destroy the people of God and His Church (Ps. 2); but we believe in a much greater "conspiracy" and that is the triumph of the Kingdom of Jesus Christ, which has been placed over all the world now and forever. "All dominion has been given to ME [Christ] both in heaven and in earth . . ." (Matt. 28:18).

We must be prayerfully pressuring our government officials, reminding them that homosexuality is a sexual perversion that should never receive special legal protections. The human rights of all individuals, homosexuals and non-homosexuals, must be and are already protected in existing laws. And, in fact, to institute special laws to protect sexual deviance results in "[taking] away the rights of those who are in the right" (Isa. 5:23). That is the reality in San Francisco. We must remind our lawmakers that they themselves are "ministers of God" before they are the servants of the people, and they will someday have to give an account of the sacred trust to which He has called them. We must remind them that the power of the Church is not in herself, nor in the ballot box, nor in political demonstrations, nor in violent upheaval of society, nor in breaking laws that are inconsistent with Scripture, but in the Spirit of Christ and His gospel to effect a true transformation in the lives of men and of society.

Christians must realize that as the Church of Jesus Christ goes, so goes the nation. As the Church is revived to do its calling and election, so this will be reflected in society as the leaven permeates and preserves the bread. There are tangible consequences to faith in Christ as well as tangible consequences to unbelief. One of the Church Fathers, Chrysostom, referred to Christians in a community as the "saviors of the city,"[1] not because they were so talented and gifted but because of Christ in them.

We believe that Christians should not only be pressuring public officials and sharing the gospel, but that they have an obligation to run for political office and that when they do, to clearly state their faith and their objectives in seeking public office.

The Future Demands Active Christians

What is your responsibility toward homosexuals and the gay political movement in light of all that we've written? One of your primary obligations is this: not to let a righteous anger against their sin cause you to forget their need of Jesus Christ. As angry as we've been over the years for all that's been done to our church and family because of our stand, we have attempted to remember that the oppressor is a sinner in need of the forgiveness of our Lord.

Ministry to the homosexual community is of the utmost importance if we're to effectively reach them. Such a ministry is two-fold: both spiritual and political. We cannot minister to their physical and spiritual needs without also opposing gay legislation and encroachments in our public schools and private businesses, etc. At times it may seem self-defeating to present yourself both for and against them: *For them*, in that you should show the compassion of the Savior toward them and not personal animosity; *for them*, in that you as a Christian are opposed to "queer-bashing" as they call it—*for them*, in that you will defend their human rights before God; *for them*, in the sense that you have the remedy for their enslavement to sin; *for them*, in that you can sympathize with such enslavement, for you yourself "once were one of them"; *for them*, in that God loves sinners and is anxious to save sinners who call on Him; *for them*, in that you really do care for them in Christ.

Against them, in that you're consistently opposed to any

---

[1] John Chrysostom, "Concerning Statues," from "Homilies of St. John Chrysostom"; Philip Schaff, Ed., *A Select Library of the Nicene and Post-Nicene Father* (Eerdmans Publishers: Grand Rapids), Vol. IX, 1968, p. 343.

policy or practice that contributes to the moral breakdown of the family and the community; *against them*, in that it is to their best interest that the nuclear family must be especially defended so they can have their own healthy families according to God's holy ordinance; *against them*, in that you oppose de-Christianizing sex education and stand for abstinence until marriage; *against them*, in that their cause for rampant wickedness will itself be their own destruction and the destruction of society around them; *against them*, in that they, in their present unrepentant state, are under the wrath of God.

Give some serious thought to what you can do to establish a Christian counseling ministry to gays, or minister to AIDS patients, or collect food for an AIDS food bank, or even start an AIDS food bank through your own church.

As much as we might wish otherwise, the gay rights movement is not going to spontaneously disappear over night. There are hundreds of men and women who need love and compassion in order to help lead them out of this destructive lifestyle. There are plenty of resources available for your church to become a minister of the gospel to the homosexual population. Will you be the catalyst to make it happen?

Ministry is vitally important. That's the genius of the Christian faith: ministry, i.e., service to others in the Name of Christ. A ministry that has an actively principled, and determined righteous indignation against the gay rights agenda and yet, a compassion for their lost souls.

There is a wicked force already taking root in your community. It is a spiritual force as described in the words of the Apostle Paul, ". . . wrestl[ing] not against flesh and blood but against the rulers, against the power, against the world forces of this darkness, against the spiritual forces of wickedness in the heavenly places . . ." (Eph. 6:12). In many communities, that force has already surfaced, having taken control of your human relations or civil rights commission, your school board, your human relations department at your office, your health department, or your city council. It's only the gospel of Christ that can discern that force and effectively counteract it.

"For Thine is the kingdom, and the power, and the glory, forever. Amen" (Matt. 6:13).

Appendix

Resources on Homosexuality and AIDS

A word about this resource list: we should probably enter a disclaimer at this point to say that although an organization, book, video or cassette is listed here, we do not necessarily agree with the proposals or ideas shared in these materials. We provide this list only so that you can investigate a number of different perspectives on homosexuality, AIDS, and ministry to those seeking to leave a dangerously self-destructive lifestyle.

Ministries and Clinics

EXODUS INTERNATIONAL is the best-known nationwide resource for information on ministries to homosexuals. Exodus keeps a listing of approved ex-gay ministries throughout the United States and publishes a newsletter. If you're unaware of a Christ- centered AIDS or ex-gay ministry in your area, contact Exodus. Write to: Bob Davies, Exodus International, P.O. Box 2121, San Rafael, CA 94912; (415)454-1017

THOMAS AQUINAS PSYCHOLOGICAL CLINIC is run by Dr. Joseph Nicolosi. His clinic practice is primarily involved in helping struggling homosexuals leave the lifestyle. Nicolosi's address is: Thomas Aquinas Psychological Clinic, 16661 Ventura Blvd., Suite 816, Encino, CA 91436; (818) 342-8324.

GENESIS COUNSELING SERVICES was founded by Joe Dallas, a leader in Exodus International. His counseling service is located at 2745 E. Chapman, Orange, CA 92666; (714) 744-3326.

AMERICANS FOR A SOUND AIDS/HIV POLICY is a public policy group founded by W. Shepherd Smith. Smith's organization provides expert testimony and materials urging a compassionate yet rational response to the AIDS epidemic. His group has also been instrumental in urging churches to form ministries to AIDS patients. For more information on the work of ASAP write: ASAP, P.O. Box 17433, Washington, D.C., 20041; (703) 471-7350.

AIDS MINISTRY BOOK AND VIDEO RESOURCES

- Greg Albers, *Plague in Our Midst: Sexuality, Aids and the Christian Family*, (Lafayette, La: Huntington House, 1988).
- Counseling and AIDS, from the series Resources for Christian Counseling, Gary R. Collins, Gen. Ed. (Word Publishers: Dallas, Tx., 1990), Vol. 24.
- Paul Cameron, *Exposing the AIDS Scandal* (Lafayette, La.: Huntington House, 1988).
- Cathy Kay, R.N., "No Second Chance," video on the AIDS epidemic aimed at a teenage audience. (Available through: Jeremiah Films, P.O. Box 1710, Hemet, Calif. 92343; (714) 925-6460).
- Dr. D. James Kennedy, "AIDS: Anatomy of a Crisis," video. (Coral Ridge Ministries, P.O. Box 40, Ft. Lauderdale, Fla. 33308, (305) 772-0404.
- William Masters, Virginia Johnson, and Robert Kolodny, *Crisis: Heterosexual Behavior in the Age of AIDS* (New York, N.Y.,: Grove Press, 1988).
- Dr. Joe McIlhaney, *Sexuality and Sexually Transmitted Diseases*, (Grand Rapids, MI.: Baker Book House, 1990).
- Dr. Lawrance J. McNamee and Dr. Brian F. McNamee, *AIDS: The Nation's First Politically Protected Disease* (La Habra, CA: National Medical Legal Publishing House, 1988).
- Dr. David Pence, *AIDS: A War We Can Win* (The Committee to Stop AIDS, P.O. Box 10517, Minneapolis, MN 55458).
- Penny Pullen, "The AIDS Epidemic: A Challenge to the Church" (National Association of Evangelicals, P.O. Box 28, Wheaton, ILL 60189; (708) 665-0500.
- Dr. Robert Redfield, *AIDS & Young People* (Washington: Regnery Gateway, 1987).
- Michael Schwartz, *Gays, AIDS and You* (Old Greenwich, Conn: Devin Adair, 1987).
- W. Shepherd Smith, Jeffrey Collins and Jonathan Hunter, AIDS Ministry and Community-based Organizational Models, two audiotapes. (National Association of Evangelicals, P.O. Box 28, Wheaton, Ill 60189: (708) 665-0500.
- Greg L. Bahnsen, *Homosexuality: A Biblical View* (Grand Rapids, MI: Baker Book House, 1978).
- David Chilton, *A Christians Response to AIDS, Power in the Blood*, (Brentwood, TN.: Wolgemuth and Hyett Publishers, Inc., 1987).
- William Dannemeyer, *Shadow in the Land* (San Francisco, Calif. Ignatius Press, 1989).

Resources on Therapy or Ministry to Homosexuals

- Clifford Allen, *A Textbook of Psychosexual Disorders* (New York, N.Y.: Oxford University Press, 1969).
- Jerry Arterburn, *How Will I Tell My Mother?* (Nashville, Tenn.: Oliver Nelson, 1988).
- Don Baker, *Beyond Rejection: The Church, Homosexuality and Hope* (Portland, OR.: Multnomah Press, 1985).
- Irving Beiber, *Homosexuality: A Psychoanalytic Study of Male Homosexuals* (New York, N.Y.: Basic Books, 1982).
- Edmund Bergler, *Homosexuality: Disease or Way of Life?* (New York, N.Y.: Hill and Wang, 1957).
- Harvey Cleckley, *The Caricature of Love* (New York, N.Y.: Ronald Press, 1957).
- Joe Dallas, *Desires in Conflict* (Eugene, Ore: Harvest House Publishers, 1991).
- Dr. Frank du Mas, *Gay is Not Good* (Nashville, Tenn.: Thomas Nelson Publishers, 1979).
- Lawrence Hatterer, *Changing Homosexuality in the Male* (New York, N.Y.: McGraw-Hill, 1970)
- Barbara Johnson, *Where Does a Mother Go to Resign?* (Minneapolis, MN: Bethany House, 1987).
- Cynthia Lanning, ed., *Answer to Your Questions About Homosexuality* (Wilmore, Ky.: Bristol Books, 1988).
- Karen Scalf Linamen and Keith Wall, *Deadly Secrets* (Colorado Springs, CO: Nav Press, 1990).
- Elizabeth Moberly, *Homosexuality: A New Christian Ethic* (Cambridge, England: James Clarke & Co., 1983).
- Dr. Joseph Nicolosi, *Reparative Therapy of Male Homosexuality–A New Clinical Approach* (Northvale, N.J.: Jason Aronson, Inc., 1991).
- Dr. George A. Rekers, *Growing Up Straight: What Every Family Should Know About Homosexuality* (Chicago, Ill.: Moody Press, 1982).
- Michael R. Saia, *Counseling the Homosexual* (Minneapolis, Minn>: Bethany House Publishers, 1988).
- Charles Socarides *The Overt Homosexual* (New York, N.Y.: Grune & Stratton, 1968).
- Peter and Barbara Wyden, *Growing Up Straight* (New York, N.Y.: Stein and Day, 1968).

Resources on the Gay Rights Agenda

- "AIDS: What You Haven't Been Told," video on AIDS and the gay rights movement (Jeremiah Films, P.O. Box 1710, Hemet, CA 92343; (714) 925-6460).

- William Donahue, *The New Freedom: Individualism and Collectivism in the Social Live of Americans* (New Brunswick, N.J.: Transaction Books, 1990.)

- Dr. Brad Hayton, *The Homosexual Agenda: What You Can Do* (Colorado Springs, CO.: Focus On the Family, 420 N. Cascade, Colorado Springs, CO 80903. To order by credit card, call: 1-800- A-FAMILY.)

- Tim LaHaye, *The Unhappy Gays* (Wheaton, Ill.: Tyndale House, 1978).

- Roger Magnuson, J.D., *Are Gay Rights Right?—Making Sense of the Controversy* (Portland, Ore.: Multnomah Press, 1990).

- Dr. David Noebel, *The Homosexual Revolution* (Summit Ministries, P.O. Box 207, Manitou Springs, Colo. 80829; (719) 685-9103. Noebel's ministry is an outreach to teens to help them to develop a coherent Christian world view.

- *Perpetuating Homosexual Myths* (The Public Education Committee on Children and Youth, P.O.Box 33082, Seattle, Wash. 98133-0082).

- Dr. Judith Reisman and Edward Eichel, *Kinsey, Sex, and Fraud* (Lafayette, La.: Huntington House Publishers, 1990). Reisman and Eichel assert Alfred Kinsey's reports on human sexuality are the results of fraudulent research designed to promote a pro-homosexual and pro-pedophile personal agenda. If widely distributed and taken seriously, this book could deal a death blow to Kinsey-inspired immoral sex education programs in our public schools.

- Enrique Rueda, *The Homosexual Network* (Greenwich, Conn.: Devin-Adair Publishers, 1982). This is probably the most exhaustively detailed look at the gay rights movement ever compiled. Unfortunately, it is out of print, but a condensed version is available as *Gays, AIDS and You*, published in 1987 by Devin- Adair.

- "Sexual Orientation or Sexual Deviation?" explicit video showing the 1991 Gay Pride Parade in San Francisco (T Beeson, *The Report: A Righteous Perspective*, 42640 10th St. West, Lancaster, CA 93534; (805) 945-8783. Additional videos on the gay rights movement are also available.

- *Should Public Schools Teach Homosexuality as a Normal Lifestyle in the School Curriculum?* (The Public Education Committee on Children and Youth, P.O.Box 33082, Seattle, Wash. 98133-0082, 1989).

ORGANIZATIONS DEALING WITH RELIGIOUS FREEDOM, AIDS, MINISTRY TO HOMOSEXUALS AND THE "GAY RIGHTS" MOVEMENT

- American Family Association. Donald Wildmon, P.O.Box 2440, Tupelo, Miss. 38803; (601) 844-5036. AFA has taken the lead in fighting for better television and has lead a number of successful boycotts to remove pornographic magazines from convenience stores. Donald

Wildmon has earned the ire of the pornography industry and is routinely being sued by porn lawyers in an effort to put him out of business. AFA's recently established law center provides counsel for those persecuted for their Christian beliefs.

- Concerned Women for America, Beverly LaHaye, 370 L'Enfant Promenade, S.W., Suite 800, Washington, D.C. 20024; (202) 488-7000. CWA's legal staff provides free legal counsel in religious freedom cases.

- Coral Ridge Ministries, Dr. D. James Kennedy, P.O.Box 40, Ft. Lauderdale, FL 33308; (305) 772-0404. Dr. Kennedy's multimedia ministry includes a TV ministry, video documentaries on important social issues and a publications department which publishes a number of informative newsletters.

- Family Life Seminars. Tim LaHaye, 370 L'Enfant Promenade, S.W., Suite 800, Washington, D.C. 20024; (202) 488-7000. FLS publishes a number of informative newsletters on education, biblical prophecy and the Washington scene. Dr. LaHaye also has radio and TV programs and conducts seminars on strengthening family life. In the *Unhappy Gays*, published in 1978, LaHaye was one of the first pastors in the U.S. to warn of the dangers of the gay rights movement.

- Family First. Nancy Sutton, P.O.Box 885, Needham, Mass. 02192; (508) 359-6318. Family First is the only organization in the Northeast to aggressively confront the gay rights movement.

- Family Research Institute, Inc. Dr. Paul Cameron, P.O.Box 2091, Washington, D.C. 20013; (703) 690-8536. FRI conducts original research on gay behavior and publishes newsletters and pamphlets on dangers of the gay lifestyle and movement.

- Focus on the Family. Dr. James Dobson, 420 North Cascade, Colorado Springs, CO 80903; (719) 631-4300. Focus is multi-faceted ministry with a daily radio talk show featuring Dr. James Dobson; airs Family News in Focus daily, a hard-hitting news program; publicizes seven major magazines, including *Citizen* which deals exclusively in public policy issues and distributes books, tapes and videos to those interested in preserving the traditional family. *Citizen* is available for a suggested donation of $20/yr.

- Rutherford Institute. John Whitehead, 1445 E. Rio Rd., Charlottesville, Virginia 22901; (804) 978-3888. Rutherford has attorneys through the U.S. who will defend religious freedom. Whitehead's group is one of most successful Christian legal organizations founded to protect freedom of worship, conscience and speech.

Order These Huntington House Books !

_____	America Betrayed—Marlin Maddoux	$6.99 _____
_____	Angel Vision (A Novel)—Jim Carroll with Jay Gaines	5.99 _____
_____	Battle Plan: Equipping the Church for the 90s—Chris Stanton	7.99 _____
_____	Blessings of Liberty—Charles C. Heath	8.99 _____
_____	Cover of Darkness (A Novel)—J. Carroll	7.99 _____
_____	Crystalline Connection (A Novel)—Bob Maddux	8.99 _____
_____	Deadly Deception: Freemasonry—Tom McKenney	7.99 _____
_____	The Delicate Balance—John Zajac	8.99 _____
_____	Dinosaurs and the Bible—Dave Unfred	12.99 _____
_____	*Don't Touch That Dial—Barbara Hattemer & Robert Showers	9.99/19.99 _____
_____	En Route to Global Occupation—Gary Kah	9.99 _____
_____	Exposing the AIDS Scandal—Dr. Paul Cameron	7.99 _____
_____	Face the Wind—Gloria Delaney	9.99 _____
_____	*False Security—Jerry Parks	9.99 _____
_____	From Rock to Rock—Eric Barger	8.99 _____
_____	Hidden Dangers of the Rainbow—Constance Cumbey	8.99 _____
_____	*Hitler and the New Age—Bob Rosio	9.99 _____
_____	The Image of the Ages—David Webber	7.99 _____
_____	Inside the New Age Nightmare—Randall Baer	8.99 _____
_____	*A Jewish Conservative Looks at Pagan America—Don Feder	9.99/19.99 _____
_____	*Journey Into Darkness—Stephen Arrington	9.99 _____
_____	Kinsey, Sex and Fraud—Dr. Judith A. Reisman & Edward Eichel (Hard cover)	19.99 _____
_____	Last Days Collection—Last Days Ministries	8.95 _____
_____	Legend of the Holy Lance (A Novel)—William T. Still	8.99/16.99 _____
_____	New World Order—William T. Still	8.99 _____
_____	*One Year to a College Degree—Lynette Long & Eileen Hershberger	9.99 _____
_____	*Political Correctness—David Thibodaux	9.99 _____
_____	Psychic Phenomena Unveiled—John Anderson	8.99 _____
_____	Seduction of the Innocent Revisited—John Fulce	8.99 _____
_____	"Soft Porn" Plays Hardball—Dr. Judith A. Reisman	8.99/16.99 _____
_____	*Subtle Serpent—Darylann Whitemarsh & Bill Reisman	9.99 _____
_____	Teens and Devil-Worship—Charles G.B. Evans	8.99 _____
_____	To Grow By Storybook Readers—Janet Friend	44.95 per set _____
_____	Touching the Face of God—Bob Russell (Paper/Hardcover)	8.99/18.99 _____
_____	Twisted Cross—Joseph Carr	9.99 _____
_____	*When the Wicked Seize a City—Chuck & Donna McIlhenny with Frank York	9.99 _____
_____	Who Will Rule the Future?—Paul McGuire	8.99 _____
_____	*You Hit Like a Girl—Elsa Houtz & William J. Ferkile	9.99 _____

    * New Title   Shipping and Handling   _____
                             Total   _____

AVAILABLE AT BOOKSTORES EVERYWHERE or order direct from:
Huntington House Publishers • P.O. Box 53788 • Lafayette, LA 70505
Send check/money order. For faster service use VISA/MASTERCARD
call toll-free 1-800-749-4009.

Add: Freight and handling, $3.50 for the first book ordered, and $.50 for each additional book up to 5 books.

Enclosed is $_____ including postage.
VISA/MASTERCARD#_____ Exp. Date_____
Name_____ Phone: ( )_____
Address_____
City, State, Zip_____